Renovation Planning & Design

A Guide to Managing Renovation Projects

Davey Wooton

homeprojectcenter.com

No part of this book may be reproduced or stored in a retrieval system or transmitted in any form or by any means, electronic, mechanical, photocopying, recording, or otherwise, without express written permission of the publisher

NOTICE

Construction is an ever-changing field. Standard safety precautions must be followed, but as new research and changes in technology, tools, and materials become available, changes in procedures and language may become necessary or appropriate. Readers are encouraged to check the most current product information provided by the manufacturer of tools and materials for proper usage and methods. In addition, readers should always verify any construction language or procedure information with current and localized data from the appropriate jurisdiction for their project. Neither publisher nor author assumes any liability for any injury or damage to persons or property arising from this publication.

Copyright © 2022 Davey Wooton
All rights reserved.
ISBN-13:

Acknowledgments

Thank you to our incredible team at Wooton Construction for all their support and help in creating this book and to our fantastic clients that have inspired me to provide a tool that empowers homeowners with knowledge.

This book is intended for homeowners to look behind the scenes of construction and truly understand what goes into each remodeling project. The detailed planning involved in each construction phase can be overwhelming, but understanding the process, jargon, and standards makes the homeowner breathe a little easier.

We are a company that sets out to absolve the homeowner of uncertainties from the beginning to end of their project and beyond into home maintenance. If you would like to know more about us, please visit our website: homeprojectcenter.com, or look us up on Facebook: Wooton Construction

Table of Contents

Introduction 1

Chapter 1: Renovation & Project Planning 1

    Section 1: Introduction to Construction 1

    Section 2: Task Categories and Definitions 8

    Demolition Terminology 9

    Foundation Terminology 11

    Framing Terminology 12

    Roofing Terminology 18

    Roof Styles: 20

    Siding Terminology 21

    HVAC Terminology 23

    Insulation Terminology 24

    Plumbing Terminology 25

    Electrical Terminology 28

    Drywall Terminology 30

    Painting and Staining Terminology 31

    Trim and/or Finish Carpentry Terminology 34

    Tile and Stonework Terminology 36

    Flooring Terminology 40

    Cabinetry Terminology 41

    Countertops Terminology and Standards 43

    The Value of Your Project: 45

    Section 3: Your Role 46

  Your Role as the Contractor: 46

Chapter 2: Plans - Concepts & Drawings 47
  Section 1: Understanding your Space 47
  Section 2: Space Planning 50
  Section 3: How to Layout your Project 59

Chapter 3 - Purchasing & Hiring for your Project 75
  Section 1: Vendors & Products Overview 75
  Section 2: Vendors & Products Overview 80
  Section 3: Selecting Materials 82
  Section 4: Vendor Qualifying 89
  Section 5: Purchasing 94
  Section 6: Tradesman Hiring 98
  Questions to Ask Yourself: 100
  Section 7: Trades & Cost 103
  Section 8: Operations & Background 107
  Job Site Responsibilities 112
  Section 9: Final Decisions 114
  Section 10: Contracts 117
  Section 11: Permits & Insurance 121

Chapter 4: Scope & Budget 125
  Section 1: Budget 125
  Section 2: Create Your Scope 128
  Section 3: Making a Material List 131
  Calculating Materials 135
  Making your Schedules 138
  Section 4: Project Journal 140
  Section 5: Cleaning Out Your Project Journal 145

Chapter 5: Renovation Project Management 155
    Section 1: Building the Timeline 155
    Section 2: Scheduling 162
    Section 3: Inspections and Expectations 167
    Section 4: Setting the Site Plan 173
    Section 5: Change Orders 183

Chapter 6 Budget Management & Record Keeping 189
    Section 1: Creating a Statement 189
    Section 2: Record Keeping & Receipts 191
    Section 3: Financial Expectations 194
    Section 4: Revisiting Your Budget 197
    Section 5: Course Review 201
    Course Goals: 205

Introduction

This manual intends to enlighten the Homeowner about the world of Construction and the fundamental processes to get any project going. It is designed to give the most relevant and essential information in a practical format without being overwhelming. The purpose of this manual is to clarify the process of preparing oneself for a renovation by giving a comprehensive guide to preparing, gathering, organizing, and tracking all the pertinent information and details needed to complete any renovation or building project.

We begin this process by introducing you to the most used language of construction. This book includes condensed definitions of the terminology used in construction, whether you are renovating or building a new home. In addition, it contains essential information allowing any Homeowner to talk to their builder and tradesman to understand what is being explained or asked.

The manual will guide you through methods of creating your budgets, space planning, and materials list. Helping you find the true purpose of your project. In addition, you will be provided with instructions on hiring labor needed for the project, sourcing your materials, and verifying your restrictions before you build.

This book also walks you through the process of construction. In addition, charts and checklists are provided to help track the timelines and schedules throughout the build's progress. These processes and diagrams will help you to monitor your budget and prepare yourself for the unexpected.

The processes outlined in this book may be replicated for any ongoing project you may have and any future ones you may endeavor.

Chapter 1: Renovation & Project Planning
Section 1: Introduction to Construction

There are so many factors that go into any renovation project, small or large. In the following course, you will learn how to prepare yourself for your renovation project experience realistically. Small projects will take less time but will require the same attention and many of the same details. We will walk you through the entire process from beginning to end, educating you on the terminology and standards for every aspect of your project and beyond, giving you the confidence to execute your project.

This course aims to give you an *understanding* of the work you are doing on your home by educating you on the industry's **Terminology and Standards,** which will allow you to *communicate* proficiently with any tradesman performing work on your home. You will walk away understanding what they are telling you and why they are doing what they are doing. We will help you understand the process in which work has to happen, create efficiencies without a more significant workload, and reduce unnecessary rework. We will help you create a Project Journal to keep yourself *organized* throughout your project. You will be able to replicate this Project Journal for any other future projects as well.

We will walk you through the process of buying products that will be built into your home. This process will include keeping track of the products for their use and placement, the product's actual cost, and when to purchase your products. You will learn to make product schedules and know which ones require schedules. You can keep all your details and lists organized and easily find them when you need them.

Proper planning is the key to any project. Be patient; know that more planning done ahead of time will save you money and time. Throughout the planning process, we will discuss every part of the process in detail. Getting started on the following course, we will introduce you to commonly used terms of construction in the industry. Many of them will be used in the chapters to follow. Learning these terms will help you understand construction and the process and give you more confidence in your project. Refer to these terms when talking to vendors, tradesmen or when a refresher is needed. Think of it as a reference guide to speaking "renovation language."

Components of Projects

Each project can be broken down into four components that are necessary to have before the project gets off the ground.

- Plans - Drawings or Building plans are scaled drawings for your project.
- Designs - Surface and aesthetic selections such as colors, tile, flooring, light fixtures, etc.
- Scope & Budget - an outline of the work to be done and the cost associated with labor, materials, and other building fees
- Timelines - putting the circus together and knowing the construction process and how the Trades affect one another.

Each of these will be discussed in detail in later chapters.

Types of Construction

There are many different building types in construction, and each has its regulations, standards, and methods. However, while building any structure from the ground up, whether a grocery store or a home, there are common elements fundamental to building, and variations will be required for each.

New Build: brand new building of a structure from the ground to finished.

Remodel: any alteration or addition to an existing structure. It could be anything from a new coat of paint on the walls, gutting the kitchen and installing new cabinets and countertops, or adding a new master suite or patio.

Maintenance: repair work to any structure that has failed to restore it to its original state. The only improvement will be in the materials used.

Residential vs. Commercial

Residential: individually owned home, condo, apartment, etc., that is used as a place of residence.

Plans: for any residential remodel or new build; plans can be drawn up by the Homeowner, draftsman, building designer, or architect.

CODES: the restrictions and standards of building that need to be met for a residence in the framework and fire safety and ADA compliance will not be the same as those for a commercial property. The residential home is meant for a single family to occupy vs. a large volume of employees to consumers to use every day.

Designs: any design can be done by the Homeowner, decorator, or interior designer. The designs for a home will be unique to the individual homeowner depending on personal taste and use of the space.

Commercial: any place of business or government or municipality building.

Plans: for a new commercial property build, an architect must draw up the plans and apply the stamp. These plans may need to be reviewed and stamped by a structural engineer.

CODES: the restrictions and standards for a commercial building are scrutinized differently than a residential home. The framework for the structure will have different load-bearing standards for use and weather conditions. Most businesses are insured for not only structural damage but a loss of business as well. Whereas if your home is damaged, you can always find a secondary living space until repairs are done, and you will not lose an income because of it. Fire safety and ADA compliance are also different because of the large volume of employees and consumers.

Designs: any designs for a business can be done by the owner or an interior designer (most likely). The deigns will be for the eyes of the masses and unique to the desired business services and atmosphere desired.

NOTE: some Home Remodelers are allowed to do small commercial remodels. To do a new build of a commercial building will require a builder with a commercial license.

The Team and Players

Building Teams & Players

Contractor: the contractor puts the whole network together of the tradesmen used to do the work. The Contractor will schedule all needed tradesmen and work with the architect and designers on the project plans to ensure a complete job. He will source all the materials required for your project. Most contractors will offer you a budget for the labor and materials to complete the job. The plans are left to the Draftsman (or Architect) & the designs are up to the homeowner or a designer. It is becoming more common for the Contractor to source the plans and designs to offer you the pre-construction planning and the build. The contractor will carry insurance on all the trades that step foot on your property.

Tradesman (Sub-Contractor): This is usually an individual or company specializing in a specific trade such as framing, concrete work, tile, floor installation, painting, etc. Tradesmen typically work for contractors and sometimes directly for the homeowner. To give an example of how specialized these guys are, let's look at how many people will be involved in getting your wall up and painted.

- One guy to hang the drywall
- One guy to float the drywall
- One guy to texture the drywall (if you want texture)
- One guy to prime a paint the wall.

Because the tradesman has honed their craft and only performs their own skill set, it is crucial to know how each affects the other. When we cover the order of the construction build in Chapter 5, it will be easier to understand how the trades work together. Most tradesmen will carry insurance on themselves and their crew only. Some tradesmen may not be insured if they work by themselves.

Handyman: the handyman is a "Jack of all Trades." They are skilled at performing multiple skill sets. He can do the minor framing, carpentry, painting, electrical, plumbing, etc. He can usually handle a kitchen or bathroom alone or with a helper. The handyman handles a lot of maintenance and repair work as well. Most will not have insurance, but some will.

Pre-Construction Team & Players

<u>Architects</u>: draft scaled floorplans and building plans for any residential or commercial building. They will oversee any commercial build they design and often work with structural engineers on those projects. In addition, the architect will work with interior designers for the project's aesthetics. Each firm can provide plans for any project, but some specialize in specific types, such as commercial buildings, new construction homes, and other remodeling projects.

<u>Draftsman & Building Designers</u>: draft scaled floorplans and building plans for any residential or commercial remodeling project. They work with interior designers, and some offer design services themselves. Each firm can provide plans for any project, but some specialize in specific types, such as commercial remodels or new construction homes, and others remodeling projects. Most will focus on residential building projects, or residential remodels.

<u>Interior Designers</u>: primary focus is designing concepts for your space usage, choosing the surface materials and colors, fixtures, and colors. They will complete your look with décor, furniture, and window treatments.

<u>Decorators</u>: provide design concepts for the surface materials, usage of the space, and selection of the surface materials, fixtures, and colors. They will complete the look with décor, furniture, and window treatments.

Commonly Used Industry Terms

Square Footage: The area measurement in feet. Length in feet x width in feet = square footage. You will use this to figure flooring, drywall space, ceiling space, the tile needed for floors, shower walls, niches (indented box in shower wall to store shampoo and soap bottles), general living area, countertops, and backsplashes.

Linear Footage: This is the unit measurement of any material in increments of 12 inches = 1 linear foot. You will use linear footage to measure trim (crown, baseboard, shoe molding, door trim, window trim, siding trim, fascia, etc.).

Squares: This is a common term used in roofing to note the amount of roofing needed. Each Square represents 100 square feet.

Floorplan: Is a 2D drawing denoting all exterior walls, interior walls, doors, openings, windows, cabinetry, plumbing items (*tubs, showers, toilets, sinks, washers*), and electrical items (*lights, fans, outlets, switches, meters, etc.*), with unit measurement annotations in feet and inches. These are made using a scaled measurement. The most common are 1/8" =1', ¼" = 1', or ½" = 1'. This scale will be noted for each drawing on the lower left— or right-hand corner.

Layout: Used in building and/or design plans showing the placement of walls, doors, cabinetry, plumbing, and electrical items to scale. A layout helps create a home's design, seeing the room's space and flow.

Elevation: The visual drawing of a 3D object from the front or sides as if you were looking at the object— usually the sides of the house, cabinets, or the wall's framing.

Scope: In construction, this refers to the line-item description of work to be done by task category

Raw Materials: These materials are used to build a home with no design element. Some examples include stick lumber, fasteners, sealants, mud for drywall, and waterproofing materials in tile work.

Finish Materials: Also known as design materials. These materials are essential in their look as well as their function. These materials will finish the look or overall design of the project. For example, such items may be faucets, light fixtures, tile, flooring, trim, cabinet styles, and hardware.

Sourcing: This is the process of finding a needed or desired material, determining the manufacturer, distributor, pricing, and how to get it shipped or delivered.

Backer Materials: These materials are raw materials needed to adhere to other finish materials. They provide structural integrity as well as waterproofing. Examples are concrete board and waterproofing behind tile shower walls, the thin set under tile, plywood, and house wrap under or behind the siding.

Spec-Sheets: The specification sheets for any product needing to install. Such as a faucet, light fixture, or appliance. It will have exact measurements of the manufacturer's product and recommendations on how to install it properly. As listed on the sheet, you will need the right tools to install the product.

Site Plan: This is a plan for the job site (*the construction area*) that will involve workstations, clean-out stations, storage areas, and delivery and drop-off locations.

CODES: This is a part of the City Development and Planning Commission in any city that oversees the construction projects in the area. They uphold and maintain construction standards and practices to ensure that the construction is at a minimum standard, deemed sound and safe. This department will assist in constructing any commercial or residential building from beginning to end. For residential projects, they are involved when adding living space to an existing structure or making structural changes to the existing building.

Cut-off or Waste: A term used to indicate the quantity of materials that will either be "wasted" or no good because it is the cut-off piece of wood, tile, pipe, etc. It cannot be used for anything else and is an acceptable waste. Each project has it. Most framing, flooring, and siding materials include a 10% overage to accommodate waste and cut-off.

Section 2: Task Categories and Definitions

Task Categories:

The following terminology is for the task categories of construction. While each category involves many different and specific tasks, they are the main categories of work involved in any renovation and/or building project. Each one is listed in the order of the work performed.

Demo: The removal of building materials.

Foundation: The base on which a structure is built.

Framing: The construction of the structure. Walls, ceilings, roof, windows, and doors.

Roofing: The construction of the top of any structure to give protection from weather and temperature changes.

Siding: The outer cladding of any structure.

Insulation: The method of helping protect the interior space from outside elements such as moisture and temperature.

HVAC: Heating, Ventilation, and Air Conditioning

Plumbing: The installation of drain and supply lines for water and gas fixtures.

Electrical: The installation of electrical wires and boxes to give power supply to the structure.

Drywall: The interior wall coverings that provide protection, insulation, and fire safety for the structure.

Painting/Staining: The color coating added to walls (interior and exterior), trim, doors, ceilings, etc.

Tile Work: The installation of tile to walls, floors, etc.

Flooring: The installation of any material to cover the structure's foundation.

Cabinetry: The storage boxes in kitchens, bathrooms, utility rooms, and storage rooms. They come in many styles to suit many purposes.

Countertops: The top to the base cabinets, giving working space.

Finish Carpentry/Trim Carpentry: The installation of the finishing touch to any construction project. For example, molding pieces, bath accessories, or hardware.

Demolition Terminology

Demolition (Demo): This is the removal of any structural member (appliance, fixture, building material, foundation). There are different levels of demolition, from partial to a full gut. It cannot be stressed enough, for all demolition, the importance of gloves, hats, eye protection, and breathing masks. These will help prevent injuries sustained from wood and other stone materials flying in your face or falling on your head and protect your lungs from breathing in the dust from these materials as they are removed from the home.

Tools: brooms, shop vacuums, contractor trash bags, large dustpans, mops, and buckets

- **Hammers**: Can be used to knock nails off or pry them out. Sometimes hammers Will hold back a piece of wood or trim to get to another piece.
- **Prybars**: Small and large, used to pull back on boards, trim pieces, and take nails and/or staples out of wood. In addition, they can lift tiles or break off pieces of stone and/or tile. Prybars are useful in holding windows and doors in place through leverage while they're secured in place.
- **Skill Saw**: An electric (*corded or battery-operated*) handheld saw with a circular blade. The blades come in a variety of sizes.
- **Hand Saw**: Handheld saw with a wooden or plastic handle; long blade with "teeth" for cutting smaller pieces of wood or when electricity is unavailable.
- **Reciprocating Saw:** (*corded or battery operated*) Saw with interchangeable blades for cutting through wood, metal, stone, etc. They are commonly referred to as Sawzall by tradesmen.
- **Utility Knife**: A handheld knife that uses a razor blade for cutting through paper, cardboard, stones, drywall, or for scoring metals. The blade should be retractable.
- **Drills**: Commonly electric (corded or battery operated) tools used to remove screws and create starter holes in demolition. In construction, it is used for inserting screws, boring holes, and mixing materials with a paddle attachment.
- **Hammer Drills**: Use a motion like a hammer and use more force than a standard drill. It is used to drill through concrete and stone and remove tiles.
- **Multi-tool**: An electric (*corded or battery-operated*) handheld tool with different blades to cut through various materials.
- **Shop-Vac**: Used and explicitly designed to vacuum building materials. Uses filtered bags, that way as much dust is captured as possible.

- **Floor Scrapers**: Large handheld flat blades on a long pole are used to remove glue, vinyl flooring, etc.

- **Pliers**: Come in various sizes and grips for pulling out fasteners, wires, etc.

- **Catfish Pliers**: Have rounded edges and sharpened prongs. The sharpened prongs can cut through smaller nails, and using the right pressure, hold onto larger nails and rock to pull the nail out of the wood.

- **Blades**: Used for cutting different materials. Includes concrete/masonry blades, wood blades, tile blades, diamond blades (used for cutting glass), and metal blades.

- **Magnet Roller**: A large rolling magnet on a long pole, used to pick up all nails, staples, etc., by rolling over the surface like a vacuum.

Equipment:

- **Trash Trailers:** Might be rented or owned. On wheels with a hitch to move from to job and taken to the landfill. If you own a trash trailer, you must bring it to the landfill to empty it. You will **not** be able to throw out mattresses or couches with foam cushions. Paint cans will have to be empty and in black contractor bags. You will need to check with the vendor to find out what items are acceptable to throw away. Some materials, such as lots of concrete, will need specific equipment. Other materials, such as landscaping, carpet, and mattresses, will require specific landfills to be disposed of properly.

- **Dumpsters:** These are rentals only. Not on wheels, will require a removal and drop-off service. There are different types of dumpsters: landscaping, concrete, and building structure.

- **Excavators:** Large machines with a large, toothed bucket on one end, used for digging into the soil and debris piles to scoop up debris and dump it into the dumpster or to move large soil piles and level the ground to ready for foundation and/or future drainage or landscaping.

- **Ditch Witch:** A large machine used to dig trenches for drainage, bury pipes, conduits, etc.

- **Tampers:** Used to pack soil to make it dense and firm for foundations or pools.

- **Augers:** Machines used to dig large and small holes that need to go deep. An example would be for footings or posts.

- **Genie Lift:** A machine used to lift workers into very high places.

- **Scaffolding:** A ladder and platform system used to reach high places, allowing the tradesman to walk back and forth to work.

- **Floor Strippers:** These machines scrape the glue and/or mortar from a concrete slab.

Foundation Terminology

Foundation: The platform on which the structure is built and supported. It can be made of concrete or raised off the ground and composed of a treated lumber structure supported by metal or concrete piers.

Form: The framed perimeter of the area where concrete is poured. A series of supported lumber holds the concrete in place as it cures.

Footings: This is a deeper and wider part of the slab, meant to bear the structure's weight on the corners and the perimeter walls. Place a footing where the weight of the roof will be bearing down.

Vapor Barrier: Aa sheet of Visqueen laid down directly on leveled soil or gravel bed before pouring the concrete to prevent moisture from wicking through the concrete. The moisture can disrupt the concrete's integrity over time and cause the concrete to "sweat."

Metal Mesh: a wire mesh grid in 6x6 or 10x10 squares rolled out on the Visqueen. It gives strength and rigidity to the slab. It is meant to keep cracking and splitting from happening due to the foundation settling over time. In addition, it keeps the concrete together.

Rebar: precut metal steel rods used to help hold the sill plates down to the slab. Part of the bolt is embedded into the slab, and a few inches are left sticking out of the ground to attach the bottom sill plate. These rods will also hold two slabs together when adding foundation to the existing foundation by inserting one end of the rod into the existing slab at a 45-degree angle and pouring the new foundation over the remaining rebar.

Ground wire: a grounding wire is a copper wire tied to a rebar rod connected from inside the slab and extends out to a grounding rod next to the slab. It helps divert electricity back into the earth,

Slab: Concrete base to the structure. The ground will be excavated, leveled out, and graded for proper drainage. Sometimes a gravel bed is laid down on top of the soil.

Raised: A platform built above the ground at 12"–12' above the ground surface, depending on where you live.

Grading: the sloping of the earth to have a proper water runoff to the road or drainage ditch.

Finishes (for concrete slabs)

    <u>Smooth</u>: if carpet or wood is installed on the interior of the house, smooth concrete is needed

    <u>Broom</u> finish: the concrete is swept with a broom before the concrete fully fires to give a slightly rough texture for grip.

    <u>Polished</u>: a machine and chemicals are used to achieve the concrete's glossy look.

Framing Terminology

Framing: Constructing the walls, ceilings, roof, windows, and doors using precut milled lumber.

True: Staying in as straight of a line as possible but making allowances for unevenness or imperfections.

Plumb: Making a line straight and level using framing squares and levels.

Treated Lumber: Chemically pressure-treated lumber allows it to be exposed to moisture and weather conditions while retaining structural integrity.

Non-Treated Lumber: Lumber that has not been treated will lose all structural integrity if exposed to the weather and extreme moisture.

Structural Members: The stick lumber that makes up the walls, ceilings, roof, windows, and doors, giving support and making up the structure of the building.

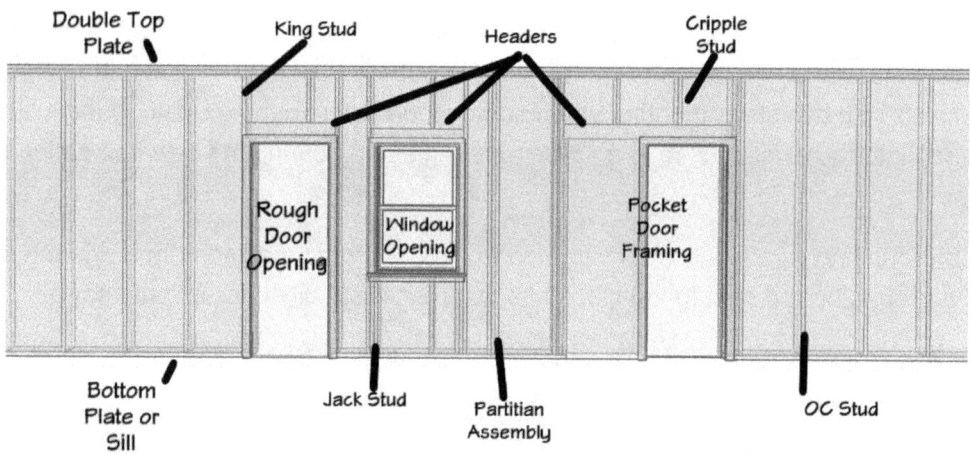

Studs: The lumber (*2x4 interior & exterior walls, 2x6 exterior walls only as a rule of thumb*) is installed vertically, making up the wall from the bottom plate to the top plate.

Joists: The support from wall to wall for a ceiling and/or the floor for a raised foundation.

Rafters: Lumber that makes up the roof. It starts at the roof (*ridge*) to the end of the eave on top of the exterior wall plate.

Soffit: The space between the rafter tail (*eave*) and the wall. 5/8" thick plywood, Hardi board, or vinyl will fill this space.

Fascia: Is the board along the end of the rafter tails. It can be concrete board, wood, echo board with a groove (*hardened wood through a treatment process*), or vinyl to clad the fascia.

Rough Opening: Is the framed opening for doors, windows, or shower pans; niches to fit the finished item. It is larger than the door and/or window installed. To get this measurement, add the finished item's size or desired opening to the finish wall product's thickness. Drywall, siding, trim work, and/or tile and backer materials.

Open Walls: The stick lumber is in place, and only the exterior plywood is attached to the studs of the framework, with the rough-in electrical, plumbing, and HVAC lines showing.

Knee Wall: Also known as a pony wall. It is a short wall, generally 36"–42" in height. It is a partition between spaces, dining rooms, kitchens, a shower wall (*with a glass panel attached*), a tub wall, a retaining wall, etc.

Niches: Any recessed sections of a wall. In living areas, they display artwork. In Bathrooms, they are used in showers and near bathtubs for shampoo and soap bottles. **Black-In:** The plywood is attached to the outside of the walls and roof, then house wrap is attached to the exterior walls, and roofing felt is attached to the roof plywood. It is the first layer of waterproofing.

Ceilings: The top surface of any room space, separating the living space from the attic.

- **Flat:** Straight across from wall to wall. The Standard is 8'–9'. New homes range from 10'–12' high in living areas.
- **Vaulted:** Raised at an angle on two sides of the room following the rafters and flat in the middle. It is not necessarily the same pitch as the roof.
- **Cathedral:** Is raised on two sides of the room following the rafters to the roof's peak (*ridge*). It is the same pitch as the roof.
- **Shed:** The ceiling will slope on only one side and then flatten out. It is to add more height to the room.
- **Tray:** The room's center lifts higher, and the room's perimeter is at a lower height.
- **Coffered:** The ceiling is framed out into several squares of equal size. Frame at the beginning of the project or use trim work to achieve the coffered design.
- **Dome** A rounded dome is framed into the ceiling, usually is one section or room is a full circle.
- **Barrel:** A rounded ceiling from one wall to another that follows the room's length.

Windows: Customarily installed during the house's framing phase to be appropriately sealed before the siding goes on. They can be installed or replaced later.

- **Sash:** The framework that holds the glass in place. There is an upper sash (top panel of glass) and a lower sash (bottom panel of glass).
- **Fixed:** The pane of glass does not move.

- **Hang:** Indicates how many of the panes of glass are operable.
    - **Single Hung:** The lower half of the window lifts and lowers.
    - **Double Hung:** Both the top and bottom panes of glass lift and lower
- **Tilt:** Indicates if the pane of glass can tilt in for cleaning purposes.
- **Mullions:** Otherwise called grids or grilles are the spacers used to break up the pane of glass. They may be internal, sandwiched between sheets of glass, or external.
- **Sill:** The bottom frame of the window.
- **Header:** The top frame of the window.
- **Jamb:** The sides of the inside frame of the window.
- **Channel:** The window's interior part that the lower and/or upper sash use to slide up and down.
- **Glazing:** The seal between the frame of the window and the glass.
- **Size:** Is usually indicated with four numbers to tell the window's width and height, in that order. Example 1: 3050 is 3'0" wide x 5'0" tall. Example 2: 2648 would be 2'6" wide x 4'8" tall.

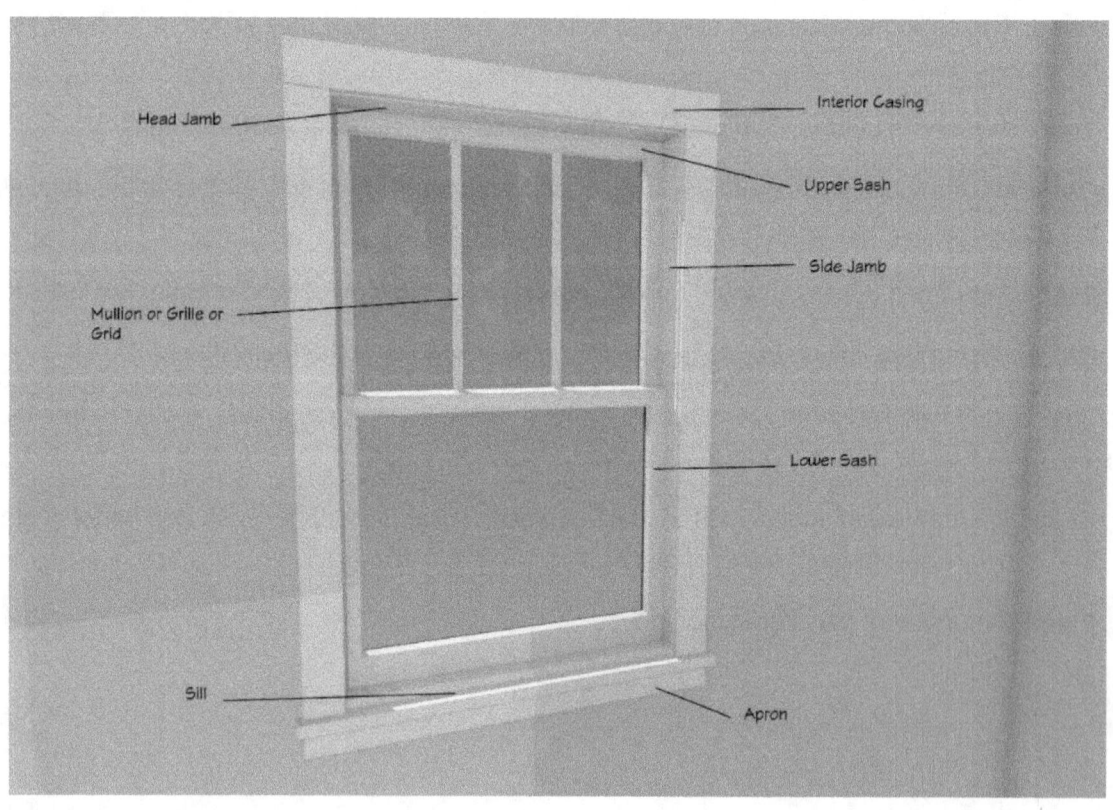

Doors:

- **Exterior Doors:** The doors on the exterior walls of the structure. They are exposed to weather conditions. Exterior doors are installed during the framing process before the siding goes on. It can be installed later, but it will require more work.

- **Interior Doors:** The doors inside the structure. They will not be exposed to any weather conditions. Interior doors are installed after the drywall is complete, along with the rest of the trim work.

- **Jamb:** The sides of the door frame.

- **Header:** The top of the door frame.

- **Stop:** The small trim in the middle of the jamb makes the door unable to swing.

- **Swing (*pivot*):** The direction the door pivots on its hinges.
    - **Left Hand:** When standing outside the door, it will open away from you to the left.
    - **Right Hand:** When standing outside the door, it will open away from you to the right.
    - **Inswing:** The door opens into the room or inside the house.
    - **Outswing:** The door opens to the outside of the room or the house.

- **Size:** Usually indicated with four numbers to tell the door's width and height, in that order. Example: 3068 is 3'0" wide x 6'8" tall.

- **Sidelights:** The fixed panels on either side of the door are glass, with either no grills or several to break the glass into panels. Sometimes, decorative glass is used in the sidelights.

- **Threshold or Transition:** The bottom part of the frame for the door. For exterior doors, the threshold slopes away from the house's interior. A transition is also the change of flooring from one room to another. Example: the shift from the bathroom to the bedroom and/or hall. Thresholds and transitions come in wood and metal options with different colors and finishes.

- **Bore:** The hole cut in the door to fit the lockset.
    - **Single Bore:** For one handle.
    - **Double Bore:** One for the handle and one for the deadbolt.

- **Strike Plate:** The plate on the closing side of the jamb that the door bolt from the lockset extends into, helping to keep the door closed.

- **Mortis:** Refers to the carved-out indent in the jamb for the hinges and strike plates.

- **Hinges:** The pivot points that are fixed on the door jamb, allowing the door to pivot. Available in rounded or square edging with many options for colors and finishes.

- **Hollow Core:** A molded door that is hollow inside.

- **Solid Core:** The door does not have any hollow spaces.
- **Fiberglass:** No rot, fiberglass. If dented, it will not rust or rot.
- **Steel:** No rot; however, if dented, it will usually rust.
- **Wood:** Solid core wood. If the wood is overexposed, it will rot. It needs upkeep on the exterior surface.
- **Styles:** The names of the different types of doors lets you know how the door functions and what look the door has.
  - **Barn Door or Library Door:** Slides side to side in front of the door opening. The sliding hardware is attached above the door frame on the wall—of any material and chosen design.
  - **Sliding:** Either only one or both panels will slide from one side to the other. It is used for exterior and interior applications.
  - **Pocket:** The door slides back into the wall. A particular frame is used during the framing process to accept the door. It has a track at the top for the door to slide open and closed.
  - **Bifold:** The door is in two sections that "fold" to the side. They are usually used in Closets.
  - **Double Door:** Two doors that open in the middle and swing open to the outside.
  - **French Doors:** Exterior doors (*typically*) swing out simultaneously with no center style.
  - **Patio Doors:** Exterior doors with one side fixed (*non-opening*) and one side that swings open.
  - **Pivot:** Standard door that swings open and is hinged to one side.
  - **Café Doors:** A set of doors that swing in both directions.

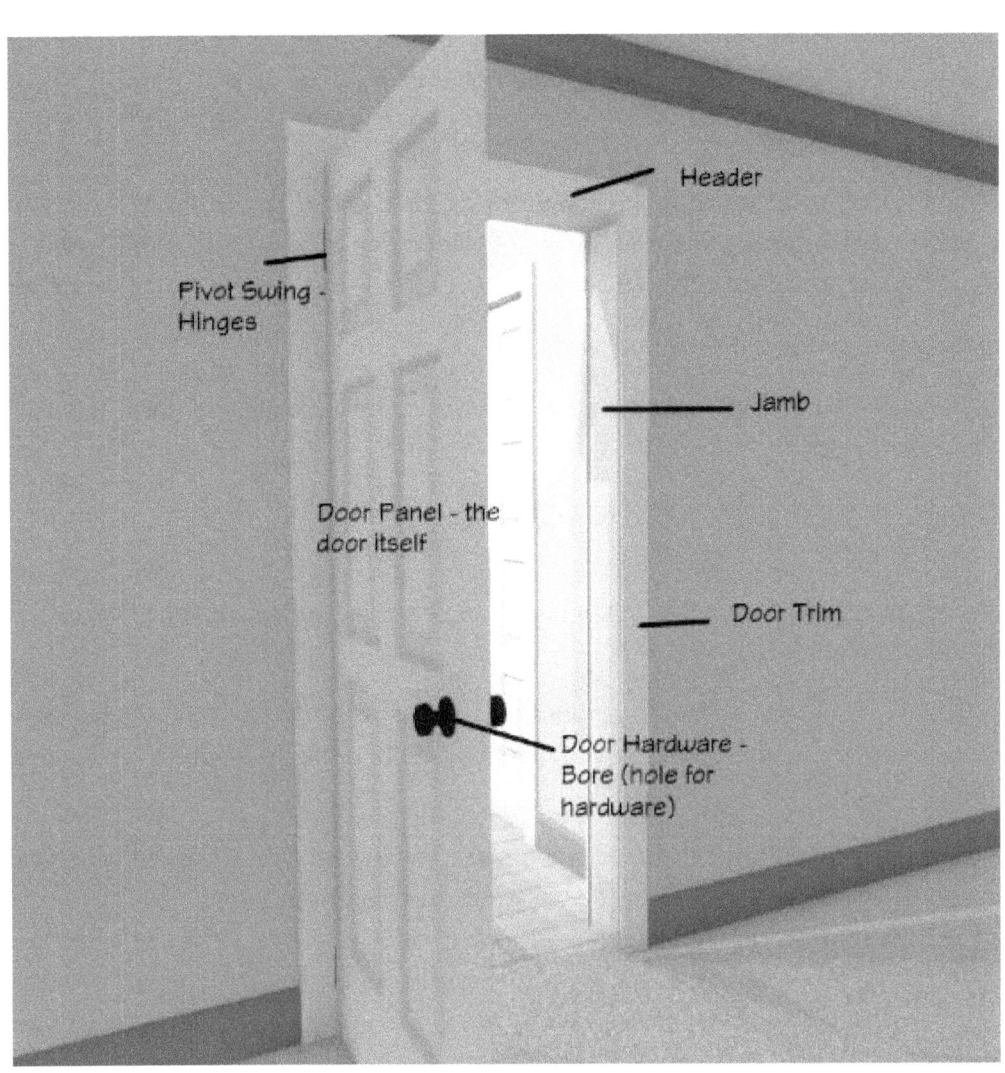

Roofing Terminology

Roofs: The angled structure protects the house from weather and temperature changes.

Valley: The mitered corner where two roof planes meet at the bottom.

Ridge: The top or apex of the roof, where all the rafters connect on both sides.

Pitch: Denotes the amount of slope the roof has. The higher the pitch, the steeper the slope. The number indicates many inches of the rise there is for every 12 inches of length. Example: 3 on 12 pitch (*written 3:12*) rises 3 inches for every 12 inches horizontal distance.

Eave: The roof overhang from the structure's external walls.

Underlayment: The roofing felt (*3' wide rolls*) is attached to the decking using button cap nails. It is laid horizontally from the eave to the ridge.

Shingles: The asphalt materials attached to the roofing felt on the roof. Made in 2'x3' sheets laid horizontally, starting from the bottom edge (*eave*) in a staggard pattern to the top (ridge).

- **3-Tab Shingles:** A single layer of granular materials on a fiberglass matt base. They are used on roof pitches of 2:12 and higher.

- **Architectural:** Multi-layer shingle made of fiberglass, organic materials, and asphalt. A heavier matt base than the 3-tab shingle. They are used on roof pitches of 3:12 or higher. It helps the watershed on high-pitch roofs.

- **Luxury shingles:** multi-layer shingles made with fiberglass and asphalt. They are made to imitate cedar shingles with lots of dimensions. Helps the watershed on high-pitch roofs.

- **Cedar Shakes:** Individual cuts of wood made from cedar. Used on roofs with a 4:12 pitch or higher. HIGH maintenance.

Metal: Sheets of metal about 16" wide and cut to the desired length to cover the roof. Some metal roofs require a purlin strip to be attached to the roof first before connecting the metal.

- **Purlin strip:** A 1"x1" strip of treated wood, cut to the desired length between the underlayment and the metal.

- **Corrugated:** The metal is wavy and is attached using screws with rubber gaskets. The screws and gaskets are exposed to the elements and will degrade over time, causing leaks.

- **Standing seam:** Metal sheets that are flat for about 12" and then a small ridge. This pattern is repeated. The sheets attach with screws with rubber gaskets where each sheet overlaps the next, concealing the screws. As a result, it has a much longer life and far less leaking than a corrugated roof.

Penetrations: Anything protruding from the roof on its normal sloping plane.

- **Roof jacks:** Pipes that come out through the top of the roof. They are the extension of the plumbing vent's stacks required for your bathroom, laundry, and kitchen drains.
- **Vent hood cap:** The cap for the vent hood in the kitchen.
- **Fireplaces:** Most true brick fireplaces are built separate from the house framing and have their own footing. They will need proper flashing to help the water and ice move off the roof and not leak down the chimney's sides.
- **Skylights:** Large square or rectangular windows put into the roof.
- **Solar tubes:** A small tube capped with a plastic dome to let light into a space like a skylight, but with less risk of leaking.
- **Dormers:** A structure protruding vertically from the main roof of the house. They will be roofed to match the house and usually have a window. Dormers allow for more headspace in a second-story room and/or attic. They can be part of the home's original construction or added later. Dormers will vary in size and style depending on the house's architecture.

Roof Styles:

- **Flat:** The slope on the roof is only up to 10 degrees, just enough to have water move to the ends of the roof.

- **Gable:** Double-pitched roof on two sides of the roof, and the building's end wall goes up to and follows the roof lines to the ridge.

- **Hip:** Multiple sloped roofs, sloping on all roof planes. If the whole roof is hipped, all sloping sides intersect at the ridge.

- **Gambrel:** Part barn, part gable roof but will have multiple pitches from the ridge to the eave (*soffit*), leaving the end wall to go up to the ridge.

- **Lean-To or Shed:** A single-pitch roof that slopes in one direction from top to bottom. They are used on sheds, awnings, additions, and patios.

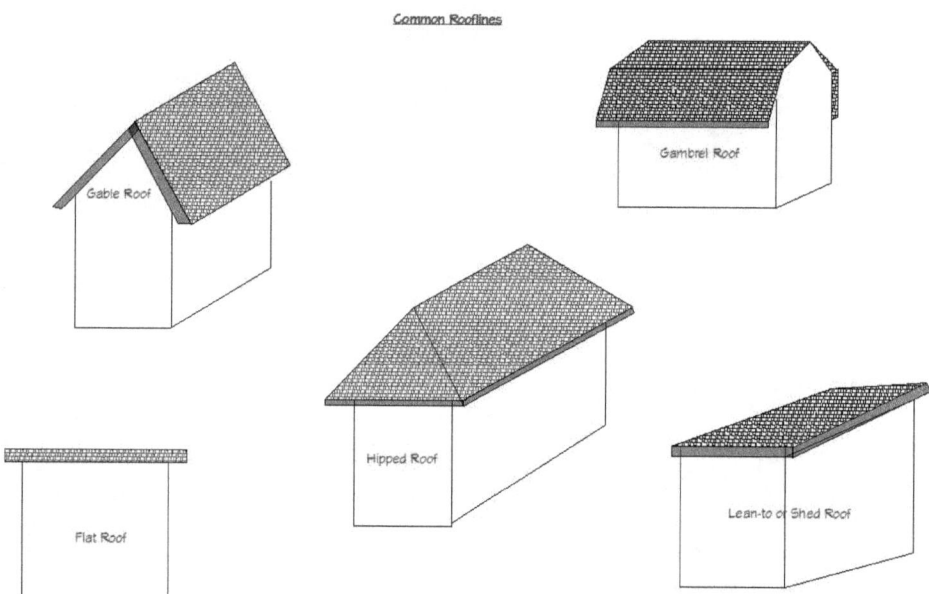

Common Rooflines

Siding Terminology

Siding: The outer cladding of a structure. The façade or facing of the building. The following are the most used siding materials.

- **Concrete Board:** The concrete boards are attached with screws or nails made for the concrete panels.
    - **Lap:** The boards are cut in 4"–12" widths and come in 10' or 12' lengths. They attach by lapping each board over the other, starting from the bottom of the wall and going to the top. The seams are staggard along the way. It will have either a smooth or woodgrain texture.
    - **Panel:** A sheet of concrete board in 4'x8'–4'x 10' sizes. It will have a smooth, woodgrain or stucco texture. They are attached vertically, butted up to each other. Caulk the seams or use trim to cover the seams.
    - **Board and Batten:** Panelboard, hung vertically with 1x2 strips of lattice trim of wood or concrete board pieces to cover the seams. Trim pieces are placed over seams every four feet apart and every twelve to twenty-four inches in between the four-foot wide panels to add decoration.
    - **Shaker:** 2'x3' sheets molded to look like shaker wood pieces. They are attached with screws or nails and lapped over one another from the bottom of the wall to the top.
    - **Trim:** 4"–8" wide, 10'–12' lengths, ½" – 5/4" thick boards used to border the top, bottom, and corners of walls, doors, and windows as well. Trim comes in either a smooth or woodgrain texture.
- **Wood:** Exterior cladding made of wood.
    - **Lap:** Wood cut into 4"–12" wide boards at 10'–12' in length. Each board laps the previous board, starting from the bottom of the wall to the soffit.
    - **Panel:** 4'x8' and 4'x10' plywood sheets attached to the house wrap. The seams are covered with a trim, caulked, and painted.
    - **Shaker:** Small rounded-off pieces of wood butted horizontally against each other, lapping vertically, starting from the bottom of the wall to the soffit.
- **Brick:** Man-made masonry product attached to the outer house wrap using brick ties and mortar—heat, moisture, and temperature resistant.
- **Stucco:** A mortar-type product applied on concrete board, applied in a 3-layer system consisting of a scratch coat 3/8" thick, a brown coat 3/8" thick, and a finish coat 1/8" thick. Usually, a concrete board is under the scratch coat. A colorant is applied to the topcoat before it goes on or is painted after.
- **Vinyl:** A plastic man-made sheet designed to imitate lap siding that protects the house's outside walls from rain and sun exposure. Available in many different designs and colors.

- **Concrete:** Solid concrete walls. Either they are made from solid concrete formed and put together or from cinder blocks filled with concrete after formed.
- **Log:** Precut logs notched and stacked one on top of the other.
- **Shaker:** 4″–8″ individual pieces of wood staggered in a row and lapped one on top of the other. Stamped concrete boards are available in the shaker look.

HVAC Terminology

HVAC: Heating, Ventilation, and Air Conditioning

Full Unit: One unit calculated to condition the air for a space of varying sizes, to condition the amount of space in the home. The whole unit is composed of many parts. The main components are the condenser, compressor, and air handler.

Condenser: (*outside unit*) Air conditioner condensers are heat-exchanging devices. The condenser rejects heat from the air conditioner system to the surrounding air. At the same time, the evaporator absorbs heat from the space that needs to be cool. In our case, it is from indoor air.

Compressor: (*outside unit*) An air conditioning compressor is the part of the air conditioning system that compresses cool, low-pressure gas into a hot, high-pressure gas. The compression of this gas helps keep the area cool.

Air Handler: (*in the wall or attic space*) Moves the air from the return across an air conditioner's evaporator coil, also called the evaporator core. That is where the cold air is produced. The evaporator coil is located inside or near the air handler, where the blower fan blows the conditioned air out of the registers.

Trunk Lines: (*ductwork*) Are the tubes running from the central unit to the registers in the attic and between floors?

Registers: The holes cut in the ceiling, floor, or wall, covered with metal, multi-directional vents to allow the cooled or heated air into the room.

Mini-Split: It is somewhat of a hybrid of a window unit and a full unit for heating and cooling areas and allows you to control the temperatures in individual rooms or spaces. Mini-split systems have two main components—an outdoor compressor/condenser unit and an indoor air-handling unit (*evaporator*).

Window: A small unit placed in a window to heat and cool a small space. Always check the box recommendations for the square footage you want to cover.

Insulation Terminology

Insulation: The materials to help protect the interior space from outside elements like moisture and temperature; the material used to wrap electrical wires to prevent the current from being passed to and through other materials. Used in between walls, floors, attic spaces or attic ceiling, under subfloors, around windows and doors, and wrap plumbing pipes and water heaters.

- **Roll Batten:** Fiberglass packed, different densities for different protection levels with a thick paper backing. It is installed between exterior wall studs and ceiling joists (*attic side*). Attached with staples if there is a paper backing or cut and placed to the desired length if there is no paper backing.

- **Blown-In:** Tiny fiberglass bits in different densities for different levels of protection, blown into the spaces between wall studs and ceiling joists. If used between wall studs, a mesh is stapled to the studs, cut back around outlets, and a hose is inserted at the top of the wall while the insulation fills the space using a machine. Blocks of insulation are fed into the machine, broken up, and blown through a large tube.

- **Foam:** A liquid foam that expands and hardens once it hits the air. Foam comes in different densities for different levels of protection.
    - **Open-Cell:** Soft foam sprayed in a thin layer quickly fills up with tiny air holes to expand up to ten times its original size.
    - **Closed-Cell:** A more rigid foam with some tiny air holes to none, allowing no air to pass through. This application is usually in metal buildings and roofs.

- **Sheet:** A sheet of Styrofoam 1/4"–1" thick. It can be cut to the desired size and offered in various densities for different levels of protection.

Zone	2x4 walls	2x6 walls	Attic	Floors	Crawlspaces
7	R13 – R15	R19 – R21	R49 – R60	R25 – R30	R25 – R30
6	R13 – R15	R19 – R21	R49 – R60	R25 – R30	R25 – R30
5	R13 – R15	R19 – R21	R49 – R60	R25 – R30	R25 – R30
4	R13 – R15	R19 – R21	R49 – R60	R25 – R30	R25 – R30
3	R13 – R15	R19 – R21	R49 – R60	R25	R19 – R25
2	R13 – R15	R19 – R21	R30 – R49	R13	R13 – R19
1	R13 – R15	R19 – R21	R30 – R49	R13	R13

Plumbing Terminology

Plumbing: The pipes, tanks, fittings, and other apparatuses required for the water supply, heating, and sanitation in a building.

Rough-In: The series of piping, tanks, and connections under the structure, allow for drainage and supply lines to all necessary valve sets.

P-Trap: A U-shaped pipe that holds water, preventing odorous sewer gases from rising into the house. Regular water line use is required to ensure water stays in the trap's bottom. If the house is not in use, flush toilets and run faucets at least once a month. They are on every house's sink, shower, and tub.

Finish: The "pretty" fixture attached to the end of the supply or drain lines on sinks, sink fixtures, toilets, tubs, showers, and tub fixtures.

Cleanouts: A capped pipe attached to the sewer line to allow for cleaning out the debris. Found on the outside of the house along the line that leads out to the main public sewer line.

Water Heater: The tank of water that heats the water for all fixtures in the house.

Fixtures: (*faucets*) The finished valves for showers, tub, sinks

Valve Set: The piece of the water supply line where the flow of water is turned on and shut off. It will also mix the hot and cold-water lines coming to the supply line.

Drain: The point at which the water leaves the building through a series of pipes to the main drainage line

Toilets: Are seated fixtures mounted to the wall or floor to remove body waste from the home.

Shower Fixtures: Valve sets and spouts used inside the shower area.

Tub Fixtures: Any valve sets and spouts used for tubs.

Sink Faucets: The valve set and spout used for a sink. These are typically centered between the wall and the sink edge.

Shower Pans: The bottom flooring of the shower. Shower pans are molded from a solid surface, or a pan is made and then finished with a tile.

Curbs: The transition from the interior of the shower to the outside of the shower.

Tubs: For soaking and bathing while sitting down or reclining. The typical size is 60" long x 15" high x 30"–32" deep. However, there are many more sizes available. Be sure to check with your vendor if a larger tub is preferred.

- **Apron:** Will fit in between two walls or cabinets and have a molded front.
- **Decking:** The top rim of the tub, usually 2"–3" wide. The decking can be molded with the tub or built around any tub and surfaced with water-resistant materials (*tile or solid surface material matches the countertops*). If the decking is made around a tub, it is usually 12" wide or more, depending on the preference.
- **Overflow:** The built-in "drain" for any tub, toward the top rim of the tub. It is built into the tub to help drain it if the water level is too high. This keeps the tub from overflowing.
- **Drop-in:** The tub will have a deck built around it and "dropped" into the decking with the top flange overlay on top.
- **Garden tub:** A large soaking tub that can be jetted or non-jetted. It can be a drop-in or an apron tub.
- **Freestanding:** The tub will stand alone, away from the wall, with all sides exposed.
  - **Clawfoot:** Will have feet at the bottom of the tub.
  - **Pedestal:** Sits on top of a solid base.

Sinks: Bowls that hold water for kitchens, bathrooms, outdoor kitchens, and laundry rooms. They come in various sizes, shapes, materials, and colors. For example, a typical bath vanity size is 16″–20″ wide x 5″ deep. Standard dimensions for a kitchen sink are 30″–36″ wide by 8″–12″ deep.

Styles:

- **Drop-in:** The bowl mounted on top of the countertop.
    - **Undermount:** Mounted under the countertop with silicone and flanges. Used only on solid surface countertops.
    - **Vessel Bowl:** A single basin sink sitting on the countertop.
    - **Pedestal:** Single basin sink attached to the wall with a column-type base.
    - **Wall-Mounted:** Is a single basin sink attached to the wall. The drain and supply lines are exposed.
    - *Apron* **(farm sink):** Large basin with a front that comes down the front of the cabinet.
    - **Single Basin:** No division inside the sink.
    - **Double Basin:** Having two wells inside the sink for water.
        - **70/30:** Divided into 70% and 30% of the sink.
        - **60/40:** Divided into 60% and 40% of the sink.
    - **Bar:** Smaller, single basin used on a bar for rinsing—12″–18″ wide.
    - **Utility/Laundry:** Large, deep, single basin used to soak clothes and sheets.

Materials:

- **Stainless Steel:** *(most used)* A family of iron alloys that contain Chromium composition that helps prevent the rusting of the iron elements. It may also have metals such as Nickel and Molybdenum to help prevent corrosion and increase integrity. The lower the gauge of stainless steel, the thicker the steel. For instance, 18 gauge is thicker than 20 gauge.
    - **Applications:** *under-mount, drop-in, apron*
- **Porcelain:** Is cast from China clay and a silicate material into a solid form. It is then coated with a hard-shell glaze to prevent moisture from entering the porcelain. It chips easily when heavy pots are dropped on it and can scratch over time.
    - *Applications: drop-in and apron*
- **Quartz:** Cast from a quartzite, sand, and colorant mixture to form a solid sink. Non-porous and hard to scratch.
    - **Applications:** *under-mount, drop-in, apron*
- **Stone:** Natural stone formed and honed into a solid sink. Non-porous and durable. It may scratch easily.
- **Copper:** This can be either pure copper or mixed with other elements to offer a long-lasting finish and resists rust and/or corrosion. It may scratch easily.

Electrical Terminology

Electrical: The power supply for any structure.

- **Panel:** An electrical panel is also called a *load center*. It is a metal electrical service box that accepts the home's main power and distributes electrical current through various circuits and fixtures within the house.
- **Gang:** The box inside the wall that houses the wires for the switches and outlets; available in 2" deep to shallow boxes of 1" and ½" deep.
  - **Single gang:** Holds one switch or outlet.
  - **Double gang:** Contains two switches or outlets.
  - **Triple gang:** Contains three switches or outlets.
  - **Four gang:** Holds four switches or outlets.
  - **Pancake:** Shallow (1/2" deep), different sizes, round metal or plastic "box" used to hold the wires for lighting fixtures in either the ceiling or the wall for sconces.
- **Circuits:** Are located inside the panel with a dedicated area of the home wired directly into it. Each circuit can shut off individually for work in a room, or if there is an overload of power to that circuit, it will shut off automatically to prevent arching and possible fire.
- **Junction boxes:** Where all the wires from different rooms are joined in one location and connected to the primary panel.
- **Conduit:** The plastic or metal piping used to house electrical wire for protection also acts as a safety barrier.
- **Rough-in Electrical:** The installation of panels, circuits, wires, junction boxes, conduits, gang boxes, outlets, and switches.
- **Finish Electrical:** The installation of the light fixtures, fans, outlet and switch cover plates, and appliances. They should be tested with light bulbs when installed.
- **Outlet:** Power source where outside appliances, large to small, are plugged.
  - **Duplex:** Standard outlet with three-prong input available for both inputs.
  - **GFCI:** (*Ground Fault Circuit Interrupter*) Outlet with shut-off and reset capability, usually installed in all wet areas of the house, such as kitchens, baths, and outdoor kitchens. Usually, only one GFCI is required in each room.
  - **Appliance:** Each appliance will sometimes require a specific outlet type. Look up the owner's manual for your model to ensure you purchase the right cord and install the correct outlet.
- **Switches:** Manually operated circuit breaker to turn on lights and outlets.

- **Single pole:** Operates only one fixture.
- **Three-way:** Gives the ability to turn on and off lights from two different places. Three-way switches can control one fixture or a series of fixtures.
- **Four-way:** Gives the ability to turn on and off lights from three different locations but only controlling one light or a set of lights (*recessed or pendant*).
- **Dimmer:** Gives the ability to control the amount of light coming from the light fixture from dim to bright.
- **Three Function:** (*Multi-function*) Used to control a fixture. Example: heaters, vents, and lights for bathrooms.

- **Lighting:**
  - **Recessed lights:** Mounted inside the ceiling to be flush with the surface of the ceiling. The recessed light consists of a housing (*inside the ceiling or attic space*), the light kit (*inside the housing*), and the beauty ring (*the trim kit on the outside flush to the ceiling*).
  - **Flush mount lights:** Mounted to the ceiling or wall without hanging from a down rod or chain.
  - **Pendant lights:** Lights hanging from the ceiling with a down rod or a chain.
  - **Wall-mounted:** Mounted to the wall.
    - **Vanity lights:** Lights made to hang over the bathroom sink area.
    - **Sconce lights:** smaller lights, usually in hallways and/or on either side of the mirrors for and vanity mirror or an art piece. The patio will also have sconce lighting.
  - **Security:** A bright light outside the house, with either a motion detector, direct switch, or both, to light up an area at night to deter trespassers.
  - **Utility:** Bright lighting in areas that require a lot of light to work, like kitchens, workshops, sheds, and laundry rooms.
  - **Soffit:** Small, 4" recessed lights in the soffit to light up the house's exterior.
  - **Undermount:** Mounted under cabinets and/or shelves to give light to countertops. If hard-wired into the wall, it may be switched to a dedicated dimmer switch.
  - **Landscape:** Solar or hardwired lights in steps or posts or along pathways, gardens, trees, or specific areas.

Drywall Terminology

Drywall Sheets: Boards made from a mixture of plaster, wood pulp, and/or other materials used on the interior facing of the walls and ceilings of a home or different structure.

Standard Drywall: Is used inside the home (standard drywall sheets). Drywall offers insulation and a small sound barrier. The most common sizes are ½", and ¼" ½" is generally used in new construction.

Seams: Where two sheets of drywall meet. They should be butted up against each other.

Tape: A paper or fiber strip used to cover the drywall's seam to give it a smooth appearance and seal the drywall once the mud is applied.

Mud: The joint compound used to attach the tape to the drywall and smooth out the drywall's seams to prep it for paint or wallpaper. It also gives texture to a wall or ceiling surface.

Floating: Uses the mud to smooth out seams and cover screw heads and/or other small drywall blemishes. Standard floating will require more than one coat or "pass." Each pass is floated, sanded, and then floated and sanded. Use a finer sandpaper grit with each sanding to get a smoother finish. After floating is complete, the walls should have the first coat of primer to show any blemishes in the mudding. Another floating may be done before painting if necessary.

- **Wallpaper:** May only require one pass if floated correctly and is smooth after sanding so that no bumps or bubbling occurs under wallpaper.

Skim: A light coat of mud to remove roughness or texture.

Texturing: An application of drywall mud on the entire surface of the drywall to hide flaws or as part of the design (*usually on ceilings*).

Patching: (any blemishes or holes in drywall) Having the damaged drywall replaced, taped, and floated. The drywall will be cut back to the nearest stud to fasten to the stud (*to make sure it does not bow out from the wall or ceiling*).

Abatement: The removal of the top layer of surface material. If a wall or ceiling is not the desired texture, it can be removed and smoothed out. In the drywall standards, this is usually referred to when discussing popcorn ceilings. The popcorn texture is abated, and a smooth surface is applied.

Painting and Staining Terminology

Painting: The color coating on the wall, ceiling, trim, doors, and windows.

Prime coat: Sealer put on the wall and ceiling to help the paint adhere to the surface.

- **Base:** If using acrylic paint on drywall, use an acrylic primer. When using oil-based paint for trim, use an oil-based primer. DO NOT use an oil base on top of a water-based one; it will bubble and need to be sanded and recoated.

- **Color:** If covering a dark color with lighter paint, use a grey primer (*tinted light or dark, depending on the paint color*). If covering a light color with light or dark color, use a white primer.

- **Base Coat:** The first coat of paint applied to the wall or ceiling.

- **Topcoat:** The final coat of paint.

- **Sheens:** The amount of shine the paint finish will have.

    - **Flat:** no shine at all, hard to clean any smudges or marks
    - **Eggshell:** very low shine, easy to clean
    - **Satin:** very low shine, easy to clean
    - **Semi-gloss:** somewhat of a shine
    - **Gloss:** very high shine, easy to clean

- **Base:** The makeup of the paint.

    - **Acrylic:** A water-based, not as hard of a shell on the final coat.
    - **Oil:** Oil-based, has a hard shell when cured after seven days.

- **Faux Finish:** The painting technique used to create a desired finish to the surface. For example, to mimic stone, simple glazing, or "age" wood. It usually requires a trained tradesman and several layers of paint and top coating.

- **Clear-Coat:** Apply a clear sealer, allowing the surface color to come through. It will darken the color slightly. Sealers come in different sheens, flat to glossy.

- **Saturation:** The depth of color in the paint.

- **Flashing:** The noticeable difference in the sheen in a particular spot, usually when a touch-up is done in higher sheens. The higher the gloss, the more prominent the flashing will be. The entire area will need painting to make the flashing disappear.

- **Holidays:** An area where the paint did not take to the primer. The primer coat will be slightly visible through the first coat of paint. It can occur because of many reasons. An additional coat of paint will remedy the holidays.

Standard Sheens & Bases		
Sheen	**Area**	**Base**
Flat	Ceilings	Latex
Eggshell	Walls: *Bed, Bath, Kitchen, Living, Dining, Laundry & Hallways*	Latex
Satin	Walls: *Bed, Bath, Kitchen, Living, Dining, Laundry & Hallways*	Latex
Semi-Gloss	Trim Work, Doors, Windows, Cabinetry	Oil-Based
Glossy	Rarely used: furniture for the lacquered look	Oil-Based

Staining Terminology: A colorant is added to the wood surface to either change or enhance its natural color. A topcoat or sealer is typically applied to protect and seal the wood. It is NOT necessary in all cases to apply a sealer when used for an interior application in a conditioned area.

- **Wiping:** (liquid) A rag is dipped into the can of stain and wiped on the wood. The more layers of stain applied, the darker the stain. Apply a topcoat sealer after the stain dries.

- **Penetrating:** (liquid) Used on interior woods previously stained and/or stripped and for very dense woods like oak and mahogany, making it harder for the color to "take" to the wood. Apply by using a rag or brush to the wood surface, then wipe clean after sitting for as long as you like. The longer it sits on the wood, the darker the stain will be. Repeat this process several times to achieve the desired color.

- **Brushed:** (liquid) Very watery in the can. Apply using a brush or roller to the wood very liberally and use a rag to wipe off the excess stain. The longer the colorant sits on the wood, the darker it will be. It may require several coats. A topcoat sealer will be applied when dried.

- **Gel:** (thick gel) Use a rag or brush to apply on the wood. The longer the stain is on the wood, the darker it will be. It may be used on fiberglass with a topcoat applied when dried.

- **Sealing:** A clear coat used to seal wood and paint, typically used on stained or natural woods.

    - **Wax coat:** For use on wood only. An applied wax that seals the wood makes it moisture resistant and conditions the wood—offered in different sheens of matte and satin.

    - **Clear Coat:** Is used for wood. Epoxy or polyurethane, either oil-based or water-based, seals the wood, giving protection and giving depth to the wood's color with or without stain.

    - **Sheens:** the amount of shine on the finished coat

        - **Natural:** little to no shine in the finish topcoat
        - **Satin:** a minimal amount of shine to the finish topcoat
        - **Semi-gloss:** a small amount of shine to the finish topcoat
        - **Gloss:** high shine to the finish topcoat

    - **Interior uses:** Trim, furniture, and doors. If the wood is in an area that will receive a lot of abuse (*foot traffic, bumping into*), use an oil-based clear coat and apply several coats. It forms a thicker and harder topcoat for protection. However, an oil-based clear coat may "yellow" over time, especially if exposed to sunlight.

    - **Exterior uses:** Use specialty coats to stand up to rain, snow, exposure to sunlight, and temperature differences.

Trim and/or Finish Carpentry Terminology

Trim/Finish Carpentry: The finishing carpentry touches of any construction job.

- **Trim:** Is installing any moldings for walls, ceilings, doors, windows, cabinets, stairs, and flooring.
  - **Crown:** Is the molding used to trim the wall to the ceiling. Many different styles and sizes are either painted or stained.
  - **Step Crown:** Uses multiple moldings to create a large molding with a look and style. Many different styles and sizes are applied in steps or layers. In addition, it may be painted or stained.
  - **Transitions:** The molding installed between two different types of flooring or where the flooring changes direction. Transitions are generally at a doorway or wall opening.
  - **Baseboard:** The molding used to trim out the wall to the floor. Available in many different styles and sizes. It may be painted or stained.
  - **Shoe:** The molding used to trim out the baseboard to the flooring. Many different styles and sizes, either shoe base (*it is taller than it is wide at its base*) or ¾ round (*3/4 of a full circle in shape*). It may be painted or stained.
  - **Casings:** Molding used around openings between rooms. Many different styles and sizes. It may be painted or stained.
  - **Paneled:** The molding used to divide a wall, section of a wall, or ceiling into square or rectangular sections. A single molding or multiple moldings gives different looks and styles, depending on the desired effect.
  - **Door:** The molding on two sides and the top of the door frame on both sides of the door. Many different styles and sizes. It may be painted or stained.
  - **Window:** The molding on both sides, top, and bottom of the window. The window may have a sill (*a flat "shelf"*) at the bottom and the **apron** molding under the sill. It can also have no sill, and the molding will look more like a picture framing. Available in many different styles and sizes. It may be painted or stained.
- **Bath Accessories:** Wall-mounted hooks and hangers to hold bathroom essentials—a wide variety of styles and finishes.
  - **Toilet Paper Hanger:** Should be near the toilet, either wall-mounted or a freestanding stand.
  - **Towel bars:** Available in many sizes and finishes to hang drying towels.
  - **Towel rings:** Used for hand towels near sinks. Available in many styles and finishes.
  - **Towel warmers:** Wall-mounted, near the tub and/or shower. Available with temperature controls and timers.

- **Towel racks:** Freestanding or wall-mounted to hang drying towels.
- **Robe Hooks:** Available in many styles and finishes.
- **Shower Doors:** Glass doors that open and close to keep water in the shower. Available in many sizes and finishes. Standard dimensions may be ordered and installed with a 1"–2" variance. Other showers must be measured (*template*) and made especially for the space. Depending on the design, it will take anywhere from 2–4 weeks, sometimes longer.
  - **Pivot:** The door will swing on the hinges.
  - **By-pass:** Both panels of glass move side to side.
  - **Sliding:** One fixed panel and one moving panel (*side to side*).
  - **Framed:** The shower door and any panels framed with metal will include headers and thresholds.
  - **Frameless:** There is no framework around the glass except the hinges, wall brackets, and support headers.
- **Shower Rods:** Used to hold curtains and liners. Available in many sizes and finishes.
  - **Adjustable:** A tension rod that will adjust to the space provided.
  - **Fixed:** Screwed into the wall as a permanent fixture.
  - **Curved:** Rod is curved outward to allow more space for the liner and curtain, either adjustable or fixed.
- **Mirrors:** Comes in many shapes, sizes, and finishes. The vanity mirror size will depend on the height of the vanity light and the sink faucet. For vanities, the most common types of vanity mirrors are fixed, hanging, or medicine cabinets. Medicine cabinets can either be recessed or flush mounted to the wall.
- **Hardware:** Handles doors and drawers for opening and closing. Available in many sizes and finishes.
- **Countertops:** The finished top of the kitchen and bathroom's base cabinets. Many different materials and colors.
  - **Laminate:** A laminated product made of sheets adhered with heavy-duty glue to a base usually made of plywood.
  - **Granite:** Solid natural stone surface, honed to shine or a leathered finish, many different colors.
  - **Marble:** Solid natural stone surface, honed to a shine.
  - **Tile:** A tile of choice adhered to a concrete board surface.
- **Backsplashes:** The material mounted between the countertop and upper cabinet or just above the countertop in baths and kitchens.

Tile and Stonework Terminology

Tile Work: The installation of any tile on walls and floors. Tile consists of many different substances, such as porcelain, ceramic, glass, metal, natural stones (*marble, travertine, granite*), terra cotta, slate, or brick. The average thickness of a tile is 3/8" thick. However, it can run up to ½" thick depending on the size and material. Tiles are cut into specific shapes and sizes for different applications (*discussed below*). All tile needs a sub-structure to attach. For example, a structural wall with waterproofing backer materials, concrete, or a raised flooring structure that is prepared to accept tile.

Stonework: The application of brick, stones, and large pavers to walls and floors. Brick and/or stone are used to create walls and floors (usually exterior applications), whereas tile needs a sub-structure to attach. Brick and stone will be of varying sizes and thicknesses.

Tile Backer Materials: These are used to adhere tile to and ensure waterproofing behind the tile.

Hardi Backer Boards: This is a concrete board attached to the studs around the shower and overlaps the shower pan or tub flange lip using screws designed for the Hardi backer board.

Schluter Systems: Shower pans, a plastic Kerdi (*a thin orange sheet hung using mortar*), shower benches, and niche inserts. Kerdi needs to be applied with a thin-set mortar and allowed to dry.

Red Guard/Hydro Ban: A liquid vinyl rolled over the Hardi backer board, Kerdi, and shower pan to prevent leaks. Apply a thick layer with no gaps or open spots. It must be allowed to dry overnight before tiling.

Laticrete Hydro Board: Moldable shower pans, wallboards, and benches. It is screwed to the studs or drywall using screws designed for the Laticrete hydro board.

Laticrete Sealant: A caulk-like sealer to run along the seams and all screw heads of the hydro boards. Once the sealant is applied, it is ready to start setting the tiles—no wait times for drying.

Thin-Set: This is the concrete mix designed especially for tile setting. There are different types for different applications that vary in drying times. It is heat and moisture-resistant and can level out uneven areas. It is usually left to dry overnight before grouting.

- **White Modified Thin-Set:** Is always used with glass tiles.
- **Modified Thin-Set:** Has an additive to strengthen the bond of the tile to the wall and/or floor.
- **Non-Modified Thin-Set:** Has no additive and is generally used in drier areas.

Thin-set is generally applied about 3/8" thick. Each tile setter will have their own preferences, and each floor will require a certain type of setting depending on the floor level.

Tile Materials: Tiles are made in a variety of materials and sizes. Each material has a different porosity and various applications.

Marble: Very porous and soft. This natural stone is cut and honed (*polished*) to varying degrees of shine or leathered texture on the surface. The more honing a stone receives, the harder the surface becomes, making it less likely to stain. As a result, marble has a medium color variation with a softer "veining" throughout the stone.

- **Application:** It is usually used on a backsplash, shower walls, floors, and a room's main flooring. If the stone has a gloss, it is not ideal for a shower floor to walk on when wet and soapy. If the finish on the stone is NOT honed to the point of a high gloss and has a texture, it may be used on the shower floor. The most common application is as a countertop. It will scratch and be susceptible to heat exposure, damaging the top surface and requiring re-honing the surface like a countertop. Typically used in wet areas but not in high-heat areas.

Slate: A natural stone that is made of layers of stone stacked and pressed together. It has a high color variation and is a softer stone. Highly susceptible to chipping and cracking when exposed to temperature variations, heavy traffic, or hit.

- **Application:** Used on interior/ exterior main flooring in living areas, patios, walkways, and paths. If used on the interior, the slate will need sealing and resealing every 1–2 years, depending on floor use. It may be used in high-heat areas and is not typically used in wet locations unless sealed.

Terra Cotta: This is very porous but hard. It is a reddish-orange substrate with a glazed color or painted decorative surface. Highly susceptible to chipping and cracking when exposed to temperature variations. It may be used in high-heat areas and is not typically used in wet areas.

- **Application:** Is installed on floors in kitchens, bathrooms, living areas, patios, and walkways and applied to backsplashes for kitchen and bathroom vanities.

Travertine: Natural stone that is very porous and soft. Medium variation color. Highly susceptible to chipping and cracking. It may be used in high-heat areas and is not typically used in wet areas because it is porous.

- **Application:** Floors in living areas, kitchen, backsplashes, and patios. Backsplashes for kitchen and bathrooms.

Brick Paver: Man-made product, porous and very hard. Either cut from whole bricks or made to mimic bricks. Highly susceptible to chipping and cracking. It may be used in high-heat areas and is not typically used in wet areas because of being so porous.

- **Application:** Is installed on walls, backsplashes, and flooring in living areas, laundry, and bathrooms. It is an uneven surface and will need sealing for interior applications. Seal every 8–10 years or if yellowing takes place. It is installed in outdoor patios and walkways and NOT used in showers since it is so porous and needs so much upkeep with sealing.

Ceramic: Is dense and hard. Most ceramics are glazed with a color and/or decorative pattern. Highly susceptible to chipping and cracking. It may be used in high-heat areas and is typically used in wet areas.

- **Application:** Typically used in flooring for living areas, bedrooms, laundry, and bathrooms. It may be used for shower walls, vanity, and kitchen backsplashes if sealed.

Porcelain: Is very dense and hard. It is a man-made material with through-body color, meaning if the tile ever chips, the color below is the same as the surface and does not change its integrity. Some porcelain tiles' colors are only an inkjet image on the surface. If the tile is chipped, it will show much but does not interfere with its integrity. Not very susceptible to chipping or cracking. High variation in color and surface texture. They are used in wet areas mostly. It is used in high-heat areas as well.

- **Application:** Is installed in living areas, kitchens, bathrooms, shower walls, backsplashes, outdoor patios, walkways, and countertops.

Glass: Man-made, very hard, and dense. Least porous and usually has higher price points.

The backing of a glass tile may be painted, or the glass itself may be colored. Not very susceptible to chipping or cracking. High color and texture variation.

- **Application:** Typically used as wall tiles in showers or backsplashes.

Recycled Glass: The glass is melted, molded, and colored to mimic other materials, such as marble. It has a texture that is not slick. It is often molded into small mosaic tiles, but larger sizes are also options.

Tile Sizes*:*

- **Large:** 24"x48", 12"x24", 4"x48" or 36" plank, or 4" x 10".

    Application: Floors and some walls.

- **Square:** 36"x36", 32"x32", 24"x24", 20"x20", 18"x18", 16"x16", 12"x12", 6"x6", or 4"x4".

    Application: Floors, walls, and some backsplashes.

- **Mosaic:** 3"x3", 2"x2", 1"x1", ½"x½", or any combination of these sizes.

    Application: Shower wall accent, shower niches (*shampoo boxes*), shower floors, and backsplashes.

Tile Styles:

Chevron: Patterned where two tiles come to a point in a repeated pattern. Large to mosaic.

- **Application:** For walls, backsplashes, floors, shower walls, and shower niches (*shampoo boxes*).

Penny: Small ½"–1" round tiles (*approximately the size of a penny or a nickel*).

- **Application:** For shower walls and floors, backsplashes, and main flooring.

Picket: The straight thin tile with points at both ends (*to mimic a picket fence*). Large to mosaic.

- **Application:** For walls, shower walls, niches (*shampoo boxes*), and backsplashes.

Subway: 3"x6" tile, either a flat surface or beveled. Most people refer to rectangular tiles as subway tiles, but a true subway tile is a 3"x6" tile.

- **Application:** For shower walls, niches (*shampoo boxes*), and backsplashes.

Tile Bullnose: The same tile you use for the field, except one end has been rounded off and polished. Not all tiles have a bullnose option. You will need to check with the vendor to ensure it does. These tiles will come in a different size than the field tiles (usually 3x12 or 3x6, sometimes 2x12 or 2x6); they will be considerably more expensive than the field tile and will have to be ordered NOT by the square footage, but by the exact number you will need for edging.

Tile Pencil Trim: A decorative tile that has a finished edge. Not all tiles come with a pencil trim. Instead, you may pick a specific trim that is not in the "family " of the field tile but coordinates with it. Although these tiles will come in a different size than the field tiles (*usually 1x12 or 1x6, sometimes ½x12 or ½x6*), they will be considerably more expensive than the field tile and will have to be ordered NOT by the square footage, but by the exact number, you will need for edging.

Grouts and Sealers: Grouts come in various colors made of cement, mortar, and colorant. Once the tile is selected, select the grout color at that time.

Tile Patterns: Different designs will call for laying the tile in different patterns. The most common are as follows:

- **Straight bond:** All seams line up straight.
- **Staggered:** The seams are staggered either every other tile or every third tile.
- **Chevron:** Tiles are on a diagonal, with every other row going in the opposite direction to the row next to it. The tiles are cut at 45 degrees on each end to touch together, creating a point.
- **Diagonal:** The seams are laid on the diagonal to the room layout.
- **Herringbone:** the tiles are laid perpendicular to each other, either at a 45-degree angle or 90-degree angle.
- **Diagonal:** the tiles are set at a 45-degree angle to the room.

Flooring Terminology

Wood:

- **Real wood:** Milled to the desired thickness and width in many wood species.
- **Engineered:** Layered wood compressed in the desired thickness and width. The top layer is solid wood, and the lower layers of a composite of different woods layered in different directions giving the board strength. It resists warping.
- **Laminate:** A synthetic product laminated together is a desired thickness and width colored and patterned to mimic real wood. It resists warping and scratching.
  - **Installations for wood, engineered or laminate:**
    - **Glue Down:** Glued straight to concrete or subflooring of plywood.
    - **Nail Down:** Nailed to a subflooring of plywood.
    - **Floating:** Clicked together with tabs and grooves on the planks' sides to create a solid floor that does not adhere to the concrete or subfloor. Use padding under this flooring. The padding can be sound-absorbing, cushioning, and/or water-resistant.

Vinyl: Synthetic plastic sheets and tiles in different styles, textures, and colors.

- **Sheet:** Cut to length and comes in 12' and 15' widths. It can be glued down or applied as a floating floor.
- **Plank:** Cut into planks in 4' and 3' lengths or 4"–6" wide planks. Available in glue-down or click-lock floating applications.
- **Tiles:** Cut into 12"x12", 12"x24" tiles that glue down.

Concrete: A smoothed-out slab that can be either sealed in its natural color, stained or painted, and then sealed.

Epoxy: A specific surface coating that can be colored or have colored flakes added to the mixture that will seal the concrete. Moisture-resistant, chemical-resistant, and stain-resistant.

Paver: Bricks cut into thin tiles to be applied like tiles with mortar for adhesion and grout.

Carpet: Tightly woven threads in many colors, textures, and materials; 12' and 15' widths cut to desired lengths.

Tile Work: The installation of any tile on walls and floors. Tile contains many different substances, such as porcelain, ceramic, glass, metal, natural stones (*marble, travertine, granite, etc.*), terra cotta, slate, or brick. The average thickness of a tile is 3/8" thick. However, it can run up to ½" thick depending on the size and material. Tiles are cut into specific shapes and sizes and used for different applications. All tile needs a substructure to attach. For example, a structural wall with waterproofing backer materials, concrete, or raised flooring structure is prepared to accept the tile.

Cabinetry Terminology

Cabinetry:

- **Base:** The lower cabinets attached to the wall.
- **Upper:** The wall cabinets attached to the wall above the base cabinets.
- **Island:** Freestanding base cabinets not attached to any walls
- **Peninsula:** A freestanding base cabinet attached to perimeter wall cabinets on one side only.
- **Pantry:** A full-height unit from floor to ceiling with either pullout shelves, drawers, or adjustable shelves.
- **Full:** The same as a pantry unit with different purpose storage.
- **Shelves:** Inside the cabinet to stack items.
    - **Roll Out:** Has slides allowing it to be pulled out and pushed into the cabinet. It will have small sides, so items do not fall off while in motion.
    - **Fixed:** The shelf is fixed into the cabinet.
    - **Adjustable:** Holes cut into the side of the cabinet interior and shelf pins placed into the holes, allowing the shelf to be placed in any setting and moved later.
- **Shelf Pins:** The pins are in the holes on the side of the cabinet that holds the shelf in place.
- **Hinges:** Allows the door to swing open and closed.
    - **Self-Closing:** At a certain point in the pivot of the door, the hinges will pull the door closed.
    - **Soft Closing:** At a certain point in the pivot, the hinge will offer a slight resistance to close the door gently without slamming.
    - **Standard:** Allows the door to pivot with no resistance.
- **Bumpers:** Clear plastic bumpers stuck to the back of drawers or doors so they do not slam against the cabinet's face frame.
- **Slides:** The drawer's mechanism allows it to slide open and return to the cabinet.
    - **Self-Closing:** At a certain point in the drawer's return into the cabinet, the slides will pause the closure and softly pull the drawer into the cabinet.
    - **Soft Closing:** At a certain point when closing the drawers, the slide will offer resistance and close softly with no slamming.
    - **Standard:** Opens and closes the drawers with no resistance. It allows the drawer front's slamming, which can damage the cabinet's drawer front or face.

- **Hardware:** The pulls or knobs used to open and close the doors and drawers.
  - **Pulls:** A handle in various lengths: 3", 5", 7", 10", and up, with two screw holes.
  - **Knobs:** A round or square piece. One screw hole.
- **Frameless:** The cabinet box will show no face frame because the doors and drawer fronts will cover the entire face frame.
- **Framed:** (traditional) The cabinet front will have a face frame made of stiles and rails for the doors and drawer fronts to rest on; the frame will show.
- **Face Frame:** The front of the cabinet that shows behind the doors and drawer fronts, with cutouts for doors and drawers.
- **Stile:** The vertical part of the face frame.
- **Railing:** The horizontal part of the face frame.
- **Overlay:** The doors and the drawer fronts rest on the face frame.
- **Full Overlay:** The doors and the drawer fronts will cover the face frame.
- **Inset:** The doors and drawer fronts are flush inside the face frame.

Countertops Terminology and Standards

Countertops:

Fabricators: The vendors with the equipment to cut the solid surface slab to fit the countertops, including the cutouts for appliances, sinks, and polished edging. Most fabricators will sell solid surface material (*natural stones, Quartz, Silestone*).

Wholesalers: These vendors sell slabs of stone. They do not fabricate the stone. You will have to find a fabricator of your own. They will, however, deliver the slab to the fabricators for you.

Solid Surface: A slab of solid material, man-made or natural stone. 2cm–3cm in thickness. It has different ratings in tiers 1–3 and exotic.

- *Tier* 1: speckling in color
- *Tier* 2: less speckling and some veining
- *Tier* 3: more veining with slight speckling
- *Exotic:* mostly veining, not as commonly found as the tier 1–3 stones
- **Materials**:
    - **Granite:** Natural slab from a quarry. Wide range of colors and styles. Very dense. Resistant to moisture, heat, and light changes the stone's integrity. They are used for interior and exterior uses.
    - **Soapstone:** A natural stone from a quarry. NO speckling. Wide range of colors and styles. It is a soft stone that is susceptible to showing scratches. It is resistant to moisture, heat, and light, changing the integrity of the stone. They are for interior use.
    - **Marble:** Natural slab from a quarry. NO speckling. Wide range of colors and styles. It is a soft stone that is susceptible to showing scratches. It is resistant to moisture, heat, and light, changing the integrity of the stone. They are used for interior and exterior uses.
    - **Dolomite:** A mix of granite and marble. Natural slab from a quarry in a variety of colors and styles.
    - **Quartz and Silestone:** A man-made slab manufactured to imitate stones. It is EXTREMELY dense and will not scratch or crack easily. Completely moisture resistant and heat resistant. However, repeated exposure to heat daily in the same spot will, over time, change the stone's color to a yellowish color. It will yellow in direct sunlight if outside every day. They are not for exterior uses. HONED finish only.
- **Finishes**:
    - **Honed:** Polished to a shiny, slick surface. It creates a seal for the stone.
    - **Leathered:** The honing is not as deep and leaves the surface with a slightly bumpy surface and matte finish. It feels like a piece of leather. It will give the same stone a difference in color.
    - **Matte:** Honed to a smooth surface that is not shiny at all.

- **Edging:** The edge styles of the countertop are finished in many ways. The customer will choose their preference. The following are the most common types.
  - **Bullnose:** rounded over
  - **Eased:** the corners are softened but remain "squared."
  - **Beveled:** is an angle cut to the edge and straight down
  - **Ogee:** curved cut put into the edge
  - **Chiseled:** rough cut, jagged/unpolished

Wood: Painted or stained with MULTIPLE coats of the clear coat or wax finish.

Concrete: Formed up and concrete poured, sanded down, and refinished multiple times to achieve a smooth surface.

Laminate: A man-made sheet in varying colors and styles applied to a plywood base with glue—moisture resistant. Do NOT put hot pans and pots on the surface; it will cause the laminate to separate from the plywood base, bubble, and eventually crack. If moisture gets through the crack, it will delaminate the plywood base.

Backsplashes: This is the covering on the wall between the countertop and the underside of the wall cabinet. The backsplash may go from the top of the countertop to the ceiling or the ceiling trim to create a more dramatic effect. Backsplashes are a place to get creative. Depending on the desired result, it can become a feature or blend into the background.

The Value of Your Project:

The value will depend on the purpose of your project and how much you want to put into it. Here we will discuss the difference between your project being your forever home or an investment property that you either resell or rent out.

Forever Home: This is the home you do not plan to move out of until you either go to the nursing home or die! The materials you use in this home will typically be items you want to last a long time and be of the highest quality. They will improve your lifestyle quality as you live in the home and give you the most pleasure. The items you will spend the most money on will be:

- Countertops
- Plumbing faucets
- Light fixtures
- Doors and windows
- Flooring
- Tiled showers
- Glass for shower doors
- Appliances
- Roofing
- Hardware

Investment (Flip House) or Rental: This is a house you may see as an opportunity to update the inside and outside, then sell or rent out to a tenant for a profit. These can be tricky to invest in, but they can be worth your time and investment with the right preparation. The property could have also been an inheritance you may need to sell. You will want quality products on a mid-level budget to increase the possible profit. Your colors and choice of fixtures should be as neutral and mainstream as possible to appeal to a larger pool of buyers. The areas to concentrate on are:

- **Kitchens**:
  - **Countertops:** Tier 1 granite with a subway tile backsplash. A timeless look at a modest cost.
  - **Cabinets:** Consider painting existing cabinets a white or soft gray to remain neutral but have a fresh look.
  - **New Hardware:** Stainless steel or satin nickel will have a neutral effect but a fresh look.
- **Bathrooms:**
  - **Shower/Tub Walls:** Subway tiled shower walls. At least one bath (usually the hall bath) with a tub.
  - **Countertops:** Tier 1 granite with matching 6" backsplash.
  - **Sinks:** Oval white under-mount; this is a clean and fresh look.
  - **Faucets:** Stain nickel, single handle.
- **Flooring:** Install a "wood" laminate, vinyl click lock, or porcelain tile throughout the house. Neutral in coloring. Carpet only in the bedrooms, if at all.

NOTE: For rental properties, you will need to replace items regularly, so consider using durable products. This consideration will apply to floor products, especially.

Section 3: Your Role

Your Role as the Contractor:

The first thing necessary to begin your project as your own contractor is to have a clear vision of what you want from your project. Knowing how you will use the space you are creating for yourself and your family and the added benefit to your lifestyle will need to be kept in mind throughout the process. Remember that this is your home and sanctuary. You are calling the shots, hiring the tradesmen, and hand-selecting the products going into your home.

Set your expectations with each tradesman of how you and your home will be treated and handled. You will be creating the schedule of work to be done. Communication will be invaluable and essential to keeping everyone in the loop and the progress going. There will need to be daily checks on progress, the arrival of products, and updates on all changes.

Do not be intimidated by setbacks or changes needed to complete your project. When planning out your process, try to make a contingency plan for if a product does not arrive on time, the weather prevents work from being done, or a tradesman must reschedule. You may have to wait for the work to be completed before moving on to the next phase of work. For instance, install the countertops before the sinks and faucets.

In the following chapters, we will discuss and walk you through the entire process in depth and in more detail. There is a supplemental manual for Renovation Language to study along with this course. It breaks down into sections according to the different task categories. Study along with the Chapters to deepen your understanding of construction, how it works, and what to look for as you complete work. You can study the entire manual or the sections that apply to your project. This course will help bridge the communication between you, your tradesmen, and vendors and give you the knowledge to move forward in your renovation with confidence in a job well done.

Chapter 2: Plans - Concepts & Drawings
Section 1: Understanding your Space

As mentioned in Chapter 1, the value of your project is important to know, and we will dig a little deeper here to understand your space. Defining the Purpose of the Space is vital to staying on task throughout the build. The following are different reasons for remodeling or building new homes. The purpose will dictate the Budget to a degree. It will affect the decisions you make in space planning, aesthetic designs, and where to invest your money to achieve the optimum result.

Investment Properties: These homes are purchased to either rent out or renovate and sell for profit.
- *Rentals* - you may choose materials that can hold up better to much heavier traffic, knowing that multiple families will be using the house that is not their own. Also, the color pallets for all your surface finishes will be much more neutral to appeal to the masses.
    - Most commonly replace items:
        - Cabinets
        - Flooring
        - Countertops
        - Showers, tubs, and toilets
        - Painting and repairing walls
- *Flips* - you may choose materials that are priced in the lower to mid-range to maximize the profit margin when you sell the house after renovating. Again, your color pallets for your surfaces will remain neutral to appeal to the masses. However, you may spend a little more on countertops and flooring to get multiple offers. Again, these will be items potential buyers don't want to spend additional money on after buying the house.
    - Most resurfaced rooms
        - Kitchen - cabinets and countertops
        - Bathrooms - showers, vanities, and countertops
        - Living areas - paint & flooring
    - Color & Décor
        - Modern look to appeal to as many potential buyers
        - Clean neutral walls; keep the space clean and airy looking
        - Window treatments are optional; again, don't be too bold with these
        - Using contrasting colors in the right places can make a big impact
            - Accent walls
            - Backsplashes

Forever Home: this is the home you plan to leave only when you no longer have a choice, either by God or your kids! You will spend more money on the materials to last you a long time and plan it completely to fit your lifestyle and needs. Your floor plan color choices will reflect your style and personality.

- Surfaces Selection - you now have to wait until the kids have moved out or have inherited the family home that has not been touched in the last few decades. Certain components of the house, like cabinetry, flooring, and countertops, may be past their time of usefulness and need replacing.
    - Most updated spaces
        - Kitchens - cabinets, countertops, layout, flooring, and lighting
        - Bathrooms - showers, cabinets, countertops, layout, and lighting
        - Living areas - flooring, painting, lighting
        - Life changes: now that you have reached a certain point in your life, you use your house differently than you have before. Several reasons for this could be working from home vs. an office, having more kids, kids have moved out, and you entertain more (or less), parents have moved in, wanting to rent out a section of the house for additional income.
    - Most repurposed spaces
        - Kitchens - cabinets, countertops, layout
        - Bathrooms - cabinets, countertops, layout, or additional bathrooms needed
        - Additional bedrooms, bathrooms, and patios
- Color & Décor - this is your chance to shine
    - Paint colors that reflect your personality and make a happy space for you
    - Upgrade to more durable long-term surfaces
        - Countertops
        - Shower tile
        - Flooring
        - Cabinetry
        - Hardware
        - Wallpaper accents
        - Lighting

Special needs: you or someone in the house may have special needs that dictate replacing tubs with walk-in showers or pedestal sinks vs. a cabinet base sink.
- Most altered rooms
    - Bathrooms - showers, vanities, and amount of space.
    - Bedrooms - create more space and flooring
- Space Design is most important!
    - Need to meet ADA requirements
    - Wheelchair accessibility
        - Bathroom Vanities
        - Showers and tubs - room to get in easily on your own or with a caretaker
        - Kitchen cooking - this could be as easy as rearranging the contents of the cabinets to be more accessible. Some surfaces may need to be lowered or adjusted.
        - Doorways throughout the house will need to accommodate walkers and wheelchairs. You may have to replace the flooring and doorways so wheelchairs or walkers can be used.
- Surface Selection
    - You will be more likely to choose materials that can stand up to abuse because of the possibility of being hit by wheelchairs or walkers and the likelihood of having an additional caretaker in the home.
    - You may also have to use harsher cleaning chemicals because of health issues.
    - Floors may need to be changed to eliminate transitions

Whatever you define as your purpose for your space, write it down and keep it somewhere for future reference. As you plan your project, it can be quite easy to get lost in some details and lose sight of why this all started. By reminding yourself of the purpose often, you will make better decisions on the floor plan and the materials you use in the space. It will also help when there is a sacrifice to make in the floor plan or materials. Another thought for you to consider is that if more people see the space, you tend to use prettier surfaces and fixtures, and if more people use the space, you will also choose more durable products.
Keep in mind the following when defining the purpose of the project

How much do you want to allocate to the project?

What value does the project give to your home?

What value does the project add to your lifestyle?

Is the project fulfilling a need? Or a desire to improve your lifestyle?

Section 2: Space Planning

If you are unsure if you need to hire a decorator, designer, architect, or draftsman, use these professionals' following descriptions to determine if your project will call for it.

In this section, we meet the **Pre-Construction Team**. They help take ideas and dream lists and turn them into drawings, designs, and budgets.

Designers and Decorators: Designers can be an enormous asset in planning a project. The designer will help you get your project together with a clear vision of the entire renovation and how it fits in with the rest of your home. The benefits of a designer are the following:

- Create the most use out of your space
- Pull together the look and flow of your space with the rest of your home
- Create the best look for what you want
- Help to understand the lighting in your space
- Choose everything from paint colors, lighting, cabinetry, hardware, door styles, adding beam work (*or other special features*), tile, window treatments, furniture, and placement of everything for the room itself and its function, including the furniture pieces.

The one thing most designers do NOT typically deal with is the structure. You will need a contractor, architect, or engineer to answer questions about load-bearing walls or moving the plumbing or electrical lines. Many designers will offer a 1-hour consultation if all you need is to pick out colors, place lighting, and create the desired effect of your space, ensuring you are going in the right direction. Each revision of plans is an additional cost.

Architects and Draftsman: To determine if you will need an architect or draftsman, use the following guidelines:

- Changing structural wall placement or eliminating any structural walls
- You are adding a room and/or roofing to the existing structure
- HOA requires an architect to do drawings
- You are adding a second story to the existing home, and you will need to submit a Plot plan to your HOA and CODES office.

All CAD drawings will follow CODES requirements. The software program has the standards for building any framing, roofing, plumbing, and electrical. If your HOA requires these drawings, you may be able to get them from a home design firm, a contractor, a draftsman, or an architectural firm. Different sets of drawings may be required, so check with your HOA to determine their specific needs. Architects and draftsmen will offer other packages of drafted plans from very basic overviews to detailed elevations from all angles with full foundation, framing, roofing, plumbing, electrical schedules, and layouts. The cost will go up for more complicated or more drawings needed. Talk to them about what you will need before beginning. Check around for architects and draftsmen who will consult you to determine your needs. Be clear with an architect or draftsmen on what you want because each revision is a new cost.

If you have determined that you will need professional drawings created, you will need to understand how to read drawings and floorplans created by architects, draftsmen, and designers. Being able to read your plans will assist in making a comprehensive materials list and will narrow your choices in your selections of contractors and vendors to use for your project.

Drawings of Your Project (*Floorplan*): This is the first step. All measurements, material lists, and work requirements are determined from the drafted plans. The most crucial part of beginning this undertaking is getting the drawings as detailed as possible and finalized for your renovation. You may use different avenues to get your drawings completed; architects, draftsmen companies, contractors, or you may choose to do your own drafted plans.

Different Types of Drawings: You may have two main types of floor plan drawings: **Hand Drafted** and **CAD** (*Computer Assisted Design*).

- **Hand Drafted** drawings use an architectural ruler, graph paper, and a pencil to draw your house plan.
- **CAD** drawings are created using architectural software. It can design both in 2D and 3D models. There are several available online applications that you can download and do your drawings. If you use an architect, they will provide you with whatever drafted plans you choose and include elevations and layouts. The cost of these will vary depending on the detail you want and the number of options you wish to have.

Components of drawings and Building plans

Full Floor Plan: Overview of the walls (*placement and measurements*), rooms, doors, and windows (*size and placement*), plumbing, electrical, and cabinetry placement. You will have to specify the type and measurements you wish to see.

Overview: 2D floor plan, "bird's eye" view of the space or home.

Elevation: the vertical perspective of a wall (interior or exterior) as if you are standing looking at the wall.

Layout: page of a building plan set to include 2D overviews, elevations, notes related to the project, and a specific Task, such as a plumbing layout, electrical layout, roofing layout, etc.

Scale: A drawing made using proportional measurements to represent the actual size of all objects on paper. A typical scale used in construction blueprints is every ¼ inch is equal to 1 foot (¼"=1'), or every ½ inch equals 1 foot (1/8"=1'). For inches, annotate using quotation marks (") and the apostrophe for feet ('). The scale used will be noted on the hand-drawn or CAD drawings.

Notes: this is a dialogue box on the page with specific notes and instructions pertaining to the project for the builder.

Specifications: this is a dialogue box listing the materials to be used and the quality of work to be expected.

No matter the source, you will need detailed drawings to include the following:

- **Wall Lengths:** measured to the ¼" to include interior and exterior walls.
- **Note Ceiling Heights:** You will need to calculate the square footage of drywall required and get a quote for the drywall hanging, floating, and painting labor.
- **Door Openings:** Correct size and placement. Measure the following:
    - The distance from the nearest wall to the opening of the door
    - The size of the door opening—from inside jamb to inside jamb
    - The height of the door—from the finished floor to the inside opening of the top header
- **Windows:** Correct size and placements. Measure the following:
    - The distance from the wall to the opening of the window
    - The size of the window opening—from inside jamb to inside jamb
    - The height of the window opening—from inside jamb to inside jamb.
    - The distance from the floor to the bottom sill of the window
- **Cabinet Placements and Sizes:** The usual locations will be the bathrooms, kitchen, and laundry—Mark all the bases, uppers, pantry units, islands, peninsulas, etc.
- **Room Labels:** Label each room, and annotate the house's front, driveway, and rear on the drafted plan. By marking the rooms accurately, kitchen, bathroom, bedrooms, living areas, laundry, garage, etc., you will quickly see the space's flow, and your design will make more sense.
- **Plumbing Placements:** For the sinks, tubs, showers, dishwashers, washing machines, water heaters, drains and vale sets, fridge water lines, pot fillers, etc.
- **Electrical Fixture Placements:** Lights, fans, switches, outlets, heat/light/vents, light/vents, can lights, all security lights, dryers, and appliances *(refrigerators, ovens and/or ranges, vent hoods, etc.)*.
- **Rooflines:** If you are adding any roofing, have at least one plan dedicated to the roof plans to include the pitch, measurements, ridge lengths, rafter lengths, soffit overhangs, and fascia sizes.
- **Notations:** Any special notes of placement of any electrical, plumbing, cabinetry, and/or demolition that may need special attention.

Floor Plan Symbols Framing & Electrical, Plumbing

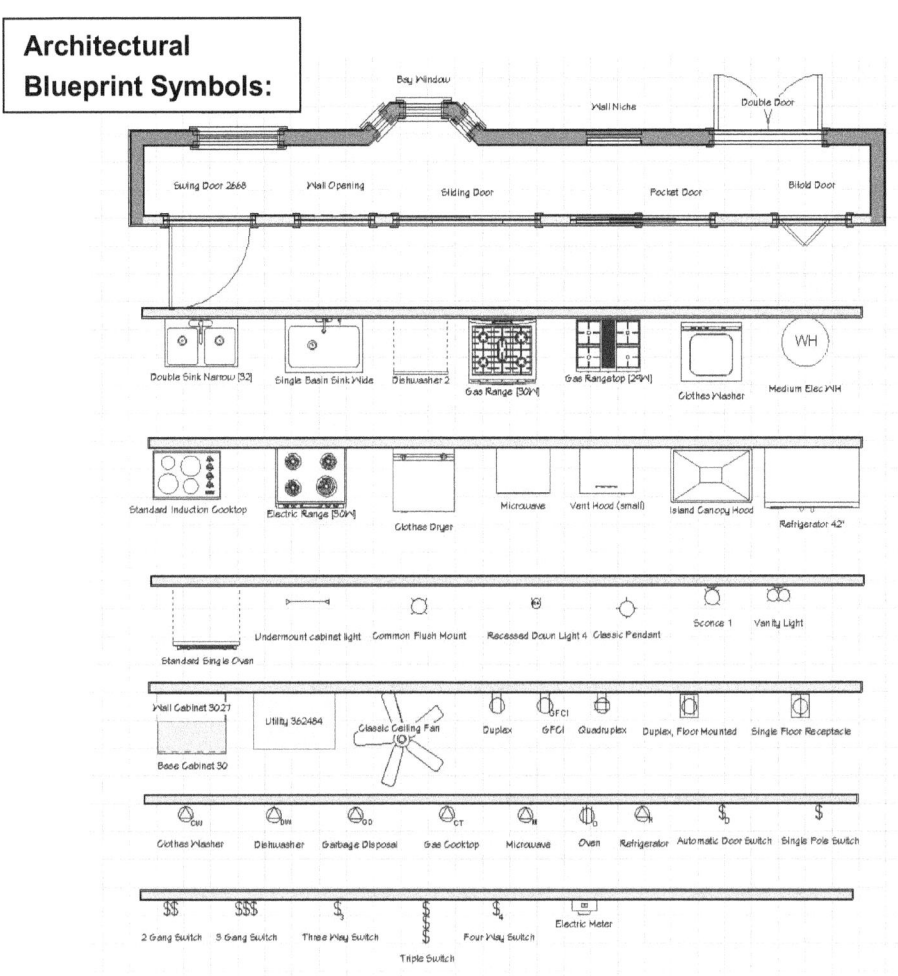

Full 2D Floor Plan

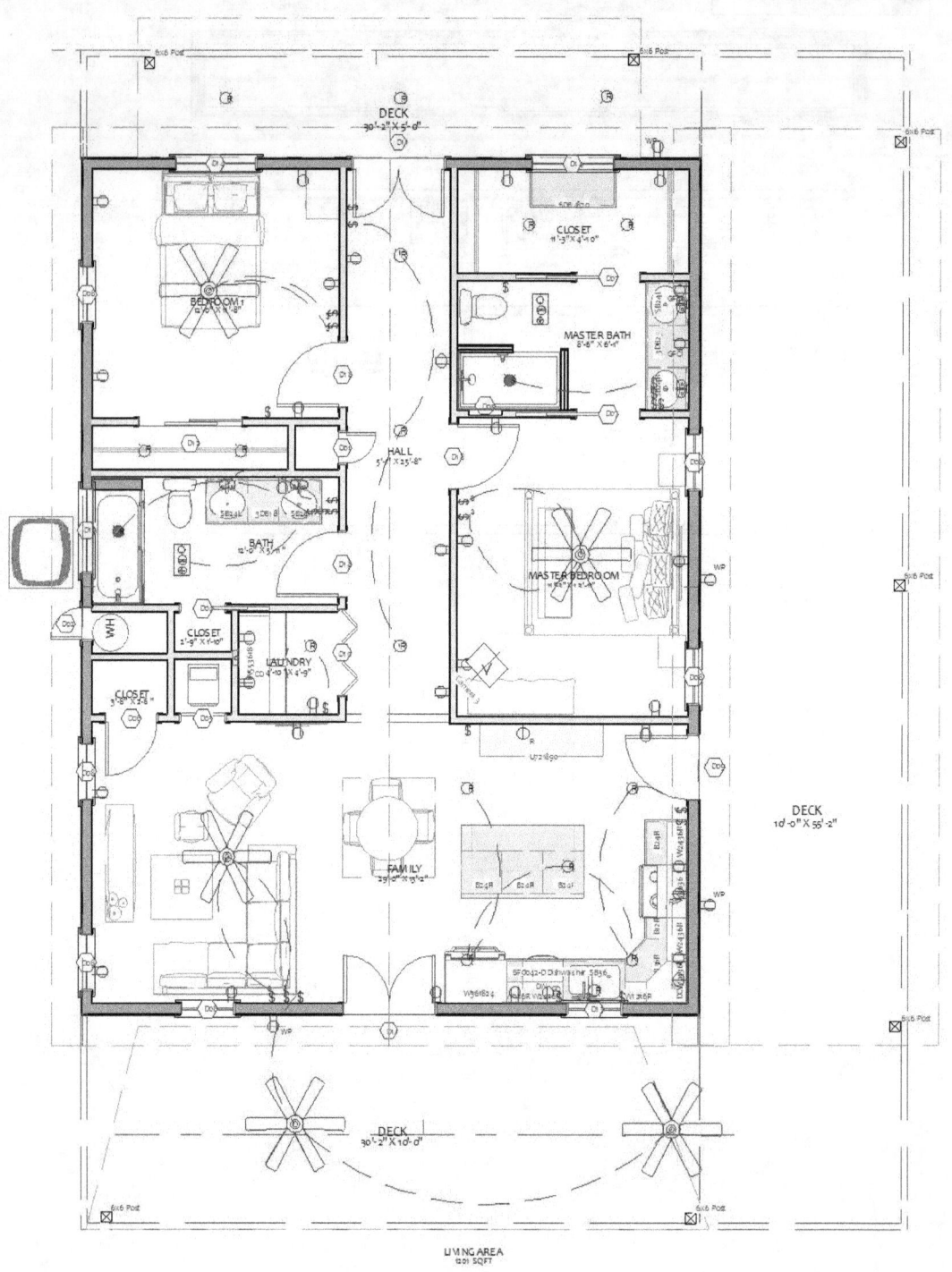

Layouts: Show a snapshot of a section from a plan for a specific task: framing, roofing, electrical, plumbing, cabinets, etc. They can include a 2D overview with measurements, schedules, elevations, and special notes for your project's construction.

Layouts: Electrical

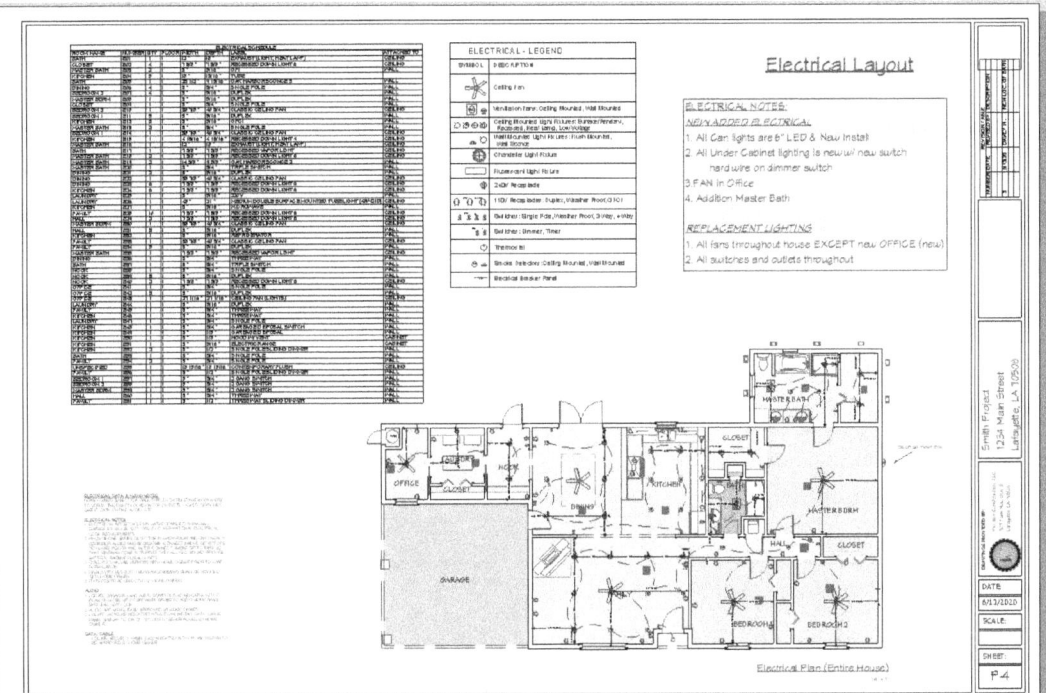

Layouts: Plumbing

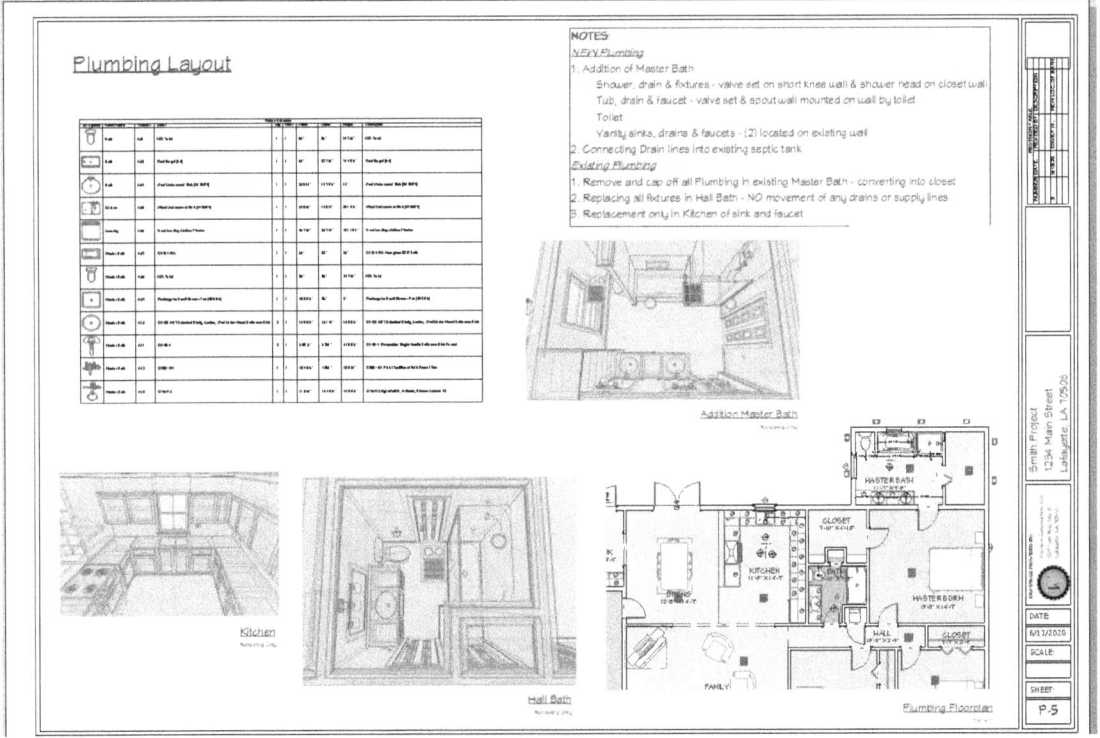

Layouts: Cabinets, Elevations

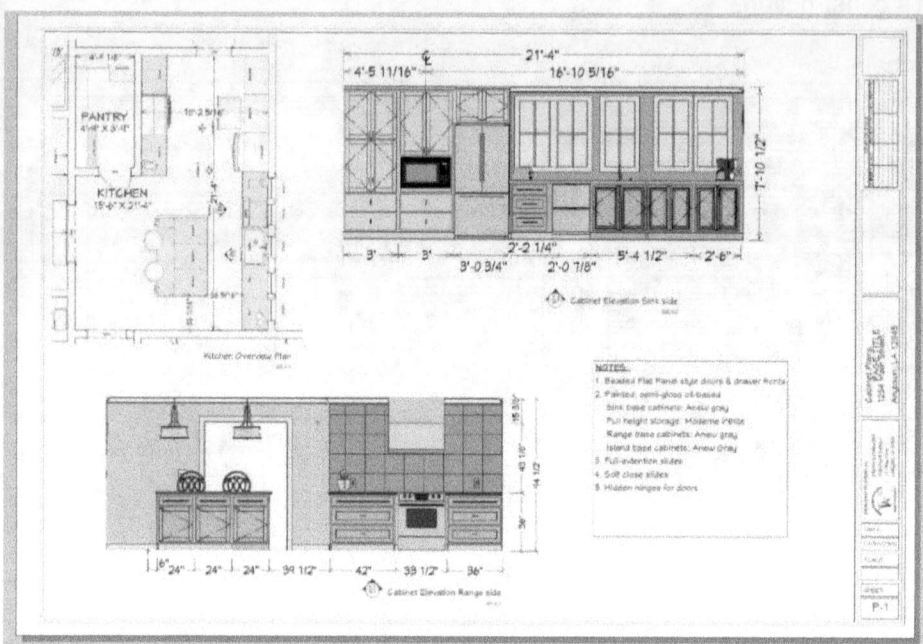

Designers will also provide 3D renderings and designs. Most of these will not have the measurements, but they will show you what the design will look like and how the space will feel. If you are visual and need pictures, it will be worth paying a designer to draw these up.

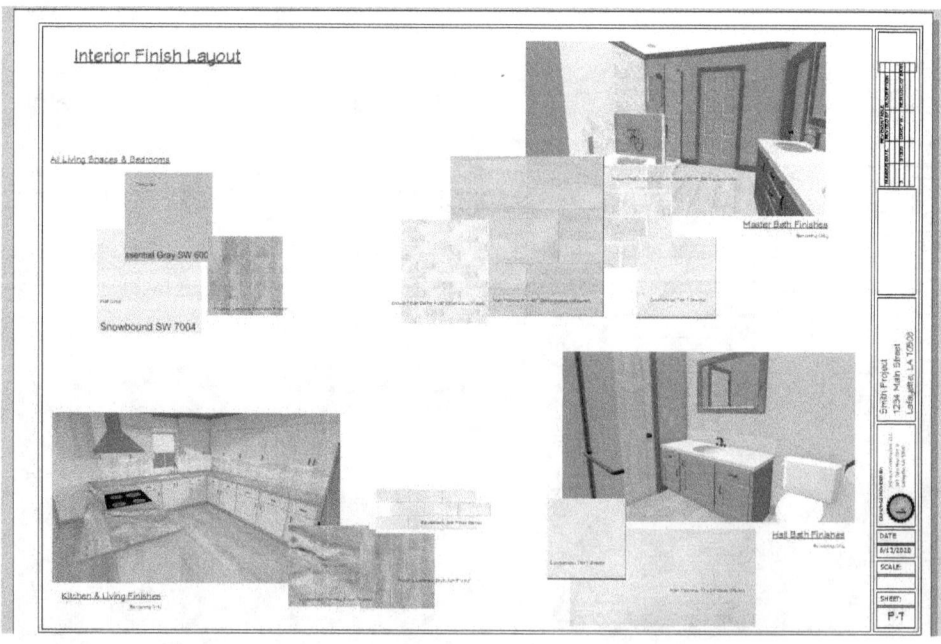

Roofing Overviews: Shaded areas can indicate added or new roofing.

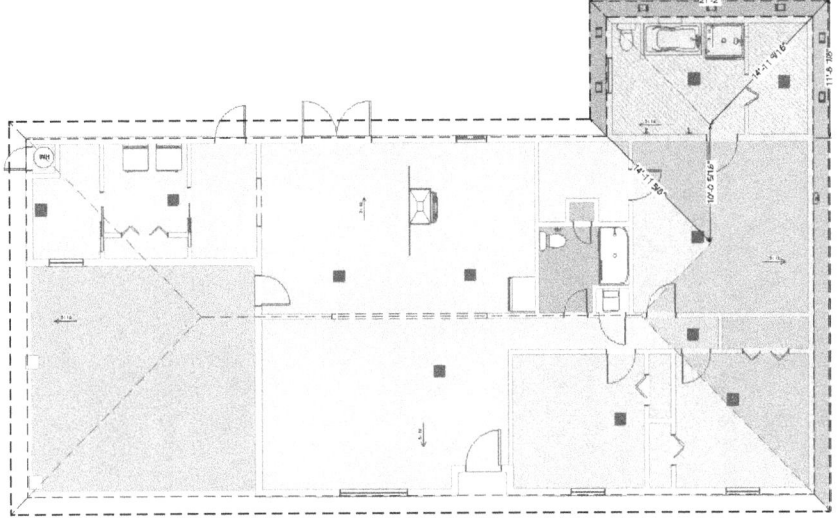

Each roof plan will show the pitch, exterior measurements for the rooflines, and ridge lengths.

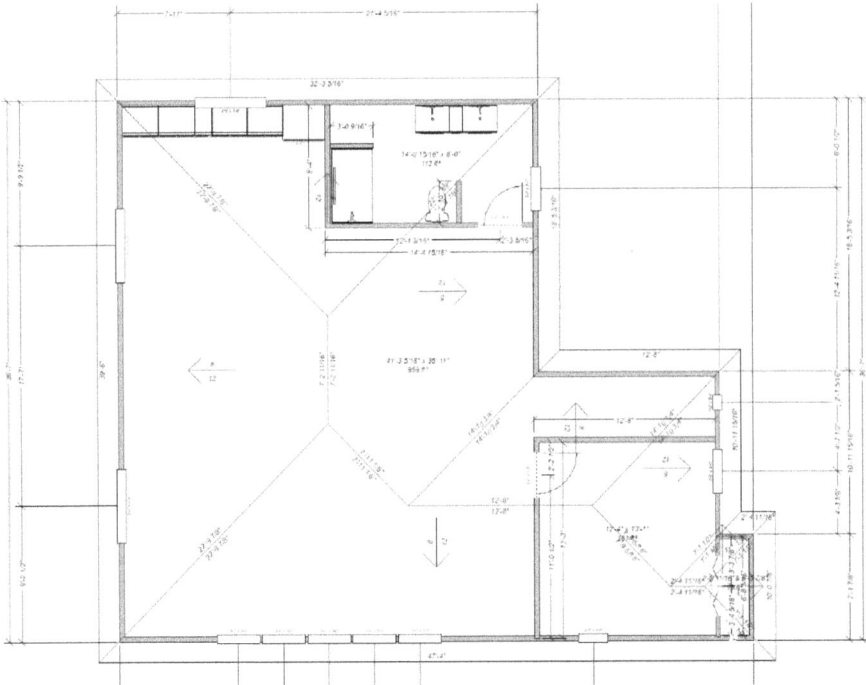

Framing Elevations: These drawings indicate wall plates, as well as the ceiling, wall, and roof framing. It will give detailed measurements for your tradesman to follow or, at the very least, have an excellent idea of the project.

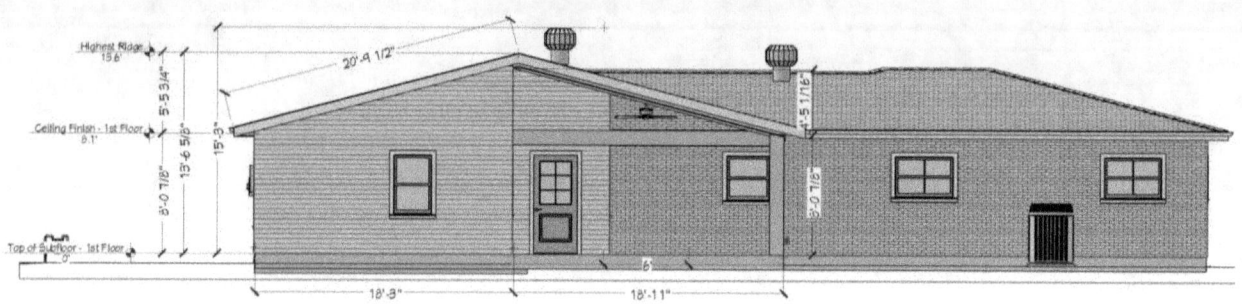

Section 3: How to Layout your Project

Room Layouts and Their Use: Determine the room so you and your family can naturally move around without feeling too tight or encumbered by the surroundings. Make the room work for you, and not have to work around the room. The placement of a cabinet and/or appliances could cause people to crowd certain parts of the room. It could also cause a particular part of the room to be empty and seem useless, which will feel like wasted space. It is important to put great thought into the placement of cabinets, plumbing, electrical, and appliances to fit your and your family's lifestyle. Let us walk you through the process of understanding room layouts and general space planning. We will first discuss each component's function, standard sizing, and general rules of placement.

Mapping out your Space on Paper:

Getting the proper measurements for your space is critical. To make your drawings, you must understand how to read a tape measure and an architectural ruler. It will help you take the actual space and scale it to a drawing on paper. From this drafted plan, you will make your Scope of work and a material list of the items you need.

- First, map out a rough drawing of your space on graph paper by drawing the room's general outline and the rooms you are remodeling. Your first drawing is just getting measurements and placements to see the space with which you are working. You will then take this rough drawing, choose a scale of ¼" or ⅛" that will work best for you, and do an accurately scaled draft on graph paper.
- Draw in the following components using the symbols for the architectural blueprints to represent each component.
    - Interior walls
    - Cabinets—base, upper, and full-height units
    - Sinks
    - Mark the outlets and switches you currently have
    - Appliances
    - Doors
    - Windows
- Using a tape measure, pick a starting point, any corner of the space, and measure. Working clockwise or counterclockwise around the room, hold your tape measure tight, ensuring it is not bent or bowed. If your tape is not tight, it will give you wrong measurements and, in some cases, false hope to use the space like you want to. Once you start measuring in one direction, keep moving in that direction.
    - Walls first—the total length from drywall surface to drywall surface
    - The distance of the windows and doors from the walls and to each other

- The size of the doors and windows
- The cabinet lengths and depths
- Note the thickness of the walls
- Note ceiling height

Most tape measures have lines on them denoting a specific measurement. Each line is a "tick" on the tape. Every inch will have 16 "ticks," each one is $\frac{1}{16}$ of an inch. Larger lines will mark ¼" and ½" notations. NOTE: some tape measures will have the "ticks" marked for you. Many of these have standard and metric measurements. Be aware of what you are using. You will need to decide how exactly you would like to measure.

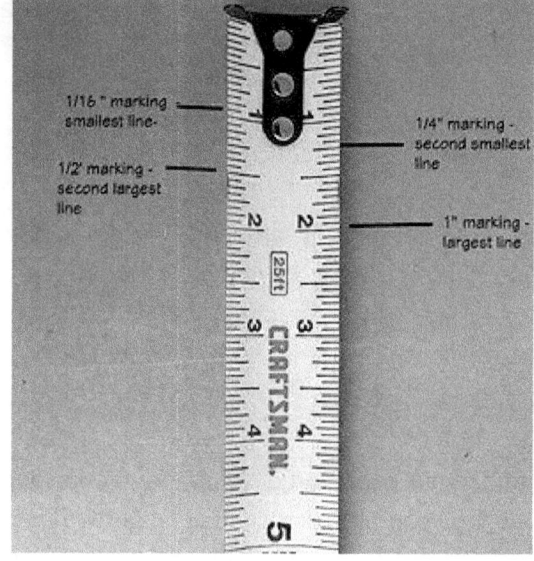

When you finish the rough draft, it will look like this:

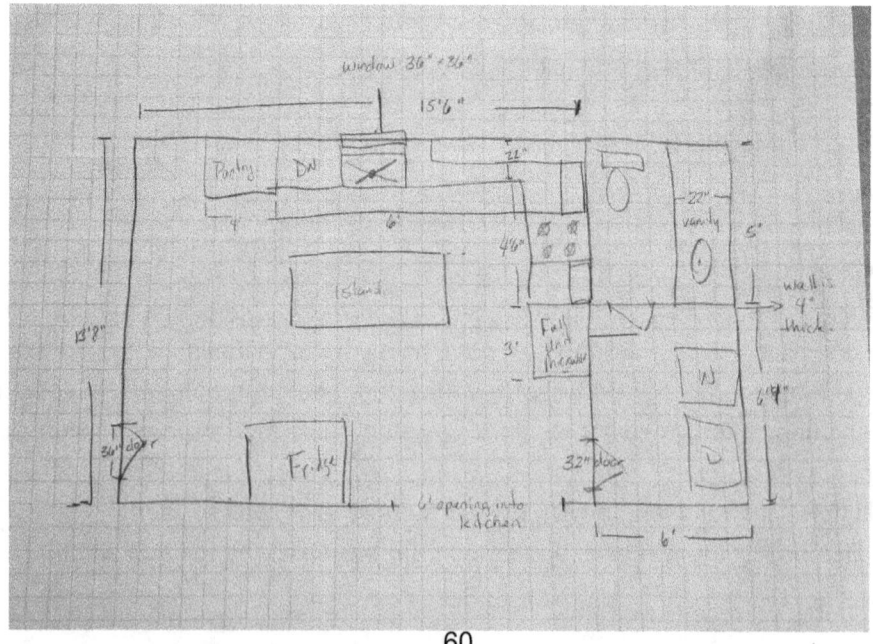

You can now take this rough drawing and, using an architectural ruler, draw a scale drawing of the space. If you use the ¼" side of the ruler, then each foot will be ¼". This same rule applies to the scales ⅛", ½", etc.

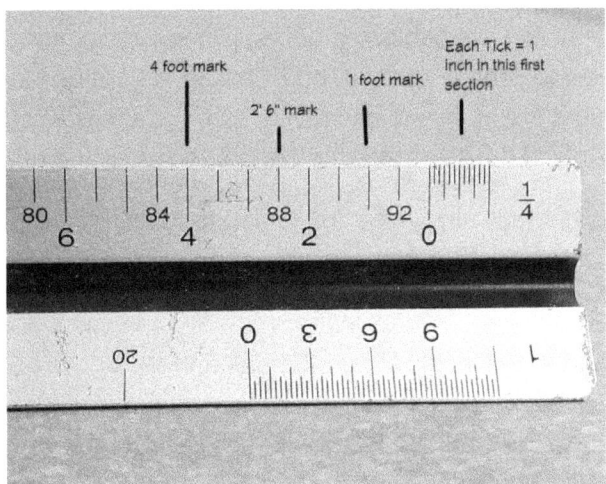

You will use the small ticks to measure out when you have 13 feet 4 inches. You will place the small ticks at the beginning of the wall or segment on the fourth tick from the 0 mark, then draw your line from that fourth tick to the 13-foot mark. You will be reading the ruler upside down. When drawing your walls, account for the thickness of the walls. This will matter when making a material list or ordering materials. Interior walls are approximately 4" thick, and exterior walls are 6"-9" thick.

Your scaled drawing might look something like this:

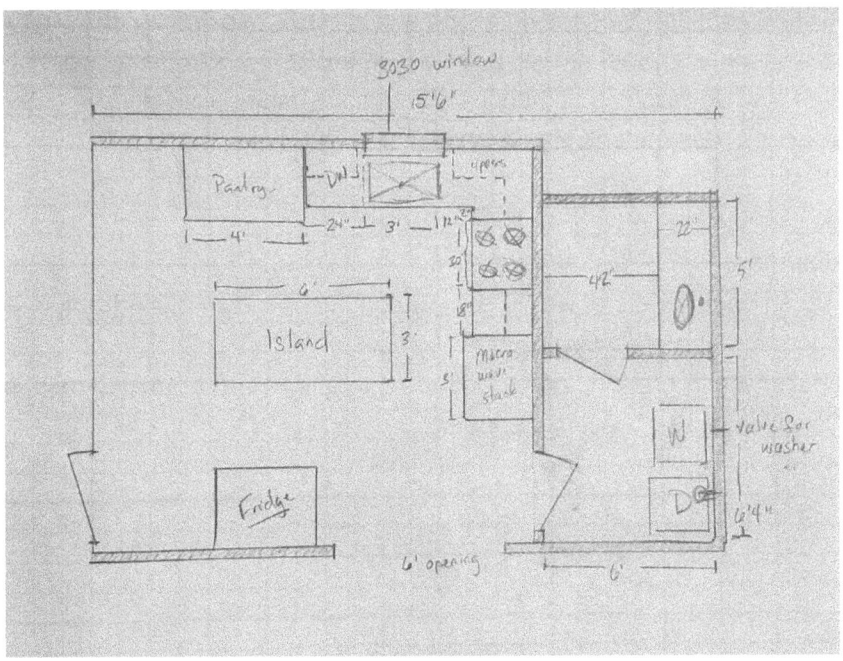

Component Placement

With the initial outline of your space complete, now is the time to start the layout of your rooms. When doing a room layout, the main items to consider are cabinetry, doors, windows, plumbing, and electrical placement. Each will determine how to use the space. The following are suggestions and recommendations to consider when placing doors, windows, cabinets, plumbing, lighting, and appliances in your room—it includes the standard measurements of the items and the sizes needed for their use.

<u>Cabinetry</u>: Placement of your cabinets will always be first for the function they provide (*storage*) and then for the room's flow (*walk-through traffic*).

- **Kitchen Cabinets:**
    - **Base Perimeter Cabinets:** Generally for work areas and storage areas for small appliances such as toasters and blenders.
    - **Islands and Peninsulas:** For cooking, food prep, and service areas. They are also used for base storage and/or the sink/ cleaning area. There should always be at least 3' of walking area around the island and between the perimeter cabinets and walls.
    - **Refrigerators** are accessible to the "cook" and the family coming into the kitchen for drinks and snacks while not interfering with the food preparation.
    - **The "Work Triangle":** This is the placement of the range/cooktop, the sink, and the refrigerator in a triangular arrangement, increasing your efficiency and making it easier to move back and forth from one to the other while cooking and cleaning. They are the main components used in the preparation of meals and the cleaning of the kitchen.
    - **Microwaves:** Are in a dedicated wall cabinet, island, or countertop, but always convenient for the whole family to use.
    - **Sinks and Dishwashers:** These usually go hand in hand with placement. Make sure when placing your sink and dishwasher they are close in proximity. The dishwasher should have room to open the door while standing at the sink. If the dishwasher faces an island or a perimeter cabinet, there should be enough space to open the door fully.

- **Bathroom Cabinets:**
    - **Vanities:** Placed on a perimeter wall, leaving enough space to walk in front, use the sink, and have every door and drawer open fully.
    - **Linen Cabinets:** Are to one side of the bathroom that is not on a walking path. In some cases, these are closets instead of built-in cabinets.
    - **Vanity Towers:** Shallow cabinets placed on either side of a sink or in the middle of two sinks

- **Doors:** The entry and exits are essential to the walking paths people will take in and out of the room. These walk paths will need to remain clear of cabinetry, furniture, or any mechanical items in the home.
- **Windows:** These are important to allow natural light in the room and the easement for a fire escape. The size of the windows will also dictate furniture and/or cabinet placement. The different applications of windows are as follows.

    - **Lighting:** To bring natural light into the room, making it an inviting and airy feeling.
    - **Kitchens:** Over the sink is the most common, and if there is a breakfast nook.
    - **Dining:** The room has an exterior wall with enough windows for lighting and the scenery outside.
    - **Living Rooms:** Give the light and airy feeling and include outdoor scenery.
    - **Bathrooms:** Small high windows just to let in light while maintaining privacy.
    - **Bedrooms:** Enough windows to let light in but not interfere with the furniture placement: You need to have at least one window that opens so you can get out of a fire and/or a firefighter can make their way in during a fire.
    - **Entry Foyers:** Windows placed on top of the door and to the door's sides.
    - **Fire Escape:** Any rooms that face the exterior walls that do not have doors leading to the outside. The window needs to be large enough to be a fire escape easement, and the window's opening needs to be 36"x36" when fully opened. It can be a single-hung, double-hung, or casement window, but it must be operable. This allows a person to escape the room and the firefighter to get in with their equipment.
    - **Attics:** If the attic has a window in it, it needs to be big enough to crawl out in the case of a fire or a fireman needs to make their way in during a fire.
    - **Dormers:** these project from the main roof of the house. A bedroom window needs to be big enough to crawl out in case of a fire.

Plumbing: Placing the bathroom and kitchen plumbing can also affect the room's walk path and use of each fixture.
- **Tub/Showers:**
    - **Shower door (*pivot*):** Enough room for the door to swing open and not hit the toilet.
    - **Shower door (*sliding*):** The opening is not in front of a toilet or cabinet.
    - **Faucets:** Place the valve set where they can be reached to turn the water on before stepping into the shower. It does not have to be in line with the showerhead if you have a shower valve and/or handheld showerhead, but if you have a tub spout, it does have to be in line with the spout. Place tub deck faucets with the spout over the rim to fill (either to the side, front, or corner of the deck), but not be in the way of stepping in the tub.

- **Toilets:**
  - **Knee Space:** To comfortably get on and off the toilet, this space should be at least 3' side to side and about 4' from front to back. Room for the toilet paper hanger and/or where it will hang or stand.
  - **Private Room With a Door:** You will need a 3'x4' interior wall space MINIMUM to stand in front of the toilet and sit on the toilet.
- **Sinks:**
  - Enough space in front of the sink to wash your hands or brush your teeth.
  - Enough space for the mirror and light fixture to hang above the sink.
  - Center the base cabinet directly below the sink.
- **Sink Faucets:**
  - **Rear Sink Placement:** Should be the center of the sink side to side and from the back of the sink to the backsplash.
  - **Side Placement:** Is done either because of the cabinet's design or the need for handicapped access. You can roll a wheelchair up to the sink and not have to reach the back to turn it on and use it.
  - **Wall placement:** spout length needs to reach over a fill sink; center spout with sink drain.

Electrical: Place your lighting according to the needs of the space and room usage.

Bathrooms Lighting & Exhausts:
- **Vanity Lighting:** Will need lighting near mirrors, either a wall sconce above the mirror and/or can lighting over the sink workspace.
- **Shower/Tub Lighting:** If adding a light over the shower, CODES dictates it to be a light/vent. The vent will turn on when the light is in use. It looks like an ordinary can light with a cover. Tubs are only allowed a light/vent, no chandeliers or hanging lights in accordance with CODES.
- **Heat/Light/Vents:** Usually placed near the shower/tub area to draw moisture and offer heat when getting out of the shower. The vent should run for at least twenty minutes after a shower to ensure the moisture gets out of the bathroom. The use of space heaters is acceptable, but be careful not to place them near any fabrics in the room and ALWAYS turn them off when not in the bathroom.
- **Vent/Lights:** Generally used in a water closet (toilet room) and over showers. In showers, the vent/light removes the steam's moisture, and in the toilet closet, it removes odors.

Kitchen Lighting:
- **Utility or Task Lighting:**
- **Pendants:** Are over sinks or an island, and a dimmer switch is for mood lighting when entertaining.
- **Under-Cabinet Lighting:** is used for the prep areas and on the perimeter cabinets. These are put on a dimmer switch if you desire to use ambient lighting or a night light when not using it for prep.
- **Overhead Lighting:** Can light set on a dimmer is becoming a standard. Recessed lights allow light to be cast throughout the room without casting shadows.
    - One over the standing area for the refrigerator doors.
    - One over the standing area for the range or cooktop. (*if there is no vent lighting*)
    - One over the standing area for the sink.
    - Light up the perimeter.
- **Vent Hood Lighting:** This will depend on the vent hood you choose. Most now come with LED lighting in different settings.

Living Room/Family Room Lighting: Commonly, recessed lighting is to spread light evenly in the ceiling space, and a fan is placed in the room's center. Sometimes a fan is not desired, but a chandelier or centerpiece lighting is preferred. Again, all lighting can be put on dimmers to adjust the lighting according to the space's use (*gaming, movies, or dance party!*).

Theater Room Lighting: Will have wall sconces for ambient lighting and switched on a dimmer.

Dining Room Lighting: A centerpiece light (feature light) is usually over the dining room table. It can hang lower than most lights because it is not on a walking path. Just be sure it's not in the eye line and is switched on a dimmer when sitting at the table.

Hallway Lighting: This will all depend on the length and shape of your hallway. Does the hallway turn, or is it straight?
- Can lighting on a dimmer switch.
- Ceiling mounted light on a dimmer or a 3-way switch.
- Wall sconce lighting if the hallway is tall and wide enough (*4' wide and 8'–9' high or more*).

Bedroom Lighting:
- **Recessed:** Is lighting throughout the space for even lighting with a fan in the center of the room.
- **Fans:** Some people may prefer the fan with a light kit and not install recessed lights. In this case, you may have the option to have the light and the fan on separate switches.
- **Chandeliers:** A feature light usually on a down rod and very decorative. It will be on a dimmer switch.
- **Flush Mount:** A light fixture that is fixed flush to the ceiling. It may be on a dimmer switch.
- **Closet Lighting:** Usually is a small flush mount light or can lighting. It is a utility light and is generally only needed as a light source. You may have a large closet with high ceilings where you can use a feature light like a chandelier, but this is not typical.

Garages, Storage, and Laundry Rooms:
- **Utility Lights (*shop lights*):** In a standard garage, four utility lights at 4' long evenly placed in a square is a generous amount of light for working in the space. You may prefer only two utility lights at 4' long placed over the "cars" if the only light you need is to park.
- **Can Lighting:** This is becoming more popular, especially with LED can lighting. These lights may have covers over the light, just like any exterior light.

Exterior Lighting:

- **Patios:** Covered can lighting will be used and spread evenly over the ceiling space, and a featured light *(pendant or chandelier)* or two, depending on the patio's size, style, and use. Patios should also have at minimum two fans to move air and keep it from becoming stagnant. The rule of thumb is to use four recessed lights for every fan to reduce the strobe light effect.
- **Security Lights:** Are at all corners of the home and near the entries to the house. These are generally motion sensor lights.
- **Soffit Lighting:** Small recessed lights in the soffit light up the house without shining directly at people walking up to the house. It helps illuminate the home without being intrusive.
- **Landscape Lighting:** Installed in steps and along pathways and gardens.
- **Exterior Sconces:** Lights near the entry and garage doors.
- **Post Lighting:** Used for decks and patios that have no cover. It illuminates the area without being intrusive to the eyes.

Outlet Placement:

- **Kitchens and Baths:** Near all water sources, there must be at least one GFCI (*Ground Fault Circuit Interrupter*) outlet installed.
    - **Backsplashes:** One or more GFCI.
    - **Under-Cabinet Outlets:** Are used in kitchens to not interfere with the backsplash.
    - **Islands:** If an Island is attached to the floor, it will need at least one outlet In compliance with CODE regulations.
    - **Peninsulas:** One outlet on the end of the cabinet or the wall of the peninsula is attached.
    - **Appliances:** Each has its own: check the <u>Manufacturer's Guide</u> for the type of plug required.
        - Range and/or Cooktop
        - Vent Hood: standard outlet
        - Microwave: outlet on its circuit
        - Fridge
        - Washers
        - Dryers
        - Disposals
        - Water Heaters
        - Window Units

- **Living Rooms, Bedrooms, Dining Rooms:**
  - **Wall-Mounted:** At least two on every wall (4'–6' from the end of the wall), more if desired. A standard outlet height is 12" from the floor. If building a mother-in-law suite, place the outlets higher at about 36"–40" so there is no bending over to plug in small appliances.
  - **Floor Mounted:** Near the furniture placement of end tables. These all have covers and are generally in a living room with an open concept floor plan and are very large. The furniture will be arranged in the center of the space, with walking paths around it. Outlets are recessed in concrete.
- **Outdoor Kitchens and Patios**
  - **Soffit Mounted:** Outlets for holiday or party lighting.
  - **Outdoor Kitchen:** In the backsplash and at least one must be GFCI.
  - **Island:** Must have an outlet if fixed in place to the floor.
  - **Appliances:** All are to have their own outlet.
    - **Grill with starter**
    - **Burners**
    - **Refrigerators**
    - **TV Outlets:** Mounted in the wall where the TV is mounted.

<u>Switch Placement</u>: Placed upon entering and exiting the room and/or space.
- **Hallways:** Usually will have a 3-way or 4-way switch. It will depend on how many different places you want to turn on and off the lights. Ask your electrician.
- **Bedrooms:**
  - Single switch to turn on all lights and fans at once
  - Two switches—one for lights, one for fan
  - One switch for the closet lighting
- **Kitchens:**
  - One switch for overhead lighting—dimmer
  - One switch for any featured lighting—dimmer
  - One switch for sink light, near the sink—dimmer
  - One switch for under mount cabinet lighting—dimmer
  - One switch for disposal—mounted on the wall or button switch on a countertop
- **Dining:**
  - One switch at every entrance to the dining room—dimmer
- **Garage, Storage, and Laundry Rooms:**
  - One switch upon entering and exiting a room
- **Bathrooms:**
  - One switch for the vanity light, sconce, or pendant—dimmer
  - One 3-function switch for the heater/light/vent
  - One switch for the light/vent over the shower
  - One light for can lighting (if any)—dimmer

Standards & Measurements

Standard Measurements: Before placing your cabinets and furniture, it is helpful to know the standard measurements of the products you will be putting in your home. Of course, there will be exceptions to the following measurements, but these are just guidelines to use when planning your space.

Cabinets: The following are industry standards; however, they may be changed if needed to fit your project.
- **Base cabinets:**
    - **Height:** Is 36" in kitchens and becoming more of a standard in bathrooms. The height of bathrooms in older homes is 30" high. Newer homes have a 36" standard height for vanities
    - **Depth:** 21"–22" and up to 24" deep AT MOST
    - **Length:** Determined by the space you have
        - Sink base for a kitchen is 36" wide
        - Sink base for the bathroom is 21"–24" wide
        - Range or cooktop space is 32" wide if you have a large cooktop or range, adjust according to the appliance's measurement

- **Wall-Mounted (Uppers):**
    - **Height:** 30"–42" high
    - **Depth:** 12" deep, specialty cabinets—18" deep
    - **Width:** Determined by the space you have
        - Over the fridge—42" wide
        - Over the range—if cabinets are installed over vent hood; 31"–32" (*or the width of the appliance you are using*)

- **Islands and Peninsulas:**
    - **Height:** 36" high
    - **Depth:** 24"–31" deep—you can have a double island at 48"–60" deep. 60" is the most an island should be The space in the middle will be unusable if it gets any larger. If using a stone for the countertop materials, you will need a seam in the stone to fit larger island pieces. Items in the middle of the island will be difficult to reach
    - **Length:** Will be determined by the space available
- **Full Height Storage:**
    - **Height:** Is the ceiling-to-floor height up to 9' high? Anything over that will require ladders
    - **Depth:** 18"–24" (*anything deeper, items will be difficult to reach*)
    - **Length:** Will be determined by the space available and needed

Closet Shelving:

- **Top Shelf:** 72" from the ground, 12" deep
- **Second Shelf with Rod:** Is 36"–40" from the floor, 12" deep. Hangers take up about 20" of space from the wall, so install the rod towards the front of the shelf.
- **Shoe Racks:** From floor to ceiling or top shelf, 12" deep and 8" apart from each other in height.

Cabinet Hardware:

- **Knobs:** Single hole
- **Pulls:** Are 3", 4", 5", 7" and up. The measurement is from the center of the screw hole to the center of the adjacent screw hole.
- **Placement:**
    - **Knobs:**
        - **Upper Cabinets:** Centered on the lower corner opposite hinges.
        - **Base Cabinets:** Centered on the upper corner opposite hinges.
    - **Pulls:**
        - **Upper Cabinets:** Vertical/lower corner opposite hinges.
        - **Lower Cabinets:** Vertical/upper corner opposite hinges.
        - **Trash Can Drawers:** Horizontal/upper style, centered.

Countertops:

- **Width:** Is the base cabinet's depth plus a 1"–1 ¼" overlay from the cabinet's edge.
- **Thickness:**
    - Stone or solid surfaces—2 centimeters, 3 centimeters
    - Tiled surfaces—½" thick with a 1" edging

Appliances: There are variations in sizes for all appliances. However, these are the most common sizes. Check with the manufacturer on the size you have chosen.

- **Oven:** (wall mounted) 24", 27", or 30" wide by 30" high and 30" deep
- **Ranges:** Are slide-in cooktops and ovens; 30" wide by 36" high. Most will come with adjustable feet to ensure you can level the appliance to look even with the countertop.
- **Refrigerators:** 36"–39" wide by 70" high
- **Dishwasher:** 24" wide by 32"–34" high

Door Openings:

- **Width:** 18", 20", 24", 28", 30", 32", 36", 48" double, 60" double, or 72" double
- **Height:** 68" and 96" (6.5' and 8')

Windows:

- **Width:** 18", 20", 24", 30", 32", 36", 48", 60" double
- **Height:** 24", 36", 48", 60", 72"

Tubs: (most common) 60"x30"x15"
- **Width:** 48", 60", 72"
- **Depth:** 28", 30", 32"
- **Height:** 15", 17", 18", 20"

Shower Pans: (most standard) 60"x32"x3"
- **Width:** 36", 48", 60", 72"
- **Depth:** 30", 32", 36", 48"
- **Height:** 3", 4" curbs

Faucet Spreads and Heights:
- **Kitchen:**
    - single hole
    - double holes (spout and sprayer)
    - triple hole (spout, sprayer, valve)
- **Bath Sink Faucets:**
    - Single hole: a single spout with a small single handle for the water supply that controls on and off as well as hot and cold.
    - 4" OC (On Center); one complete unit mounted on a decorative plate. The supply valves are 4 inches apart; measuring from the center of one outer valve to the center of the other outer valve with the spout in the center.
    - 8" OC (On Center) (Widespread): typically, three individual pieces The supply valves are 8 inches apart; measuring from the center of one outer valve to the center of the other outer valve with the spout in the center.
- **Bath Shower Valve:** Single valve set, height usually 36"–42", from the floor; a place where it can be turned on easily.
- **Bath Shower Head:** 72"–80" high off the floor
- **Roman Tub Deck Faucets:** The valve, spout, and sprayers will always be separate and installed in any configurations that work with the tub and decking setting. A standard setting is:
    - sprayer
    - hot water valve
    - spout
    - cold water valve

Sink Widths and Depths: Rectangular, circular, and oval shaped

- **Kitchen:** Double sink (evenly, 60/40 split, 70/30 split, apron, or single basin)
    - **Length:** 30", 36" from side to side
    - **Depth:** 8", 10" top to bottom
    - **Width:** 20", 22" from the front of the cabinet to the back walls
- **Bar:** single basin, double basin
    - **Length:** 18", 20", 24", 36" from side to side
    - **Depth:** 8", 10" from top to bottom

- **Width:** 20″, 22″ from the front of the cabinet to the back wall.
- **Bath:** Rectangular, circular, and oval shaped
    - **Length:** 16″, 18″, 20″, 24″ from side to side
    - **Depth:** 5″, 8″ from top to bottom
    - **Width:** 16″ to 23″ from the front of the cabinet to the back wall

<u>**Toilets:**</u> round and oblong shaped
- **Round:** 26″ from front to back
- **Oblong:** 29″ from front to back
- **Height:** 15″, 16 ½″ high to top of the seat from floor, 30″ from top of the tank to the floor
- **Width:** 20″–24″ wide from side to side of the tank

Knowing these measurements and placement options will significantly help place the products in your home to be most effective for using the space and help you choose your final product.

Planning a Kitchen:

Base cabinets will need to offer enough countertop space for prep food and store small appliances such as coffee makers and toasters.

- Creating a working triangle of the sink, refrigerator, and cooktop is optimal.
- The sink cabinet base and dishwasher will be next to or side by side. Therefore, you will need a minimum of a 36" sink cabinet base.
- The range or cooktop will be opposite or perpendicular to the sink. It will help when cooking to place dirty cookware and utensils in the sink after use. Ranges and cooktops take up a minimum of 30" wide.
- The refrigerator is the final piece of the triangle. The refrigerator is usually found on the kitchen layout's perimeter to facilitate family and friends' access at a gathering. This is so that it will not interfere with the person doing the cooking while entertaining. Typical refrigerators take up about 42" of space. Check the refrigerator measurements you intend to use while planning its area.
- Recessed lighting is used above the base cabinet to shine down just past the countertop.
- Feature pendant lighting over peninsulas and islands.
- All fixed islands will require outlet power sources.
- Under-mount cabinet lighting in areas 18" and larger, if desired at all.
- All lighting is to be on dimmers.
- Try to place a microwave off the countertop. You can place a microwave in an island or a full-height cabinet with or without an oven.
- Keep a minimum of 36" between cabinets and the island or wall for walking space. Optimal is 42" of walking space.

Kitchen Plan:

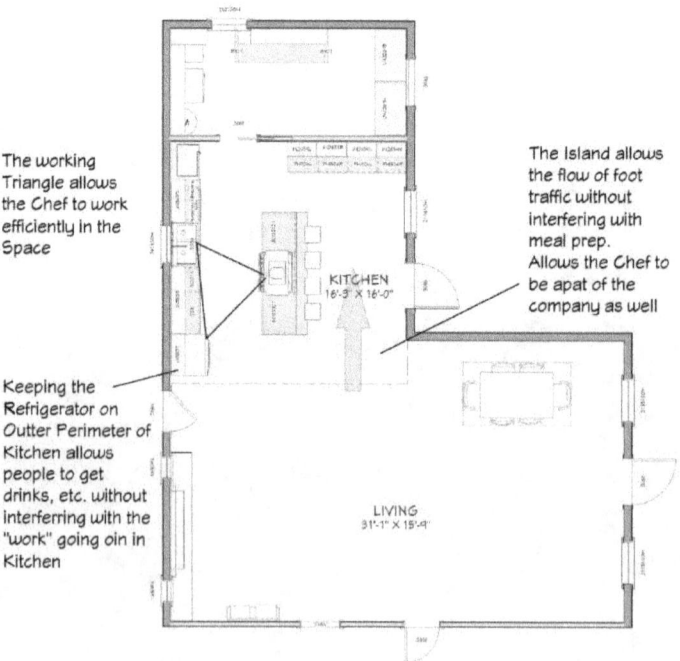

Planning a Bathroom:

Vanity tops need enough space to put in hand soap and maybe a toothbrush. They can also be as large as the space will allow you to have.

- Tubs: standard tubs are a minimum of 5 feet wide by 30" deep. You will need a minimum of 24" space in front on one side of the tub to get in and out when bathing. Sliding doors and curtains are used on tubs with a shower head to control the overspray of water. Freestanding tubs will normally be used as the feature of the room.
- Showers will be a minimum of 3'x3'. Any smaller, and it becomes difficult to move around while showering. You will need to allow space in front of the shower for the door to open, step out, and towel off.
- Toilets need a 3' wide by 4' deep space front to back to allow for the toilet itself and getting on and off the toilet. Place the toilet in the corner of the room or outside the shower/tub, away from the shower entry.
- Vanities are placed perpendicular or parallel to the shower, depending on the size of the space. You need to allow enough area in front of the vanity to wash hands, face, or other grooming. The base cabinet doors will need to open fully. Vanity sinks are typically 20" wide, though some are smaller. Be sure of the size you are using during your planning.
- Linen cabinets (*if there is enough space*) are in the corner of the bathroom's back or front.

Small Bathroom

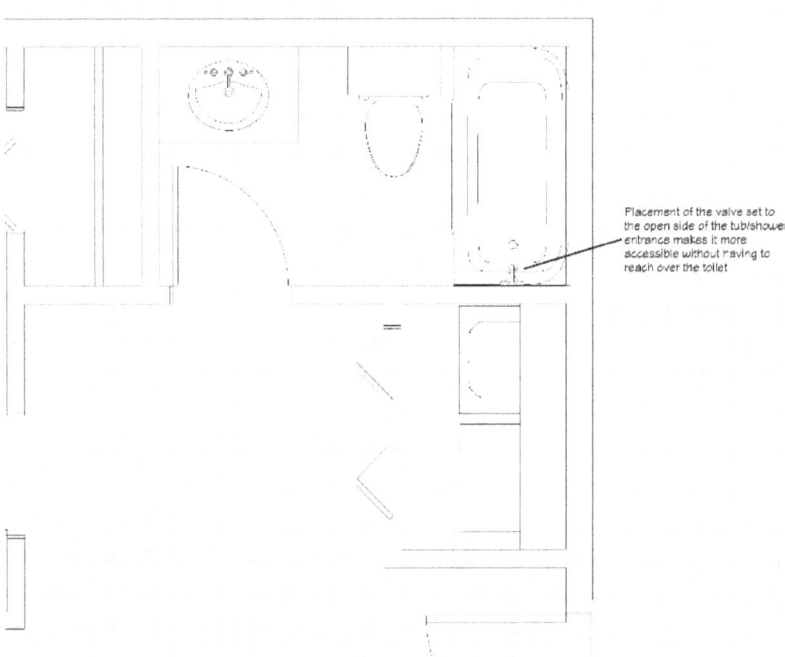

Placement of the valve set to the open side of the tub/shower entrance makes it more accessible without having to reach over the toilet

Large Bathroom

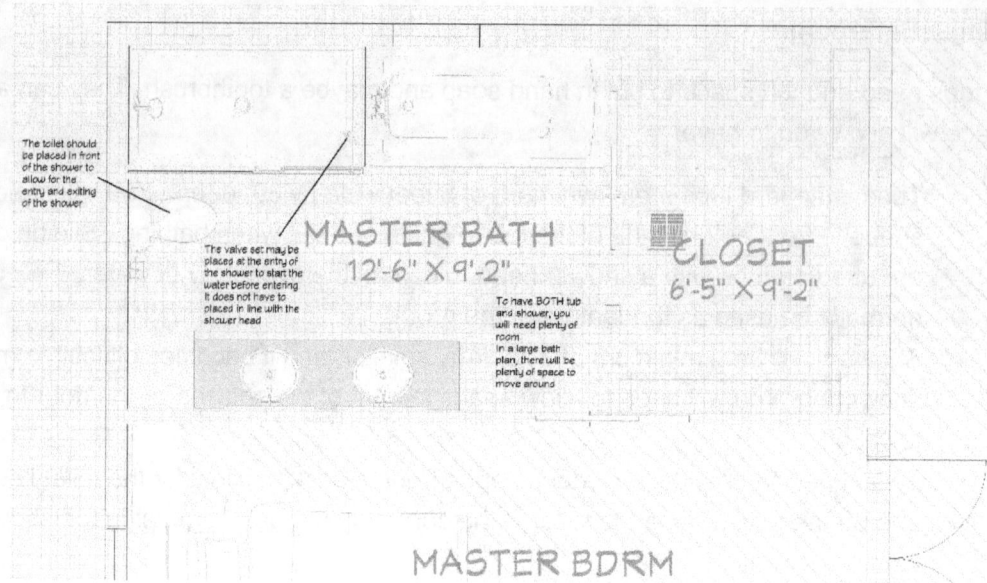

Planning a Bedroom:

- At least one or two walls with no windows and/or doors to allow for furniture placement
- Closet doors will need enough room to open fully
- One window for safety easement. It must be large enough to escape in case of a fire or allow a firefighter to enter with his equipment.
- One outlet on every wall
- Can lighting on the perimeter and fan located in the center of the room

Planning a Living Area:

- You will need to allow for walk-through traffic to get to other rooms
- Make space of about six feet wide for entertainment equipment such as televisions and gaming systems
- Fireplaces take up about a six-foot-wide space at a minimum and will need three feet of clearance in front of it
- An outlet or two is on every wall
- Can lighting on the perimeter on a dimmer switch
- A fan is centered in the room for airflow
- Arrange your seating to allow walking room in and out of the room. Place for conversation when entertaining and watching the TV.

You will now make the needed changes to your drawing if you add space or change the location of any walls, cabinets, etc. It may be a good idea to do these drawings to figure out precisely what you want to do with your room, even if you are using an architect or draftsman. It will help to keep the cost of revisions to a minimum and make furniture selection easier.

Chapter 3 - Purchasing & Hiring for your Project

Section 1: Vendors & Products Overview

The 2 main types of design in construction are Floorplans (Space) and Aesthetics (Surfaces)

In the last chapter, we covered your Floorplans. Making sure the structure and placements work for you is the 1st step in making your vision come to life. You should now have a scaled drawing of your project, and we can make it gorgeous!

The two main components of your aesthetic design are Surfaces and Fixtures

<u>Surfaces</u> are the core of your overall "look" for your home. They are the finish materials that reflect your personality and create your sanctuary.

<u>Fixtures</u> are those components that are fixed to the walls, ceilings, and floors.

These two components complete your design and give you form and function. In selecting your surfaces and fixtures, the 2 most important factors are color and shape.

Surfaces

- <u>Paint colors</u>: color and sheen will need to be chosen
    - Walls - sheen is typically eggshell or satin
    - Ceilings - sheen is typically flat or matte
    - Trim work - crown, base, shoe moldings, door and window casings, doors, cabinets (these could be painted or stained. Either way, a color will need to be chosen. Sheen is typically semi-gloss. In some cases, glossy may be an option.
- <u>Tile</u>: sizes, placement, patterns (**create visual aids for tile patterns**)
    - *Sizes*
        - Mosaics no larger than 2" in diameter on a mesh backing
        - 2x2 squares
        - 1x1 squares
        - 1 - 2-inch pickets
        - Penny tiles - the size of a penny
        - Hexagon tiles
        - Pebble tiles - flat or rounded on top with different size pebble shaped

- *Placements*
  - Shower walls and niches: typical sizes range from small mosaics to large format 12" x 24" tiles. In rare instances, a 24" x 48" may be used but is seldom used due to weight concerns.
  - Shower floors - typical sizes are any tile under 2", and mosaics are often a good choice.
  - Primary flooring - typical sizes range from small mosaics to large format 12" x 24" tiles. In rare instances, a 24" x 48" may be used because your foundation has to be perfectly level, whether concrete or raised platform, so you won't get cracking
  - Tub surrounds -typical sizes range from small mosaics to large format 12" x 24" tiles. In rare instances, a 24" x 48" may be used but is seldom used due to weight concerns.
  - Backsplashes - typical sizes range from small mosaics to large format 12" x 24" tiles.
- *Patterns* for installation:
  - Mosaics are normally on a mesh backing and fit together like puzzle pieces.
    - Penny tiles
    - Pebble tiles
    - Hexagon tiles
    - Square tiles
  - 2x4, 2x6, 2x8, 3x6, 3x8 and 3x12 subway tiles and any larger format tile such as 12x24, may be installed a few different ways
    - Staggered offset every 2 rows
    - Staggered offset every 3 rows
    - Straight bond - the grout lines are straight up and down and across.
    - Chevron - miter point together at an angle like an arrowhead
    - Herringbone - set perpendicular to one another either at an angle or 90 degrees
    - Diagonal - either straight bond or staggered at a 45 degree (more or less) in either direction
    - Vertical - rectangular shaped tile, long side from the top of the wall to bottom
    - Horizontal - rectangular-shaped tile, long side from one wall to the other

- Flooring: choose a material that best suits your project
    - *Wood* flooring - typically used in bedrooms and living areas. However, there is a growing trend to have wood in the kitchens as well
    - *Laminate* flooring - typically used in bedrooms and living areas. However, there is a growing trend to have wood in the kitchens as well
    - *Tile* flooring - typically used in wet areas but can be used anywhere inside and outside the home.
    - *Vinyl plank* flooring - typically used in bedrooms and living areas. However, there is a growing trend to have wood in the kitchens and baths as well
    - *Vinyl sheet* flooring - used mostly now in rentals or as a replacement
    - *Carpet* - typically used in bedrooms and some living areas. NEVER in a bath or kitchen.
- Countertops - (Slide 6) used in the kitchen, baths, laundry, built-in bars, service areas, and patios.
    - Solid surface; most common. Stain resistant, heat resistant, and low maintenance. * Marble is soft and can damage easily.
        - Stone
            - Granite
            - Dolomite
            - Marble
            - Quartzite
        - Quartz - (manmade) formed and colored using quartzite stone, sand and polymers, making it very durable
    - Laminate - typically used in laundry rooms or rentals or where there are budget concerns. Stain-resistant and low maintenance.
    - Tile - not used as much as it was in the 1990s because grout lines took on stains and dirt -- high maintenance.
    - Concrete - this takes time for the curing process, and not many people do concrete countertops—low maintenance.
    - Stainless steel - holds up well and is stain resistant—low maintenance.
    - Wood - typically a butcher block or spliced-together pieces with multiple layers of coating. High maintenance.

Fixtures to Choose

- Lighting - getting the lighting right will set the room's tone and increase the space's useability.
    - Utility lighting: workspaces and areas requiring more light for tasks
        - Workshop - entire space for working
        - Kitchens - over-cook prep areas and sinks
        - Baths - over sinks and in showers
    - Ambient lighting: lighting to see what's going on in the room, but can do low lighting for movie nights, entertaining, etc.
        - Kitchens - pendants and recessed lights on dimmers
        - Dining rooms - lower lighting while eating is more conducive than bright lighting
        - Living rooms - low lighting is good for watching TV are just having conversations
        - Bedrooms - typically lamps are used to read, and usually only getting dressed or watching TV
        - Hallways - need to see where you are going
- Plumbing - this is where form and function meet. The priority is to have your water and waste supply and drainage, but it can look good too!
    - Kitchens - hardest working room in the house
        - Sinks
        - Faucets
        - Pot fillers
        - Fridge water lines
        - Dishwashers
    - Baths - 2nd hardest working room in the house
        - Sinks
        - Faucets
        - Shower valves and heads and handheld sprayers
        - Toilets
        - Tubs

- <u>Cabinetry</u> - storage as well as beauty
    - Kitchens
        - Uppers
        - Base (or lower), the trend is to have as many drawer pullouts as possible.
        - Islands
        - Peninsulas
        - Pantry units
    - Baths
        - Vanity
        - Linen cabinets
        - Johnny cabinets (over the toilet)
    - Laundry
        - Uppers
        - Base (or lowers)
        - Utility (floor-to-ceiling)
    - Hardware
        - Pulls - cabinetry
        - Knobs - cabinetry and doors
        - Levers - doors

Schedules

Once the selections are made, and calculations are completed, you can make your Design Schedules. Design Schedules keep all your information about the materials you select for your home in one convenient place. It contains information such as name brands, model numbers, quantities, colors, and labeled for each specific space. They are often used as quick reference guides to double-check orders when they come in and ensure the right colors, tiles, lights, etc., are installed in the right room. We will go further into this in Chapter 4, Scope & Budget

Section 2: Vendors & Products Overview

Your budget materials can be divided into two main categories: the rough or raw materials and the finish materials. Both purchases will be necessary and will require different vendors. It will require a lot of research and a lot of conversations. In this section of the course, we will discuss in further detail the following:

- **What Questions to Ask:** Knowing what to ask your vendors will help in knowing what you are getting. You will be sure you are getting the correct products to fit your space and lifestyle. Each item will work properly, be utilized to the best of its ability, and enhance your way of life.
- **Where to Look for Specific Items:** In today's market, many options range from big box stores (chains) to local vendors and online distributors. We will explore the advantages and disadvantages of each of these options. One of the most important qualifications you will look for is the quality of the product you buy, not just the price point.
- **How to Source Products:** It is essential to know what you want. The more challenging part is knowing where to get it. We will show you different ways to look up items that may not be readily available at your local brick-and-mortar stores.
- **Standard Sizes for Products:** Knowing the standard sizes of the most common products used in your home will help you place every product in your house to make the most of your space and be the most fitting to your lifestyle
- **Discounts:** Certain local vendors and distributors will offer discounts to customers making larger purchases. We will be able to guide you in finding these vendors.
- **Local vs. Big Box Purchasing:** We will explore the advantages and disadvantages of shopping local vs. big box stores. Each has its value and benefit. Knowing their differences and commonalities will help you make the best decision to purchase your products for your home.

We will also define the difference between making purchases for your "forever" home versus an investment property. The quality and longevity of specific products will help you in making these decisions

Types of Vendors

Each Vendor specializes in a material. Some stores and/or suppliers will carry many materials, but each material type will be limited when they do. Usually, when a vendor specializes in one or two material choices, they will carry a large variety of lines in each of the materials, giving you more options. The different types of vendors you will use are as follows:

Big Box Material Suppliers: Carry lumber, plywood, fasteners, drywall, paint, plumbing supplies; both rough-in and finish (*limited*), electrical supplies; both rough-in and finish (*limited*), doors (*limited*), shutters (*limited*), tile and flooring (*limited*), cabinets (*limited*), HVAC (*limited*), Appliances (*limited*), and shower doors (*limited*).

Lumber Yard: All framing lumber, treated and untreated, beams, plywood, specialty framing components (*trusses, corbels, unusual cuts, etc.*), trim work (*crown, base, and shoe moldings, posts and columns, wood siding and lap siding, etc.*), doors, shutters, drywall, fasteners, and paint (*limited*).

Door and Window Suppliers: Are for standard and specialty doors, windows, and shutters. Specialty doors and windows are offered in many colors, materials, and styles and can fit unusual spaces and requests. Most of these are made to order.

Plumbing Suppliers: These suppliers will carry everything from the rough-in supplies to the finished products. They will offer multiple lines for each item and can order specialty items.

Electrical Suppliers: These suppliers will carry everything from the rough-in supplies to the finished products. They will offer multiple lines for each item and can order specialty items.

Mechanical Suppliers: Are for specialty items and motors for mechanical items around the house, such as generators and HVAC system parts.

Online Distributors: They will carry everything from standard items to exceptionally specialty items. You may be limited to the amount of information you can get through an online source, but if there is a contact number, always try to talk to someone about the product you have chosen to ensure you have a good fit.

Stone and Countertop Suppliers: Specialize in natural and man-made stone and surfaces. Always go in and talk to someone about their product lines. They are more than happy to talk to you. Some vendors only supply the stone but will recommend a fabricator to you.

Tile Suppliers: These suppliers will carry a vast range of tile; in some cases, it is a warehouse full of choices. It can get overwhelming. Pace yourself.

Specialty Suppliers/Carpenters/ Cabinet Makers: Always talk to these suppliers about what item you need and its purpose. They will help you get the perfect item, whether cabinetry, moldings, ventilation items, etc. In addition, they will carry laminate countertop supplies, hinges, slides, blades, fasteners, etc.

Section 3: Selecting Materials

This next section will explore the factors that decide which product to use and purchase. Your products will need to be a good fit for your project in form and function. Your budget and many other factors will dictate the quality of the materials you are buying.

- **Durability:**
    - How long do you need the product to last? Is this an item you may want to change in 5–10 years? Or is it an item you hope never to change again until it needs changing?
    - Is the product in a high-traffic area? Many flooring options we choose will receive a great deal of abuse and will need to withstand foot traffic over time.
    - Is the product going to receive a lot of abuse? Cabinets, countertops, flooring, fans, baseboards, and door casings are highly exposed items. They take abuse because of their function in the home or are the most exposed to running into or being cleaned often. Cleaning products can wear down finishes and paints on walls, trim, cabinets, hardware, faucets, and appliances.
    - Is the product going into a rental or forever home?
        - **Rental:** You must choose an item that can withstand much use and abuse. Most people do not show great care for items in rentals because it is not their own. Because a rental has a higher turnover of people and families (with pets) in the house, you will also need to pick a product that can be changed inexpensively. So, going with a substantial, but not the highest cost is your best option.
        - **Forever Home:** Choose the item that will bring you the most enjoyment for the most extended time. It is usually a higher-priced item, but you will show it the care and attention it will need to get the most use.
- **Availability:**
    - **Stock Items:** These are the most popular selling; therefore, they will be in stock. They are usually of good quality as well. Vanity sinks, light fixtures, showerheads, tile, and some flooring will fall into this category. If you need an item quickly, this will be your option. Used most often in rentals, so replacement is quicker and easier.
    - **Ordered Items:** Look at the estimated arrival time for these items and give yourself another 2–3 days buffer for the arrival. If not received on time, many items will affect the timelines of other things. These items can go on back order at any time with no warning.
        - **Sinks:** Will affect the timeline for countertop installation and the finish plumbing installation of the fixtures. The sink must be at the stone provider's location to cut the stone to the correct measurements. Never go off the spec sheet for this. If it is wrong, the stone will need fabricating again. For this reason, most fabricators will NOT cut the stone until the sink is at their facility. You have hand-selected the stone, and they want to ensure you get what you paid for and not do it twice.

- **Tile:** If the tile is not in on time, you may lose the tradesman for a period. They will move on with their schedule and must fit you back into their schedule later. This setback will also set back the plumber from installing shower fixtures and the glass provider from measuring and making the shower door (*if being made*).
- **Drywall, Lumber, Roofing:** (*building materials*) Arriving late will set back the tradesman installing the drywall, lumber, or roofing, and each tradesman that will follow.
- **Cabinets:** Will set back countertops being measured and installed, the plumber installing finish plumbing, and tile backsplash from being installed. Sometimes the boxes for the cabinets can be installed before the doors and drawers, just so the countertops can be measured (*templated*), keeping the schedule on track.
- **Countertops:** Will set back finish plumbing and tile backsplashes.
- **Price Point.** An item's cost may not always be just the money amount, but it can cost you time and cause you to make different choices elsewhere. Therefore, you will need to prioritize what items you choose. The following are just a few examples in each task category of the advantages and disadvantages to consider that can influence your decision-making regarding the cost and value of the items you are choosing for your home:
  - **Framing:** Good quality lumber will be needed for your structure to stand the test of time, weather, and properly function.
  - **Foundation:** Never go cheap on a solid foundation concrete.
  - **Roofing:** Good quality shingles and proper installation will protect all the work you have put into the house for years to come.
  - **Doors:**
    - **Exterior:** Getting the right exterior doors that will not rot or damage easily will help protect your home and help keep the weather out.
    - **Interior:** Hollow core and solid core doors are both good quality. If dampening the sound is essential to you, then the solid core doors' expense may be worth it.
  - **Windows:** Insulated Low-E glass windows may have a higher cost, but they will save you on your energy bills. They are also more durable in storms. However, getting a wood window is a higher cost, and it will cost you more over time with maintenance to protect the wood.
  - **Siding:** This is the protection for the outside of your home as well as its appearance.
    - **Vinyl:** While the least expensive, it has the lowest maintenance. No repainting, although you can paint it if you want years later. If a piece gets damaged, you can change a few pieces with little time and expense.
    - **Wood Lap Siding:** Still on the lower end of expense, will need painting and/or sealant to seal the wood, preventing mildew growth and rot. However, wood is always susceptible to rotting. It will have to be maintained about every 7–10 years. You can replace only the damaged area with little time and expense if a piece gets damaged.

- - **Concrete Lap Siding:** Has a median range price point for siding. It will last for a long time without rotting. It is usually primed and painted. Some may already arrive primed, but it is always recommended to use an exterior primer before painting. The painting will need to be maintained every 10–15 years. If a piece gets damaged, it can be replaced with little time and expense.
  - **Brick Siding:** The most expensive siding option but requires very little maintenance, usually power washing once a year. It has the most durability against damage from storms or other flying objects. However, if it does get damaged, repairs can be pricy. Like drywall, it will have to be cut back to the most solid connecting point and then reinstalled with ties and mortar. You also run the risk of not being able to get the same brick to match, especially any brick over five years old.
- **HVAC:** Getting the cheapest unit will usually result in higher utility bills, more repairs over time, and possible early replacement. It will cost more over time.
- **Plumbing:** The rough-in items are a must and have more consistent pricing. The finished plumbing will have a wide range of costs. Most name-brand lines will carry their low lines in big box stores, offering you a reduced price and higher lines in plumbing supply stores or distributors. While the product's exterior looks the same, the internal parts are of better quality in the higher lines. The faucets will last you a long time, requiring less maintenance. Unique pieces are usually more expensive because they are featured in your bathroom or kitchen. It may be one of the items you decide to sacrifice in another part of the project to get the look you desire.
- **Lighting:** The rough-in items are a must and have more consistent pricing. Finished lighting products can have a wide range of costs. Big box stores will carry the lower line items of some name-brand lighting to give you a reduced price. There is no difference in the materials used to make the light fixture; it is just the manufacturer's lower price line. Lighting stores will carry all lines from lower-price to higher-priced lines. The significant difference in the light fixtures will be the design and function. You will need to decide how much of a feature piece you want. The areas that have design feature lights are dining rooms, living rooms, and kitchens. It may be one of the items that you decide to make sacrifices in another part of the project to get the look you desire
- **Wall Coverings:** Used to cover stick framing, insulation, rough-in plumbing, and electrical in the exterior and interior walls.
  - **Wood Paneling:** The cost will vary depending on the type of wood covering you choose. The most common varieties of wood surfacing are 4x8 panel sheets of wood veneer, shiplap, tongue, and groove. The labor cost will also vary with the type of wood you are installing, but it does not offer a fire-retardant option. It can dry out over time, making it brittle, although it can be painted to seal it, increasing its longevity. It is usually not recommended to install wallpaper on wood paneling because the seams in wood paneling will show unless floated out with drywall mud which is labor intensive.

- **Drywall:** The most standard wall covering. The overall cost with mud, fasteners, and tape, is similar to wood paneling. The labor cost will vary depending on texturing to be done and the wall heights. It will take days for drywall to be ready for paint or wallpaper, whereas the paneling is ready to paint as soon as installed. Drywall needs to be primed and painted. Drywall offers insulation and is fire-retardant. It slows the rate at which fire spreads and burns. It also provides sound dampening, and sound-absorbing drywall may be hung in areas like theater rooms, music rooms, or playrooms. Drywall sheets are offered in different thicknesses and types, such as standard, moisture rock, and sound proofing. The cost will vary with each type.
- **Paint:** Both with interior and exterior paints, it is worth the expense to use name brands. Because they last a long time, clean easily, and resist flaking or cracking. Their higher lines will be applied with as little as two coats to cover more evenly and have a good depth of color.
- **Stains and Sealers:** It is worth using the more expensive sealers because they will last longer and offer more protection. Stains are available in different colors and applications, including wipe-on and penetrating. The different species of wood absorb differently, which will dictate which color and type of application you need. The tighter the grain of the wood, the harder it will be for the wood to absorb the stain. This may require a penetrating stain vs. a wiping stain. The darker the color desired, the longer the stain will remain on the wood without being wiped down between coats. Ask your paint specialist if you are in doubt.
- **Tile:** Some of the higher-priced tiles are a product of design and not necessarily the material is a better quality. ALWAYS check the tile pricing because some lines may look expensive and reasonably priced, while others may look simple in design, but the cost is beyond your budget.
  - **Glazed Ceramics:** Usually the lowest in cost. The color is applied and baked on the top of the tile. So, if chipped, the ceramic color underneath will be noticeable. It is also porous under the glazing, so it will be susceptible to moisture retention if chipped. It will allow mildew to grow, causing the tile to become more brittle over time if water gets in and dries out repeatedly. However, some of the coloring and patterns offered in these tiles are beautiful. They are best in a place with light traffic or that won't be touched.
  - **Porcelain Tile:** Very dense and moisture resistant. Some lower-priced lines have the coloring baked or painted to reduce the tile's cost. A "through body" porcelain tile will be consistent throughout the tile in color, making it hard to notice chipping or cracks. Most commonly used in showers, floors interior, and exterior.
  - **Marble:** It is at a higher cost because it is a natural stone cut into various tile sizes and shapes, from large format to mosaics. It is very durable, chip-resistant, and moisture-resistant. The finish is honed (*polished*) if worn over time from cleaning or high-traffic use. It is a soft stone.
  - **Granite:** Usually in the same price range as marble. Is a natural stone cut into various tile sizes and shapes, from large format to mosaics. It offers the same

durability and moisture resistance as marble. In addition, it can be honed if the finish wears off over time.

- **Cabinetry:**
  - **High-Density Board:** These cabinets range from low to high quality and cost. They usually are preassembled and offered only in specific, standard sizes and colors.
  - **Solid Wood Cabinets:** Are at a higher cost but will offer you the best quality. They will stand up to abuse and last you a long time. They can be made in custom sizes and styles to fit your needs and desires for use and look. They are finished with paint or stained with a sealer, but they will need to be sealed for protection from use.
- **Countertops:** The price will vary more because of the materials rather than the countertop design. However, design and size will affect the price. For example, the arched edge of an island bar extension will cost more than a straight edge.
  - **Fabricators:** The vendors with the equipment to cut the solid surface slab countertops to include the cutouts for appliances and sinks and polish the edging. Most fabricators will also sell solid surface material (*natural stones, quartz, Silestone, etc.*).
  - **Wholesalers:** These vendors sell slabs of stone; they do not fabricate the stone. You will have to find a fabricator of your own or ask if they work with one. They will, however, deliver the slab to the fabricators for you.
  - **Laminate:** The lowest in cost, chip-resistant, and stain-resistant. It is NOT heat resistant and can crack if hit too hard. The designs are now made in various patterns and textures that can mimic solid stone materials.
  - **Tile:** higher price than laminate, but still more economical than a natural stone. The designs are in a wide range of patterns and textures. However, it is heat and moisture-resistant, requiring maintenance in sealing the grout lines and the tile. It is susceptible to cracking and chipping if a heavy object is dropped on it. The grout lines are susceptible to staining.
  - **Solid Surface:** This is on the highest end of the price range. Various solid surface materials, designs, patterns, and textures exist. With this variety, there is also a wide range of pricing. Availability will also affect pricing. All the surfaces are heat-resistant and moisture-resistant. The density of the surfaces also makes them resistant to cracking, chipping, and scratching. The price ranges from lowest to highest are as follows:
    - Tier 1 granite
    - Tier 2 granite
    - Tier 3 granite
    - Man-made solid surface: quartz, Silestone
    - Exotic stones and marbles

- **Hardware:** For cabinets and doors, the price range is extensive. It is an area that will be entirely subjective for you. Your hardware can stand out as a jewelry piece for your doors and cabinets or blend in and intentionally not draw attention. Shop!

Application and Sizing: In deciding which product to buy, it is essential to consider what you are using the item for and the space it takes up in your home.

- **Purpose:**
    - **Appliances:** Can be considered tools for your home and lifestyle. They preserve and prepare food, clean your home, and maintain your hygiene. If cooking is a high priority for you and your family, then this is an area where you may spend more money to get the right appliances that work for you. All spec sheets need to be given to the cabinet maker.
    - **Cabinetry:** Has the primary use of storage but can add beauty to your home. Since your cabinetry is necessary and highly visible in kitchens and bathrooms, it is an area to consider spending money to get the most use out of them. It is also an item that may only be changed once while you live in your home.
    - **Hardware:** Is used to open and secure cabinets, drawers, and entry doors. These pieces can be statement pieces and complete the look you have designed for your space. They are highly visible on the cabinet's fronts and the doors throughout the house. You will be purchasing hardware in large quantities. It can be changed quickly in the future for a different look. The amount of money you spend on your hardware will depend on what look you are trying to achieve.
    - **Countertops:** Are used to prep and serve food. These are also highly visible and usually featured in the kitchen and bathroom's overall design. The countertops are typically chosen first, then the cabinet style, hardware, and all paint colors are selected based on the countertop choice. It is an area you will want to consider spending more money on to get the best product for your design and use.
    - **Faucets:** are a means of getting water into your home for cooking and cleaning. These are highly visible items in the kitchen and bathrooms. They can be accessories or featured items. You will also want to consider spending more money on these items to get longevity and a complete look.
    - **Light Fixtures:** Offer you light in your home. Individual light fixtures will complete a look for your space and set a mood as featured lighting. These pieces you may spend more money on than any other light fixtures in the home:
        - Dining rooms- they will anchor your table to a specific spot
        - Pendants over kitchen islands, peninsulas, and sinks; for work and design
        - Living room lighting (*sometimes*)
        - Vanity lights in bathrooms – for both work and design
    - **Stair Railing and Balusters:** While their primary function is to keep you from falling off the side of the stairs, they can tie together the whole house's look and set a tone

for the house's style. It is an item that may not be changed regularly, so spending money in this area will be necessary.
- **Tile and Flooring:**
  - **High Traffic Areas:** Should have durable, quality products that can stand up to use and abuse.
  - **Low Traffic Areas:** shower walls and backsplashes can have surfaces that do not need the high traffic area's durability. In these areas, you can focus more on style than substance.

Each has a simple purpose but can be a feature to make your home beautiful and express your family's style. Each featured item you want to be noticed in your design should be appropriately sized for the area. If it is too large, it will detract from everything else and feel out of place. If it is too small, it will look out of place and out of balance in the room.

As you can see, there are many factors to consider when purchasing items for your home, and each one will require a fair bit of thought. It would be beneficial to write down each area's purpose. Prioritize the products you want the most or that get the most use. Remember why you are doing this renovation and how you use your home. It will narrow down the possibilities for you in your research. Knowing the colors you like will narrow down the paint colors to choose and the featured items you want to see. When making decisions for your home, going with the cheapest option is not always the best decision. Choose products of quality and items that bring you joy! It is your sanctuary; you should feel your best in this space.

Use the Forms at the end of the Chapter to record your vendor choices and any contact information you need. In addition, your surface & fixture schedule and design material schedule will help you shop for the appropriate materials and vendors.

Section 4: Vendor Qualifying

Defining the Vendors Needed: You will need to determine the vendors you need for your project. You will likely have multiple vendors in each category in which work is done. Therefore, you will need to get a fair comparison and shop for the best price and quality. There are many factors to consider when choosing a vendor.

- Price points
- Delivery time
- Delivery options
- Return policies
- Discounts offered
- Communication
- Payment options

This next section will explore the difference between some of the custom specialists, big box stores, local vendors, and online distributors. Sometimes, the item you choose will decide the vendor you will use. An example would be staircase railing, newel posts, and balusters. Not every vendor carrying these items will offer the same style or material you desire for your project

Sourcing: Each type of vendor has its advantages and disadvantages. There are also different ways to source a product and find out where and how to get the product.

- **Local Shopping:** Looking up local stores and shopping for the products. You may be able to see the product in person or look through catalogs to choose your product. By shopping locally, you will have the chance to look at your product in person. It will give you the dimensions, actual color, and the ability to know if you have a good fit for your space. An excellent example of this would be lighting fixtures. Pendants and chandeliers can be deceiving just by looking at a picture of them online. To see them in person, you get the whole perspective. Pictures of plumbing fixtures can also be deceiving. It helps to see it in person to know precisely what you are getting. Another advantage of local shopping is the ability to talk to an associate with knowledge of the product line one-on-one. They will be able to answer any questions you may have about pricing, warranties, returns, shipping expectations, and/or delivery options. Finally, always request specifications and installation sheets for your items once chosen. It will help you and your tradesman install them properly.

- **Online Shopping:** You will enter the item in the search line and use the images option to look at what items catch your attention, where it's available, and/or which distributors carry them. Various apps allow doing the same type of shopping, such as Houzz and Pinterest. However, you may be limited to what you can purchase from the site. Sometimes, it may direct you to other sites allowing you to buy items. When shopping online, always look for the specifications page.

Print it out to have on hand for the tradesman to install your item. There should also be an installation guide. This page will tell you what type of carpentry will need to be done to install your product. For example, if you install a heavy light fixture, the ceiling will need extra bracing to hold the fixture's weight. To install certain plumbing fixtures, they may need to have specific supply lines run for proper connection. A disadvantage of shopping online is that you do not see the product in person to see the color finish or the dimensions. With the specification sheets, you can use a tape measure to judge the size of the product.

- **Word of Mouth:** Hearing from trusted friends and family where they bought products and their experience is always helpful. It seems to be the oldest method of shopping. These products come with a review from a source you know and/or trust and help narrow the field of choice for you. With our family, friends, and co-workers, we can also learn lessons from them; they may have learned the hard way. Having someone tell you about a product that has been installed and used is a good testimony to the quality of the product you can get. You may even be able to see the item in person if they are kind enough to have you over to look at it.

- **Local Specialists:** Will have a portfolio or web page that can show you what they can offer you. The most common local specialists will be cabinet makers (*recommended*), stone and quartz fabricators, door and window suppliers, etc. Seeing the product or at least a similar item in person is another tremendous advantage. It gives you a more accurate image of the item in your space. Most of these specialists will also have clients that may allow you to see the product in person in their house. Again, talking to someone who has this product installed in their home and uses it is the best testimony you can get. You will also explore and discuss different options with the expert for the product you are considering. You will know if these products fit your lifestyle and serve the purpose you are looking to fulfill.

Here is a quick reference guide for selecting vendors.

Task Category	Material	Vendor Options
Framing	Stick lumber, plywood	Local: lumberyard or big box
Roofing	Shingles, drip edge, flashing	Local: lumberyard or big box
Insulation	Insulation	Local: lumberyard, big box, tradesman
Siding	Lap siding, brick, stucco, metal	Local: lumberyard, big box, tradesman, stone/brick suppliers
HVAC	Units, trunk lines, registers	Local: tradesman, big box, specialist
Plumbing	Rough-in valves and supply line drains, pipes	Local: plumbing supply, big box, tradesman
Plumbing	Finish Fixtures for sinks, showers, and sinks	Local: plumbing supply, big box Online: distributors and specialists
Electrical	Rough-in lines, wire, boxes, panels, circuits, conduits	Local: electrical supply, big box, tradesman Online: specialty items
Electrical	Appliances, light fixtures	Local: electrical supply, big box Online: distributors and specialists
Drywall	Drywall, screws, mud, and tape	Local: lumberyard, big box
Painting	Paint, primers, rollers, brushes, rags, cleaners, etc.	Local: paint suppliers, big box Online: distributors
Cabinetry	Kitchen and Bath: base, uppers, islands, peninsulas, storage, and pantry	Local: cabinet maker (recommended), Big Box Online: distributors and specialists
Countertops	Solid surface, tile, laminate, wood, concrete	Local: stone suppliers, tradesmen, specialists, big box
Tile Work	Flooring, shower walls, backsplashes, accent walls	Local: tile suppliers, Online: distributors
Masonry	Siding, post caps, mailboxes, driveways	Local: brick suppliers
Trim Work	Crown, base and shoe moldings, paneling, doors and windows, casings, cabinetry	Local: lumberyard, specialty millworks supplier, big box Online: specialty suppliers
Finish Carpentry	Shower doors, bath accessories and hangers, hardware for doors and cabinetry, window treatments, wallpaper	Local: hardware specialists, big box, glassworks suppliers, paint suppliers (wallpaper), interior specialists, big box Online: specialist suppliers in each area

Questions to Ask: Once you have decided which vendors you will likely use because of the materials you need, it is time to get to know them better. Be confident with the questions you ask. There is never a stupid question. However, it is always right to ask questions if it is a concern or you do not know enough about a product. The following are the most common questions you may have for your vendor.

- **Price Point:** What is the actual cost of the item? You will need your quantities on hand for this. Knowing your square footage will be crucial for this information. A vendor can help you with the individual cost of an item and the total price when purchasing in bulk. For example, purchasing multiple doors and windows, tile, and flooring in bulk will usually have a square footage price.
- **All-Inclusive Cost:** Each product will need other setting materials to install it. For example, the tile will need a waterproofing system. Depending on the tile you choose for your wall applications, you may need a bullnose or pencil trim to finish the tile's exposed end. Another option would be a metal tile trim that gives a finished look to the tile's exposed end. You will need to have the price for all these items and decide on the type of products you are using. Your vendor can help you make this decision by showing you options to know the all-inclusive cost of tiling your shower walls, backsplashes, floors, or accent walls. It also applies to electrical, plumbing, siding, and drywall.
- **Storage and Delivery:**
    - Will your vendor be able to store your items for you until you are ready for them?
    - Is there a cost associated with the storage?
    - Is a scheduled delivery of the item possible?
    - How much will the delivery cost?
- **Product Knowledge and Relationship:**
    - How many years have they been doing business with this manufacturer?
    - Do they have a person to contact with questions and information about your product?
    - Have they seen any problems or advantages to using specific manufacturers or distributors?
    - Is there any recall they know of for the product line you are interested in purchasing?
    - Do they have a working knowledge of the manufacturer's procedures and practices in delivering a quality product?
- **Return Policy:**
    - If a product comes in broken, what is the procedure for returning it and getting a replacement?
    - If the product is not satisfactory to you because of color, finish, size, etc., what time frame do you have to return the product and order a new one?

- **Applications:**
    - Are there any recommendations on the application and/or use of the product you are interested in purchasing? For example, large tiles should be installed on the floor and would be too large to install on a wall, such as 24"x48" tiles. It can be done; however, the labor cost will go up significantly, and it will be very difficult to change out in the future.
    - Will the product be the best option for the use of your project? Certain plumbing and lighting products may have options you are unaware of but would help achieve the product's best use. For example, some plumbing products are best with handheld sprayers incorporated in the showerhead and take up less space. Some sprayers should be installed with a separate wall-mounted holder and a diverter, depending on your shower's configuration and how you would like to use it.
    - What is the priority of using the product for you? It may determine the type of product you use. Example: flooring; if the importance is holding up to abuse (kids, high traffic area, pets), then tile or vinyl plank flooring will be better than real wood or carpet that can damage easier.
- **Recommended Installers:** Most vendors, even big box stores, will have a list of installers they use to install their products. Ask for names and/or if the vendor will be one of your "tradesmen" and schedule the product's installation. You will not be able to get this from an online provider.
- **Lead Time:** How long it will take for your product to arrive.
    - **Orders:** Normally, you will have to order your product (especially flooring and tile). To schedule your tradesman, you will need to know how far in advance to order your product.
    - **Stock:** Is this an item they have in stock regularly or just a temporary promotional item?
    - How much notice will you need to provide before picking up the item?
    - Can you have anyone pick up the item? Do you have to give a name? Your tradesman may be able to pick it up for you.
- **Payment Plans:**
    - **Cash Upfront:** Do they need the full item paid for upfront?
    - **Deposits:** Will they require a portion to be paid before ordering? What is that percentage?
    - What forms of payment are accepted, cash, check, or credit card?
    - Is there financing available?

You may come up with more questions, but these are the most common and important questions to answer before beginning your project.

Section 5: Purchasing

Ordering Items: Once the scope is outlined and your tradesmen are scheduled, you will begin the purchasing process. This part can be the most fun stage of your project. Timing can be crucial to your project to move along and follow the schedule you have set as closely as possible.

- **Lead Times:** This is the amount of time it takes for your product to reach you. Having all materials and products is essential before your tradesman starts work.
    - **Stock I**tems are on hand at your local vendor or distributor.
        - **Local Vendor:** You can pick up these items anytime and even send your tradesman to pick them up.
        - **Online Distributor:** Will be able to ship it to you within a week.
    - **Special Orders:** These are items that will have to be obtained from the manufacturer or approved distributor.
        - **Local Vendors:** Can take anywhere from a few days to several weeks for your product to come in. When doing your initial research, you should find out which items will take several weeks to arrive. Order these items as soon as possible and arrange these items' storage before they need to be installed.
        - **Online Distributor:** Most items will ship within a week. You should be able to get an estimated time of shipment before ordering. If this item will take several weeks to arrive, order the item and arrange storage for it until it's time to install it.
    - **Specialty Items:** These items will be precisely measured or fitted to your project by local vendors. Such items will be the following:
        - **Cabinets:** These are generally measured and made to fit your space. They will be tailored to fit your needs. From the measurement time to the installation, time can be anywhere from four to eight weeks. It will depend on the amount of cabinetry you are ordering and the style.
        - **Countertops:** (*Solid Surface and Stone*) You will handpick these for the style, color, and specific stone piece. You will be able to choose the placement of the stone as well. If you want to show a part of the stone in an open countertop area, you can request your fabricator to cut the stone to feature this area. The time from the template (*measure*) to installation would generally be two to four weeks.
- **Back-Orders:** You may not find an item on back-order until you put in the order. It will happen with your local vendors as well as online distributors. When you receive a back-order notice, it should come with an estimated arrival time. It will rarely happen that the manufacturer will not have an estimated arrival time for you. If this happens, you will need to decide:
    - **Stick With the Original Order:** You may like the item enough that it is worth the wait. You also may be ordering the item far enough in advance. Therefore, the delay will not be an issue with scheduling your tradesman.

- **Change the Item:**
  - **Stock:** You may be able to change to an item that is in stock. You may have to change if you need the item not to lose your scheduled time with your tradesman.
  - **2nd Choice:** You may choose to order your 2nd choice, which will arrive in the standard time, allowing you to keep your scheduled time with your tradesman.
- **Items That Frequently go on Back-Order:**
  - **Doors and Windows:** There may be a high demand from the manufacturer, causing a delay in fulfilling the orders.
  - **Tile:** The demand for certain tiles and the breakage that occurs in shipping and storage will sometimes delay fulfilling the order.
  - **Wood Flooring:** The high demand from the manufacturer may cause a delay in fulfilling the orders.
  - **Lighting & Plumbing fixtures:** The high demand from the manufacturer may cause a delay in fulfilling the orders, especially in certain colors or finishes.

- **Storage:** Order all items ahead of time that you can. It is better to have the items on hand and ready to install instead of taking the risk of not having an item and slowing down the project. You will have to plan your storage with your vendors and tradesmen. The following will be items of consideration when storing your items.

- **Responsibility:** Establish who is responsible for storing any items. It will be either you or your vendor.
  - **Vendor:** You may not have enough room at your house or property to store all your items. Some vendors have the warehousing capability to hold your items for as long as you need. Others may only be able to house your items anywhere from one week to a month. When talking to your vendor, ask what they can offer you.
  - **You:** You feel more comfortable storing your items at your house. There are options for how you store these items.
    - **Spare Room:** You may have room to store all your items in your home.
    - **Shed or Storage Area:** This may be a storage shed or a garage
    - **Rental Unit:** You do not have room for all of them. You may consider getting a temporary mobile storage unit. You cannot store all your items in these if you plan to keep them for a long time. Certain items need to be stored in a conditioned environment that does not cause damage or warping.
    - **Conditioned Items:** These items will require storage in a temperature and air-controlled environment.
      - **Wood Flooring:** Too much moisture in the air can cause the wood to swell and not be installed properly or cause it to warp before installation. If the air is too dry, it can cause the wood to shrink and cause the wood to split, and crack when installed.

- **Cement Bags:** if there is too much moisture in the air, the cement will solidify in the bag, making it unusable.
- **Grout:** If too much moisture is in the air, the grout may solidify in the bag, making it unusable.
- **Drywall:** If too much moisture is in the air, the drywall may become soft and warp. It will not be able to be installed properly.
- **Doors (*wood*):** Wood doors will warp, swell, and become brittle if exposed to too much moisture, arid air, or varying changes in temperature.
- **Wood Trim:** Will warp, swell, or become brittle if exposed to too much moisture, dry air, or varying temperature changes.
- **Paint:** If paint gets too hot or cold, it can split or curdle, making it unusable.
- **Glues and Cleaners:** If not kept in ambient temperatures, they will likely become unusable.

- **Non-Conditioned Items:** These items may be stored in an on-site unit or shed. They will not be affected by humidity or temperature changes.
    - **Treated Lumber:** This lumber is made to be exposed to varying weather conditions.
    - **Light Fixtures and Plumbing Fixtures:** These items are generally made of metal and glass. They are not susceptible to weather changes.
    - **Windows:** The metal and glass will not be affected by the weather and temperature changes.
    - **Steel or Fiberglass Doors:** These doors hold up to the exposure to weather changes.
    - **Fasteners:** Most are made of metal and will not be affected by temperature changes and/or humidity.
    - **Bricks and Tile:** These products stand up to weather and are usually moisture resistant.
    - **Insulation:** It stands up and guards against temperature changes and moisture build-up.
    - **Plywood Sheathing:** While NOT meant to be exposed directly to weather, it can be stored in a unit or shed with little effect on the wood. This is because of how plywood is made. It is made from several small pieces of wood laminated together, binding it together tightly and giving it strength. This reduces the warping, shrinking, or swelling of the wood. It is used as the protective outer layer on walls and roofs before the siding and shingles (*or metal*) are applied.

Vendor Payment Schedules: Most vendors will take deposits to order your materials. Then will collect the remainder of the order when it is completed or the product arrives. Therefore, you will want to put deposits on materials and order as soon as you have decided.

- **Deposits:** Begin putting deposits on those materials that will need to be built or ordered for your project.
    - **Cabinets:** When your final quote comes from the cabinet maker so he can begin fabrication.
    - **Countertops:** You can secure the exact stone you want, and they will hold it for you, but you will need to put a deposit down.
    - **Plumbing:** Finish fixtures.
    - **Electrical:** Finish fixtures.
    - **Siding:** If unique, order brick, stone, vinyl, etc.
    - **Flooring:** May take up to four weeks to come in for select woods and/or stone products.

- **Full Invoice:** There will be some products that you will only pay for when the product arrives. It will entirely depend on the stipulations of your vendor. No deposit will be required.
    - **Framing:** The lumber materials will be paid for when you receive them.
    - **Siding:** Will be paid for on arrival or billed for on a 30-day expectation.
    - **Plumbing:** Finish fixtures.
    - **Electrical:** Finish fixtures.
    - **Drywall:** Materials.

Section 6: Tradesman Hiring

In this section, we will cover the process of hiring tradesmen and discerning which ones you will need to perform the work for your project. It will help to define your budget further and allow you to make changes as required. During this process, you will have lots of open conversations and need to be direct with what you want and expect. Most tradesmen are specialists in their field, so there will be many people you will need to interview. In the following section, we will cover the following:

- **Determining the List of Tradesman:** Each task category will require someone to perform the job. Each tradesman is a specialist in their field. A few may be harder to find than others, but we will give you tips on how to find them.
- **Getting Quotes:**
    - **Labor and Materials:** To get accurate quotes, you will have to define the work and materials you need. It will be a part of the negotiation process with your tradesmen.
    - **Getting Timelines:** In each task category, you will need to establish timelines to schedule your material deliveries and the tradesmen to perform work. We will discuss having buffer times as well.
- **Operations and Background:**
    - **Licensed and Insured Tradesmen:** There will be specific tradesmen that will have to be licensed and insured for you to hire them. Others working in specialty fields of carpentry may not need or have insurance. We will discuss which tradesmen those will be and why.
    - **Getting Referrals:** There are many ways to get referrals for tradesmen.
        - **Word of Mouth:** The most popular and usually the most trusted because we hear from family and friends that we know and trust.
        - **Web Sites:** Online services can provide reviews given by people who have used the tradesmen you are looking at hiring but can sometimes be unreliable.
        - **Vendors:** When making materials purchases, the vendor you are dealing with may have a tradesmen list they use or know.
    - **Handling Change Orders:** Change orders seem to occur most of the time in any renovation project. Whether out of necessity or design, knowing how your tradesman handles these is crucial.
    - **Hours of Operation:** You will need to know the hours during the day and how many days a week the tradesmen work to schedule the project properly.
    - **Payment Schedules:** When and how do the tradesmen expect to receive payment.
    - **Responsibilities:** In purchasing materials, storage of tools and materials, site cleanliness, site behavior, etc.
- **Final Decisions:** Make your final decisions based on experience, price point, duration of work, workmanship, ability to handle change orders, ability to work with others, and references.

Tradesman Definitions:

The following briefly describes all the tradesmen to be used on a project. First, look at the outline of the work you have determined needs to be done, and the list of tradesmen you will need to interview for your project will become very clear. Then, you will fill out your tradesmen checklist and quote form.

- **Demolition:** The removal of building materials and deposal of the materials.
- **Foundation:** Installs and removes concrete slabs and footings.
- **Excavation:** The grading of the ground includes removing any ground materials.
- **Dirt Work:** Can do excavation, fill in the dirt, compacts it, and readies it for construction. For example, removing a large tree root ball or a pool requires filling the void with dirt.
- **Framer:** The framing of all exterior and interior walls, windows, doors, ceilings, roofs, soffit, and fascia.
- **Masonry:** Install all brick and stonework (siding and steps), driveways, sidewalks, and retaining walls.
- **Wood or Lap Siding Carpenter:** Specializes in removing and hanging wood or lap siding.
- **Vinyl Siding Carpenter:** Specializes in removing and hanging vinyl siding, soffits, and fascia.
- **Plumber:** Installs all water and gas drains and supply lines. Installs all finish fixtures for water and gas products.
- **Electrician:** Installs all wiring, boxes, switches, outlets, lights, exhaust fans, appliances, panels, and other electrical needs such as garage and gate openers, motorized blinds, pool pumps, etc.
- **Drywaller:** Hangs all drywall * can be the same guy as your floater; you will need to ask.
- **Floater:** Floats out all drywall * can be the same guy as the drywaller; you will need to ask,
- **Painter:** Caulks, primes, paints walls, ceilings, siding, trim work inside and out, doors and window trim, shutters, brickwork, etc.
- **Tiler:** Will remove and install tile in showers, backsplashes, and floors inside and outside.
- **Flooring:** There are different specialists. Sometimes you find a guy who can install any flooring you need.
    - **Carpet and Padding**
    - **Wood:** Glue down, nail in, or floating floor
    - **Vinyl:** Sheet or plank
    - **Refinisher:** He will strip the wood or brick flooring you have and stain and clear coat it
- **Trim Carpenter:** Installs all trim work for ceilings, floors, doors, windows, cabinetry, and specialty projects.
- **Finish Carpenter:** *Can also be a trim carpenter, installs all doors, hardware, mirrors, accessories, etc.

Questions to Ask Yourself:
To ensure the process of hiring a tradesman, you will need the answer to the following questions:

- What work will you be performing (if any)? There are some areas that homeowners would prefer that they do themselves:
    - **Electrical:** The finish electrical only, installing lights, plates, covers, etc.
    - **Plumbing:** The finish plumbing only, installation of fixtures, etc.
    - **Painting:** You may find it enjoyable or necessary to fit your budget.
    - **Demo:** You may want control over this area or find it necessary to your budget.
- What is the value to you of having someone else perform the work? Even though you may be capable of doing the work, it may save you time and/or give you peace of mind having a tradesman do the job.
- What is the importance of a licensed and insured tradesman? It will be a must for specific fields, and for others, not so much. If a tradesman gets hurt on your property, your homeowner's insurance may cover it. We will go over this in more detail in the chapter.
- How many tradesmen do you wish to interview? It takes time to get a proper interview with a qualified tradesman. Your time is precious, and since there will be a good handful of people to talk to, you may limit yourself to 3–4 in each field.

Each of these topics will be covered in further detail in this section. Having a good relationship with your tradesmen is essential, and being prepared before talking with them will help ensure this. It will increase your ability to communicate with your tradesmen and help them understand your needs and expectations.

Suppose you hire a company (*Contractor*) that will handle multiple tradesmen and task categories of work. While being more expensive than the handyman working on his own, there is value in paying for their service. These companies will be your arbitrator with multiple tradesmen, getting quotes, scheduling the tradesmen, and handling the work schedules and deliveries. They will also make material lists, research materials for your project, and bargain with vendors. Some companies will provide you with schematics and layouts, which are also valuable to you and your project. These companies will also carry the insurance burden for tradesmen who may not be insured and fully licensed. It is important to note that this service will cost you, but it can be well worth the expense. During this process, this should be one of the considerations you make.

Tradesmen: You will need to determine what specific tradesmen will be required to complete your project. Some tradesmen specialize in the following fields, each with their crew members. There are also construction crews that can handle multiple areas of work.

- **Demolition:**
    - Concrete—slabs, sidewalks, pools, retaining walls, etc.
    - Structure—framework and roofing
    - Plumbing—rough-in plumbing to finish materials
    - Electrical - wiring to finish fixtures
    - Asbestos—need to be certified and licensed to remove asbestos (walls, ceilings, and roofing)
    - Tile and flooring
- **Foundation:**
    - Concrete and Pier
    - Leveling houses
    - New foundation
    - Driveways and sidewalks
    - Retaining walls
- **Framing:**
    - Remodeling Framing—walls, doors, windows, ceilings
    - Additions and Patios—will include doing roofs and tying into existing
    - Decks, awnings, etc.
- **Roofing:**
    - Standard roofing—shingles
    - Metal
    - Flat—there will be companies that specialize in flat roofs
- **Siding:** You may find that masonry, stone, and stucco could be the same crew, but lap or vinyl siding will be different crews.
    - Masonry and stone
    - Wood
    - Stucco
    - Vinyl: Specialist
    - Metal sheeting
- **HVAC – Heat, Ventilation, Air Conditioning**
    - Changing out or adding a full unit inside and out, along with tubing to vents
    - Cleaning out all tub lines and interior units
    - Servicing the thermostats and plenums
- **Insulation:**
    - Standard roll insulation for ceilings and walls
    - Standard blown-in insulation for both ceilings and walls
    - Foam Insulation—a specialist for ceilings, walls, sub-floors, and attics

- **Plumbing:** Licensed and insured
  - Water supply and drainage for the main house
  - Gas supply for appliances, heating systems, and fireplaces and maintenance
  - Adding and servicing pumps
  - Adding and servicing Septic tanks
  - Changing out or adding water heaters
- **Electrical:** Licensed and insured
  - Main power supply to the house
  - Rewiring of the main house
  - Replacing light fixtures
  - Replacing old outlets throughout the house
  - Adding circuits or breakers
  - Changing out or adding 2nd service of power to a house or property
  - Changing out main panels or adding sub-panels to the house
- **Drywall:**
  - Hanging drywall
  - Floating drywall
  - Texturing drywall ceilings and walls
  - Scraping popcorn ceilings
  - Patchwork
- **Tile Work:**
  - Installing interior and exterior tile for showers, tub surrounds backsplashes and flooring
  - Installing waterproof systems
  - Demo of tile and/or flooring
- **Flooring:**
  - Installation of carpet, vinyl (*sheet and plank*), wood, laminate, and tile
  - Removal of existing flooring
  - Refinishing wood and/or sealers on tile and pavers
- **Cabinetry:**
  - Installation of any cabinetry base, upper, storage units
  - Specialty entertainment or storage units
  - Reconfiguration of existing cabinetry
- **Countertops:**
  - Fabrication of stone and quartz
  - Installation of countertops, wall caps, bench seating, tub decks, etc.
  - Fabricate and install wood, steel, or concrete countertops

Section 7: Trades & Cost

Cost of Labor:

There will be the initial cost of labor for the hours the tradesman is putting into the construction. This labor rate is determined to cover their living and travel expenses, tools, and tool maintenance. There may be other costs going into a tradesman giving you a quote. Some tradesmen will want to buy their materials for the work they are doing. There will be brands they trust and know how to work with better than others. They will usually include these materials in their quote. You will need to determine whether this is the case with the tradesman when interviewing them. There will be critical questions to ask during your interview with your tradesman. After laying out in detail what the job entails for your tradesman, including drawings and a site visit, you will need to have an open dialogue with the tradesman. They will always bring their tools.

- **Quote:** Does the quote include labor only or labor and some materials? Some tradesmen will include certain back-end materials that they prefer to use. The following is only a *guideline* to talk to your tradesman about the materials that may or may NOT be included in their quote. For your project to proceed smoothly, you and your tradesman must *be clear on what materials* you are getting for the work to be performed.

Task Category	Materials included	Labor	Materials NOT included in quote
Demolition	Trash bags, brooms, vacuums	Removal of all building materials outlined	Trash trailers, dumpsters
Foundation	Concrete, lumber for forms, visqueen, metal mesh, grounding rod	Frame out and pouring of concrete	Concrete you may get
Framing	Fasteners	Frame out walls, ceilings, roofs, doors, and windows	Lumber, doors, windows, plywood, roofing felt
Roofing	Drip edge, shingles, ridge vents, roofing jacks, fasteners	Installing shingles, drip edge, flashing, and roofing jacks	shingles
HVAC	The entire unit, trunk lines, ceiling or wall registers, thermostat	Installation of unit	

Siding	Lap Siding: fasteners Stucco: base and topcoat Brick: ties and fasteners, sand and mortar	Installation of siding on exterior walls	Wood or concrete lap siding, bricks color of stucco
Plumbing	Drains, connectors, lines, pipes, rough-in valves	Installation of all plumbing supply, drain lines, fixtures	Finish fixtures
Electrical	Wire, boxes, meters, circuits, panels, switches, outlets, can lighting, and beauty rings	Installation of all wires, conduits, boxes, switches, outlets, fixtures, cover plates	Finish light fixtures
Drywall	Fasteners, tape, mud	Hanging and floating of drywall	Drywall sheets, mud
Trim Carpentry	Fasteners, caulk, and putty	Install all casings, crown, base and shoe moldings, window and door trim, caulk, and putty	Crown, base, and shoe moldings, door, and window casings, cabinet trim
Tile Work	Thin-set, waterproofing materials	Install waterproofing and tile with any trims	Tile, grout, trim pieces
Cabinetry	Cabinets, hinges, drawer slides	Install all cabinetries, including doors and drawer fronts, and install all hardware	Hardware
Countertops	All countertop materials (backsplash if desired)	Measure and install all stone countertops with edging and under-mount sinks, drill holes for plumbing fixtures	Sinks and faucets
Flooring	Glue, carpet tack strips, nails, or other fasteners	Install carpet, vinyl (sheet or plank), wood, laminate, or tile	Flooring itself, thin-set, grouts, any underlayment padding

If you want your tradesmen to purchase all the materials for you, you will have to provide the type, size, color, and other relevant information they need to get the exact items you want.

- **Discounts:** Do your tradesmen receive any discounts that may be passed along from the vendors being used? Some tradesmen will have a long-standing, good relationship with the local vendors and hold accounts with them. Sometimes, they will give you a discount on products if you purchase them through the tradesman. It will usually apply to the products the tradesman will include in the quote they give you.

- **Apples to Apples:** Make sure you are making a fair comparison when getting quotes from multiple tradesmen. The above chart will help you ask the tradesmen what materials are included with their quote so that you can be clear on precisely what you are paying for and open the discussion for who is buying the materials needed.
    - **Time and Materials:** Some will quote you BOTH the labor and materials. In this case, you will have to remove the materials from your budget you may have already considered purchasing.
    - **Labor Only:** Some will quote labor ONLY. No materials are included. You will still have to factor in the materials' cost to get your budget's actual price.

- **Material Preference:**
    - **You:** In your research for materials, you may have found certain materials you would prefer to use. Now is the time to request those to be used—siding, shingles, paint, windows, doors, grout, etc.
    - **Tradesman:** There may be materials that your tradesman prefers to use for the project. These items may be ones they prefer to work with and trust to perform well.
    - **Differences:**
        - **Vendors:** There may be certain local vendors that your tradesman prefers to use. There are various reasons this could be:
            - Line of products carried stock and specialty items
            - Quality of products carried
            - Discounts are given
            - Delivery options
            - Return policies
            - Price points of products
        - **Materials:** If there are differences in the preference of you and the tradesman, ask what factors make those specific materials preferable to use. The following will be just a few items the tradesman will prefer using. Such materials may be the following:

- **Foundation:** Concrete and vendor they use; quality and availability
- **Framing:** The stick lumber and plywood sheathing; quality and availability
- **Roofing:** Shingle suppliers; brand, quality, availability, and price point
- **Siding:** Bricks, concrete or wood lap siding, vinyl siding; quality and availability
- **HVAC:** Type of unit
- **Plumbing:** The rough-in supplies and vendor; quality and availability
- **Electrical:** The rough-in supplies and vendor; quality and availability
- **Drywall:** The drywall sheets and vendor, quality, and price point
- **Painting:** The type of paint they like to use and vendor; price point and quality
- **Staining:** The type of stain and clear coat to use; quality
- **Trim Carpentry:** The type of trim and vendor; availability
- **Cabinetry:** Hinges to use on the doors and slides on drawers; quality and availability

Talking with your tradesman will give you a better insight into your home's materials. Use the benefit of their experience and combine that with the research you have done to ensure you make the best possible decision for your project.

- **Cost Savers:** Are there any things you can do that will reduce the price?
    - Picking up materials
    - Having materials delivered
    - Cleaning up after them

Remember to keep things as open and honest as possible while talking to your tradesman. It will set the tone of expectation moving forward.

Section 8: Operations & Background

The following will be a series of questions you will want to be answered by your tradesman to make the best decision in choosing someone to work in your home. There are many factors to consider when making this decision; you are looking for someone who is the best fit, not just for you but also for the work to be done. Now that you have found out what their pricing and preferences of materials are, now it is time to ask about their operation and where you fit into it.

Experience: Aspects of a tradesman's experience to explore:

- How long have they been working in their trade? Usually, someone with anything over five years in construction has learned a great deal. Most tradesman will learn their trade by doing it, not just from books. They will have practical application experience, and that can be the best teacher. They have made and seen mistakes and learned to avoid or correct them.
- What is their area of expertise, and do they have any experience with any other field? Knowing what they are comfortable doing and their range of different skill sets is essential. In addition, you may have another tradesman that has to cancel working on your project for any of life's reasons, and you may be able to call on them to fill in and help keep the job going.
- What did they do before they began working in their field? If it was not construction, what drew them into it? It can tell a lot about their character and experience with their craft. For example, some people get into construction, thinking it is a quick buck, and find out quickly it's hard work and takes dedication and planning. On the other hand, they may have a corporate background, letting you know they are planners and aware of costs, timelines, and project and resource management.

Operation: You have three basic types of tradesmen—Contractor, Tradesman (Sub-Contractor), or Handyman. (Covered in Chapter 1)

- **Contractor:** Someone who employs other people and works for a larger company. The cost may be higher, but they will carry insurance and be licensed. Their work will also come with customer service, warranties, and guarantees. They have experience in all or most of the following task categories and will be able to handle more than one, if not all, the task categories listed:
    - Foundation
    - Framing
    - Roofing
    - HVAC
    - Plumbing
    - Electrical
    - Drywall
    - Painting

- Cabinetry
- Countertops
- Tile Work
- Masonry and Stonework
- **Tradesman (Sub-Contractor):** Someone who usually works alongside other crew members (*maybe has one helper or two*) or has multiple crews. They will have insurance and a license. Ask about warranty policies and guaranteed work. Most will have some policy in place; it just may vary. You will most likely use them in the following task categories:
    - Foundation
    - Framing
    - Siding
    - Painting
    - Trim Carpentry
    - Cabinetry
    - Tile Work
    - Masonry and Stonework
- Handyman: this is a person who usually works alone and is a "Jack of all trades." They may sometimes enlist the help of another person. They do not carry insurance, nor are they required to have a license. Ask about warranty policies and guaranteed work. Most will have some policy in place; it just may vary. You will most likely use them in the following task categories:
    - General maintenance repair work on a house
        i. Minor roof repair
        ii. Door and window repair
        iii. Trim work
        iv. Cabinetry repair or small fabrication
        v. Soffit, fascia, and siding repair
        vi. Minor plumbing and electrical work
        vii. Small flooring or tile installation
    - Full Bathroom or kitchen remodels

You may find a handyman who can handle multiple task categories or know another tradesman they have worked alongside and recommend. ***NOTE:** If the handyman is NOT insured, please check your homeowner's insurance policy to see if you are covered while they work on your home.

- **Timelines:** There will be two different timelines to consider when talking to your tradesman, the length of time it will take them to perform their part of the job and their availability. There are a few factors to consider and ask about when talking about timelines:

- **Duration:** The amount of time your tradesman will take to perform the work outlined for their part of the project. Let them know to be honest about how long it will take because it will be essential to schedule other work around them. Some tradesmen will tell you a timeline that they think you want to hear to get

the job, but you and he need to remember to look at the project with realistic eyes to avoid frustration and bad feelings in the future.
- **Change Orders:** Ask for extended times, meaning if there are any reasons for the job taking longer than anticipated. Some of these questions will not be answered until the situation arises and you can revisit the schedule.
    - What would those reasons be?
        - Unforeseen rot
        - Material breakage—new and/or old
        - Materials delays—orders and deliveries
        - Weather
    - How much time could that add to the entire timeline?
    - How much will that add to the price? (*Labor and materials*)
- **Billing**: procedures for invoicing for labor and materials
    - Do they bill weekly, take a draw as the project progresses, or take a deposit and final payment when the job is complete?
    - What materials are being purchased, and how can they be reimbursed?
    - How quickly will they need a check from you when the invoice is presented?
- **Availability:** You will need to know when and what hours they intend to work on your project.
    - **Start Time:** This is the time they will be able to begin the work initially agreed upon.
    - **Workday:** The hours during the day and what days of the week they will be on-site working on your project.
    - **Change Orders:** If a change order is needed, will they continue the work while they are there? Or will they have to schedule to come back later to complete the change order work? This will also depend on the type of change order you have:
        - **Structural Changes:** May have to be done right away, such as rot, faulty construction, or defective materials.
        - **Added Work:** May have to schedule later, especially if the change affects other work being done.
        - **Material Delays:** will they have to reschedule altogether, or will they be able to start the day the materials arrive?

- **Your Part:** If you are performing a specific part of the project, you will need to know how this will affect their timeline. Depending on the work you decide to take on yourself, other aspects of the project will be waiting on you to finish before work can proceed. The following list will tell you what areas will be waiting on you to complete if you take on a task:
    - **Demo:** Foundation and framing will wait until you are finished
    - **Foundation:** Framing will wait until you are finished
    - **Framing:** Plumbing, electrical, siding, and roofing (everything) wait until the framing is complete
    - **Plumbing Rough-In:** Insulation, drywall, and tile work wait until the plumbing is complete
    - **Electrical Rough-In:** Insulation and drywall wait until electrical is complete
    - **Drywall:** Floating, trim installation, painting, wait until the drywall is complete
    - **Painting:** Finish plumbing, finish electrical, and touch-ups will be done when everyone else is finished
    - **Trim Carpentry:** Painting, hardware installs, fixture installs for plumbing and electrical
    - **Tile Work:** Finish plumbing, 2nd coat painting
    - **Cabinetry:** Countertops, finish plumbing, tile work if using a tiled backsplash, waits until cabinetry is installed

- **Hours of Operation:** The hours of operation are very different for remodeling than for new construction. In new construction, no one is living in the home yet, so if the crew needs to work late or on the weekend to meet the deadline, they can without interrupting the family's daily life. Remodeling construction usually follows a typical work week with hours of 7:30 a.m. to about 5:00 p.m. These hours may vary depending on the type of tradesman you are hiring. Be sure to clarify the expectations when they will be in your home. There may be times you will request no work be done and reschedule because of life situations such as a death in the family, a sudden illness of a family member, or an unexpected business trip. The following questions will help you establish these expectations.

- What is the start and stop times for a typical workday?
- Are there any times they work on the weekends?
    - Do you want them in your home on the weekends?
    - Are you and your tradesman willing to work through the weekend if a deadline needs to be met?
- How many days a week do they work?
- How much notice do you give if you need to reschedule work because of a life situation?

Pay attention to holidays that fall within the timeline of your project, and ask your tradesman how much time they take off for the holidays. Most will only take off for the "big" holidays, such as Christmas and Thanksgiving. Some will also take off on the 4th of July. Depending on when the holiday falls in the week, sometimes more days are taken off than just the holiday itself. Some tradesmen will work the weekends to make up work and try to make deadlines. Always have this conversation to be prepared for any event.

- **References:** Always ask for references from people with who they have previously worked. Ask if you can visit any of the sites to see their work. A few more ways to get references are the following:
    - Facebook page you can visit or Instagram
    - Website you can visit
    - Do they have any pictures on their phone or in a portfolio you can see?
    - Are there any customers you can visit to see a similar project?

Looking at their work will speak volumes about their ability and skillsets. If you can talk to a previous client, you will get to know the work the tradesman can do and how they work, as well as any issues that may have come up and how they were handled.

- **Payment Schedules**: As mentioned in Billing, you will need to establish a payment schedule with your tradesmen. Not every tradesman will have the same payment schedule. You will need to understand with each what they will expect or need. The most common methods of payment are as follows:
    - **Deposit:** To pay for the materials they will be purchasing themselves.
    - **Weekly Payments:** For the work, usually performed on Fridays to cover labor.
    - **Final Invoice:** For completion of work.
    - **Draw:**
        - The 1st draw is to cover materials purchased.
        - The 2nd draw is to cover labor costs.
        - The 3rd and final draw—completion of work.
    - **Half and Half:**
        - First half of the quote to begin work.
        - Second half of the quote at the completion of work.

Getting the payment plan set up in advance will help you and the tradesmen feel comfortable moving forward with the work knowing the expectations. You will also be able to set your budget in order by knowing how and when the money is going out. It is best to have all the money you need for the entire project secured, plus any contingency amount you think you may spend on change orders and beyond.

Job Site Responsibilities

You will need to set expectations with your tradesman on which responsibilities you will have and which ones you will need them to take. Note each of these so you can refer to it during the project's progression.

- **Cleanliness:**
    - **Debris Removal:** Trash trailers and/or dumpsters provided by you **or** them
    - **Daily Clean-Up Expectations:**
        - Materials storage—designated areas
        - Tool storage—designated areas
        - Food items are to be removed at the end of every day
        - Facilities—port-o-lets on-site, you will need to be informed when they need servicing, and they will need to tell you unless you check it yourself
        - NO drug paraphernalia, alcohol bottles, or cigarette butts allowed
    - **Weekend Cleaning:**
        - Material storage—stored and locked away in the designated area
        - Tool storage—stored and locked away in the designated area
        - Ladder and scaffolding—completely broken down and stored away
        - All food items are cleaned and thrown away in bags
        - All flooring is swept and vacuumed if needed, and cigarette butts are picked up
- **Site Locations:**
    - **Tool Storage:**
        - You will designate the area where tools are stored (shed, storage room, etc.)
        - They are to tell all workers and make sure they adhere to this area
    - **Materials Storage:**
        - You will designate an area to store your materials
        - They are to tell all workers and make sure they adhere to this area
    - **Smoking Areas:**
        - You will designate an area where you are comfortable with smoking (*no matter where that is*)
        - They are to tell all workers, and they are to adhere to this area
- **Materials:**
    - **Orders:** You will track and verify delivery
    - **Deliveries:** You will need to be there (*or someone you trust*) to ensure proper storage and check the materials' inventory and state
    - **Back-end Materials:** The tradesman will purchase the materials they prefer. If you are buying, you will need to have the materials you are responsible for at the job site the day before the tradesman begins their work.
- **Other Crew Members or Subcontractors:** You will need to establish who you are to report unacceptable behavior to if the tradesman has any crew members.

- **Work Performance:** The tradesman who hired them
- **Site Management:** BOTH
    - **YOU:** Reporting to the tradesman if the site needs attention in cleanliness, materials, or tool storage
    - **Tradesman:** Checking to make sure of site cleanliness, material and tool storage, debris removal, and job progress

Working With Others: Sometimes, meeting project deadlines requires multiple tradesmen to work alongside each other. Some tradesmen will refuse to work alongside other tradesmen. It is not always about being difficult, but rather from the experience of being asked to do part of their work for free, or they are unable to perform the work they agreed to on time because they are stopped from doing their job. Others have no problem working alongside other tradesmen. And some cannot work alongside others due to the nature of their trade. The following is a guideline for those trades that can and cannot work with each other.

Tradesman	Able to Work With	Work Performed Alone
Foundation	Plumber—rough-in pipes	Concrete pour
Framer		Stick framing
Roofer	Anyone	Roofing
HVAC	Plumber, electrician	HVAC
Siding Specialist	Anyone	Siding
Plumber	HVAC, electrician	Finish plumbing
Electrician	HVAC, plumber, finish carpentry	All electrical work
Drywaller		Hang and float drywall
Trim Carpenter	Cabinetry	Install all crown, base, and shoe moldings, door and window molding, casings
Painter		Prep, prime, and paint walls, ceilings, trim, doors, and cabinetry (if needed)
Cabinet Maker	Trim carpentry, painting	Install all cabinetry
Countertops/Stone Provider	Cabinetry	Template and install countertops
Tiler	Painting	Install all tile flooring, walls, backsplashes
Finish Carpenter		Install accessories, shower doors, hardware, mirrors, touch-ups

Section 9: Final Decisions

Final Decisions: Now that you have done your research, it is time to decide. We will review all the aspects of making your decision about the tradesmen you will use to complete your project. There is a tradesman checklist/quote to fill out while talking to your tradesmen to keep all your information in one place at the end of the chapter. Keeping a digital file with all the pertinent information for each tradesman will help you keep better track of each one, along with the tradesman checklist/quote form as a quick reference guide. You can make a simple Excel spreadsheet to help you track this information.

- **Experience in Their Field**:
    - **Years of Experience:** Put the tradesmen in order from the most experienced field to the least
    - **Digital Files:** If you can, keep digital files for each tradesman and download pictures of their work. If the tradesman only has work pictures on his phone, ask him to send you a few images relative to the project you are doing. EX: Look at bathroom pictures if you are renovating your bathroom. Compare the craftsmanship with the years of experience. There may be one that jumps out at you that closely matches what you are looking for in craftsmanship and desired look.

- **Price Point:** The price of labor is essential to your budget.
    - **Fair Comparison:** Try to compare apples to apples in terms of the overall cost. It will not just be the labor but also the materials they may purchase. This is where the tradesman checklist/quote will come in handy. Make a note of any special notes of materials they will provide or any extra services they can provide.
    - **Warning Signs:** it is NOT always the cheapest guy that will work. It can sometimes be a warning sign it the tradesman quote is TOO low. He may be the type that will bid very low to get the job, and as soon as he starts, he will start giving you change order after change order to make up the difference. You may end up paying more at the end of the project than the highest quote you received in the interviews.
    - **Averages:** You can look up online the national average price of labor for any task you are sighing to have done—anything from demolition to finish carpentry. Remember, though, these prices you see will be a national average and not just a local average. So if your tradesman falls close to the average range, they are reasonable with their quote.
    - **Insured and Licensed:** If your tradesman is insured and licensed, they will be more expensive than an individual working for just themselves who can waive insurance and keep tax burdens down by not having employees.

- **Duration of Work**: How long the job will interfere with your daily routine is always a concern.
  - **Deadlines** can also affect your overall timeline if one tradesman gets off schedule and makes the project longer. First, you must be very clear with the tradesman. You need a realistic timeline from them to schedule another tradesman. Then, you must decide to who to give the work.
  - **Change Orders:** Your timeline can be extended by making any change orders to the project. If you do not decide within a timeframe, materials may not be delivered on time for the tradesman to perform their job. It is crucial to the project's progression to decide on the finish materials BEFORE work begins and not question what you have chosen. It will lessen the chance of change orders for design.
  - **Forever Homes:** If you are undertaking an extensive project (*most of your home, including all bathrooms, kitchen, and bedrooms*). It may take a long time, and you will suffer from fatigue; in these times, you will need to focus on the project's overall vision and know that you will be living in the home that best fits your family's needs and lifestyle. The goal is that you will only be doing this type of renovation once. It may be worth extending the timeline to get what you want.
  - **Investment Properties:** You will need the work completed as soon as possible to rent out or sell the property and recuperate the renovation expenses as quickly as possible.

- **Guarantees of Workmanship:** Most tradesmen will guarantee their work for up to a year for everyday use. When interviewing the tradesmen, this question will come up. You will note their standards of practice in their interview form. You will need to review these when deciding who to hire.
  - **Abuse:** They CANNOT guarantee against the misuse of the property, especially in rental properties with tenants.
  - **Nature:** They CANNOT guarantee work in natural disasters such as floods, hurricanes, hailstorms, windstorms, mudslides, earthquakes, hard freezes, and fires.
  - **Faulty Materials:** They will not be able to warranty work against defective materials that may have a recall. You will be doing most of the materials' purchasing; in this instance, they CANNOT back up the materials you chose and purchased by you if it fails. It is an issue with the manufacturer.
  - **Improper Installation:** The tradesman should warranty all work if the materials are installed improperly, and they fail to perform. You should expect them to stand behind their work and be able to reinstall new materials (*if needed*).

- **Change Orders:** The ability of a tradesman to deal with a change order when one arises and their process in dealing with them.
    - **Necessary:**
        - Is it in their skill set to do the work, or do you need to hire a different tradesman?
        - What and how does the cost of the labor and materials affect your budget? You may have to give up something else to get the repair work done, or you may have a contingency fund for these occurrences.
        - The time it will take to do the work will significantly affect your timeline. You may have to shuffle around other tradesmen to keep the progress going.
    - **Design:**
        - Their ability to do the work, or do you have to hire another tradesman? You may have chosen something that is outside their skill set. Example: changing from drywall to paneling or adding in wallpaper.
        - The cost of labor and materials will affect your budget. There may be something else you are willing to give up, or you may have a contingency fund for this type of occurrence.
        - The time it will take to get the work done will significantly affect your timeline. You may have to shuffle around other tradesmen to keep the progress going.

Section 10: Contracts

Contracts: Now that you have chosen your tradesmen and vendors and have your project ready, it is time to wrap up the final details to get your project started. We will discuss the following to have in place: tradesmen contracts, vendor terms for orders, and contingency plans.

- **Tradesman Contracts:** These contracts are written in different ways, but all should contain essential information.
    - **Contract Types:**
        - **Formal Contract:** May be downloaded from a legal website specific to remodeling renovation contracts or drawn up by a lawyer. The latter will be more expensive and possibly unnecessary.
        - **Informal Contract:** May be written or typed up in a document containing the needed information and signatures. Most tradesmen will have a prepared form.
        - **Verbal Agreement:** This is standard practice but can lead to confusion later in the project. A written form will help you and your tradesman stay on track with what is agreed upon.
    - **Contract Information:**
        - A description of the work to have been completed.
            - **Detailed:** The complete outline of work to include quantities, square footage, and linear footage.
            - **Brief:** A summary of the work to be done. Example: install all trim work to include crown, baseboards and shoe moldings, windows, and door trim.
        - The date the agreement is drawn up.
        - The total bid (quote) of the work to be done.
        - A deposit amount, if needed.
        - The payment plan as the work is completed.
        - The time frame in which the work is estimated to be completed. Any delays, including anything from weather, delivery times, or unforeseen circumstances to be included with a buffer time.
        - Warranty for the work completed.
            - Qualifications for rework; are any tasks to be redone because they are incorrect and at no charge? If other work is to be redone because of a change order, for structural reasons, and the homeowner's request, the warranty will be charged accordingly.
            - What does the warranty covers (*labor and/or materials*).
            - The length of time the warranty is good for after the completion of the project.
            - What determines the completion of work.

- **Material Responsibility:** A statement of which materials will be provided by the tradesman and which will be provided by you.

Whether or not you have a detailed formal contract, informal contract, or verbal agreement, the contract's information should always be noted somewhere by either documentation, email, or text. It will allow you and the tradesman to refer to it later if there are any questions about your agreement.

- **Vendor Order Agreements:** When ordering any products, it always is followed with documentation. Each order form is considered an agreement. You will be provided an order form online or at a local vendor location. Both you and your vendor will rely on these forms to ensure the proper items have arrived from the manufacturer and that the price point is correct. Most local vendors will have you sign a purchase order form before ordering any items. It is essential to take the time to review the purchase order form in detail before signing and putting a deposit down for the items. Most of us want to say we "trust" the salesman we are working with and order what is on the form without looking, but that is an unfair burden to place on that person. You are responsible for knowing exactly what you are getting for the money you are spending. You will need to check the purchase order for the following:
    - **Item Number and Description:**
        - It will tell you the exact item you are getting.
        - You may need the item number to look up specifications and installation sheets.
        - You may need the item number to order replacement parts in the future.
    - **Quantity:** Make sure you are getting the correct amount for each item.
    - **Color:** This is the most overlooked detail and the most common to get wrong on a purchase order. Always check the color! This is the most missed description.
    - **Price Point:** Is listed as only the total sum for the quantity you are purchasing or listed as BOTH the price per unit and the total cost for the amount you are ordering.
    - **Freight Charges:** This is the cost of shipping from the manufacturer.
    - **ETA:** The Estimated Time of Arrival. It helps you stay on schedule
    - **Warranty Clause:** This will tell you the vendor policy for damaged, missing, or other qualifying reasons for the return or exchange of the product, the paperwork needed, and the time frame you must make any returns and/or exchanges. It may be printed on the back of the receipt.
    - **Point of Contact:** The vendor's name, address, and the salesperson you worked with if you have any questions or if your tradesman needs to talk with the vendor.

- **Rental Contracts:** If you rent equipment, it will come with a rental agreement. In the agreement will be some of the most common rental terms, which will include the following:
  - **Condition of Equipment:** No damage to the equipment, causing it to operate improperly.
  - **Time Period:** Rentals are daily, weekly, and monthly. You will most likely be charged for a week if your rental lasts more than three days. The same goes for three weeks, and you will be charged a monthly rental. Always check the terms for the time limits with your vendor.
  - **Storage Instructions:** The rental of most machinery and power tools will require you to store the equipment when not in use. Always ask your vendor for instructions for the equipment's care so as not to void the terms of the rental agreement.

Confirmations: Now that the scope of work is complete, drawings are done, contracts are drawn up, and deposits are made on materials, you will need to confirm everything is in place with your tradesmen and vendors.

- **Tradesman:**
  - **Start Date:** Begin with your first tradesman to confirm his start date. Contact each successive tradesman at least one week before their start date to confirm the schedule is still good. Then contact them again the day before the start date. A lot happens in a week for a tradesman, and not every one of them will call you to let you know if the schedule is changing because of the long hours they are working. If you have any material delays, you must inform them and reschedule if needed. It would be best if you gave your tradesmen a heads-up on any changes made. You respect their time, and they will give you the same consideration. Calling regularly will also let them know you are staying on top of the schedule.
  - **Materials Purchases:** Always confirm what materials they are providing and what materials they expect you to provide. This is crucial to have in writing.
  - **Deposit Amounts:** Always confirm if a deposit is required and the payment they are expecting,

- **Vendors**
  - **ETA:** Estimated Times of Arrival. Confirm that the products you are ordering are coming in on time. Calling in advance will help catch if an item is on backorder or has any shipping delays. The vendors deal with a high volume of orders, and not all setbacks are caught right away. You may not receive an automatic call if there are problems. Sometimes you may find out the product came in ahead of schedule. Ask if the product has been inspected for damage, the correct color and quantity and if the entire order has arrived. Sometimes there may be one piece still to arrive, and they were waiting to call you until EVERYTHING arrived. If this is the case, you may have the option to pick up what is in or wait until everything is available.

- **Delivery and Pick-Up Times:**
  - **Delivery:** If you are having your items delivered, make sure the date is still suitable. They may be down a truck or ahead of schedule. Ask for the delivery driver to call you when they are on their way.
  - **Pick Up:** if you are picking up the items, make sure you can schedule to get them on time. If you need your tradesman to pick up your items, confirm with your vendor the pickup times.
  - **Balances:** Verify the outstanding balances, if any, and arrange with your vendor how you intend to pay off the balance at the time of pick up.

It will lessen the confusion for you, your tradesmen, and your vendors if the final decisions for every project phase are made ahead of time. If it helps you in the decision-making phase, when you reach a final decision, mark each quote, picture, and/or spec sheet with a sticky note, or write directly on the form the word "FINAL" in red, along with the date. It will remind you that the selections are made and you have reached a decision. As a result, you will be less likely to start changing your mind or second-guess the choices you have made.

In the renovation industry, this process of viewing the scope of work, material selections, and tradesman schedules is repeated several times. This process is done for every project section as the tasks are completed and the next ones begin.

Section 11: Permits & Insurance

Permits: If you are doing significant renovations to your property, you will need to apply for a permit with your local planning development and zoning CODES office. If you ever doubt whether to pull a permit, pull one! If your plan includes moving any structural walls, adding any plumbing, significant relocation of plumbing, or adding any foundation and roofing, you will need to pull a permit. If you are only changing out the finish products in the home and leaving the footprint alone, you are not required to pull a permit. It is considered updating your home and not actual renovation by the CODES office. You should be able to call your local CODES office or go online to your local Department of Development permits office. You can download an application to fill out before going into the office. Online it should tell you what is expected of you to complete your application. A couple of items you will undoubtedly need are:

- A scaled drawing of the project overview to include the entire property lines. All measurements should be marked.
- The online application is filled out.

Check with your permit office if you need to deliver the permit application to the office or if it is something you can upload and email to the CODES department. The process of getting the permit may take up to ten days. Call after about five days to ensure your application is in process. The size and cost of your renovation by the CODES office will determine the permit fee.

After receiving the permit, it must be displayed to be seen from the road. Ensure it is protected with a sheet protector and taped to a window if you display it outside. You will need to call in for all inspections when they are required:

- **Foundation:** After the form is built with metal mesh, vapor barrier, and grounding rod, but before the concrete is poured.
- **Foundation 2:** After the concrete is poured.
- **Open Wall:** All stick framing is in place, exterior plywood and house wrap are on, the electrical wires run, and rough-in plumbing is in place. BEFORE insulation.
- **Electrical:** The electrician will call in their inspection (there will be two; rough-in and final)
- **Plumbing:** The Plumber will call in their inspection (there will be 2–3 rough-in and a final).
- **Final Inspection:** The job is completed.

If you fail an inspection, the work must be corrected to meet the standards CODES has set before continuing with the remainder of the project. Then, another inspection must be called in to get a "PASS" to continue work.

Before beginning the renovation project, you may have questions about CODES standards. The local CODES office is very receptive to answering questions. In addition, you may make an appointment with one of the inspectors before beginning the project to ensure that you hold to the standards outlined by the codes department. Some concerns you may bring to them:

- **Structural Needs:** Beam sizes and lengths, the lumber sizes according to the spans you cover.
- **Plumbing** access for your plumbing lines.
- **Electrical** loads and requirements.
- **Easement Requirements:**
  - How close can you build to the property lines?
  - What type of structures can be built close to property lines?
  - How many and what size exits do you need in the rooms of your house?

These are just some examples of a FEW questions that may come up. You may have more questions; you may have fewer, but it is always helpful to call and schedule some time with a city inspector to clear up any concerns you may have moving forward with your renovation.

HOA (Homeowners Association): If your neighborhood has an HOA, you will need permission to build or make any improvements to your property. You will need similar drawings used for the CODES office to present, but you will also have to show the products you use. HOA organizations will be more demanding on renovation projects than the CODES office because the CODES office is only concerned with your construction standards. The HOA is also concerned with aesthetics. It will need to meet the standards of the neighborhood. Most HOAs have strict guidelines for the community regarding the type of materials you can use and even paint colors used on the home's exterior that will be seen from the road. *It is better to ask permission and NOT forgiveness with an HOA.* You will need to call the committee and get a detailed list of the required items. Some may want full architectural drawings and designer renderings. Others may be satisfied with less but always check with your HOA.

Insurance: When you add to your existing home, you must ensure that you are covered for damage and/or liability of injury under your current policy or may have to make changes to your policy. Some policies may be purchased while undergoing very LARGE renovations to cover your property and belongings. Different policies will cover different situations:

- **Non-Occupied New Construction:** If you will not be living in the house while renovations are being done.
- **Occupied New Construction:** You will be living there during the renovation.
- **Workman's Compensation or Liability Insurance:** Coverage for on-site workers during the renovation.

Talk to your insurance agent about what they can do to help you remain covered.

Most tradesmen will carry their insurance. You should request a certificate of insurance from their insurance agent to be faxed or emailed directly from the agent as the policyholder. Do not accept a copy from the tradesman. Getting a copy from the agent will ensure the policy is current and up to date.

Bridges: Always keep the contact numbers and information of the tradesmen you have not chosen. You may need to call on them if the tradesmen you chose first cannot be scheduled as planned or delayed you for a long time, causing your timeline to alter.

124

Chapter 4: Scope & Budget

Section 1: Budget

Before beginning your project, knowing what you are getting into financially is essential. Know that there has not been one home renovation that has ever come in EXACTLY at the original cost calculated. There will be changes to the project, and not all of them are bad. Some of those changes will help you and your family enjoy the space more. Most frustrations with home renovation projects come from the amount of money spent and seeing the value. To minimize this stress, first, ask yourself a few questions.

- How much money do you want to dedicate to this project?
- How much are you willing to spend on change orders?
- What are the priorities of the project?
- What is the overall desired result of the project?
- Are you and your spouse on the same page?

To begin building your budget for your project, you will need the following components:

Scope of work

Material costs

Labor costs

Other building fees, such as debris removal, permit fees, and elevation fees (if applicable)

Time and Availability: Another aspect of your budget is money and time. We all budget our time, and sometimes down to the very second, we lay our heads down on the pillow. Timelines are essential to keep a project moving and within a monetary budget. Budgeting your time as well as you can for your role in the renovation will help you avoid becoming overwhelmed. So, to better prepare yourself, there are a few more questions to ask and answer:

- How long do you anticipate the project to last?
- Do you have established timelines to meet, such as moving, a celebration, the birth of a child, or school holidays?
- How much time do you have to dedicate to your project?
    - Oversite of tradesmen
    - Perform any work you may be doing on the project
- How long do you think it will take to get the materials?
- Do you have space to fit dumpsters, trash trailers, and materials?

The more you understand what you can give to this project, the better you can manage the moving pieces.

Defining Your Budget: The following are all building blocks in creating a realistic budget for your project.

- **Factors of Your Budget:** When outlining the budget, several factors are involved.
  - Account for labor, materials, deliveries, shipping costs, and time.
  - Will financing be needed? Are you securing a loan for the project?
  - Architect fees for drawings and plans, if needed.
  - Permitting fees are needed to build.
  - Designer fees for design and materials selections.
  - Contractor fees for oversite and project management if you choose to hire one.
- **Defining Your Scope of Work:** This is a detailed list of the work to do for your project. The plan is made according to the task categories listed for you in Chapter 1. Use as detailed a description as possible when describing your project's work. The scope should include the following:
  - Demolition
  - Foundation
  - Framing
  - Roofing
  - Siding
  - HVAC – Heating, Ventilation, and Air Conditioning
  - Insulation
  - Plumbing
  - Electrical
  - Drywall
  - Painting/Staining
  - Trim Work
  - Tile and Masonry work
  - Flooring
  - Finish Carpentry

Start with a general description of each one for your first outline of the work you want to do for your home. When writing out what you want to do using the scope outline, you may see if you need to involve an architect, draftsman, designer, or decorator. For example, suppose you want your kitchen's complete gut to reconfigure the cabinets, lighting, plumbing, and wall placements to suit your family and lifestyle better. In that case, you may want the advice of a designer. You may enjoy entertaining, and your current kitchen is not suited to having people in the kitchen, or there is not enough food prep and serving space. Therefore you want to add on to your house, and you may consult and Architect or Building Designer to draft plans for this addition. If you want to keep the layout of the existing kitchen because it functions well for you, but it is completely outdated and needs a facelift, then designers may be useful for a consult.

Materials and Labor Costs: you will need to contact vendors and suppliers to get real costs for the items you have selected for your design. We will need to complete that picture of the cost with quotes from specific tradesmen to complete the work.

- **Vendor Selection:** Choosing between local vendors, "big box," and online vendors for your products will depend on the project's needs and/or the desired effect. There are several questions to ask and answer when choosing a vendor.
    - Delivery times
    - Price points
    - Availability
    - Customer service procedures if circumstances change
    - Communications
- **Tradesman Selection:** In choosing the right tradesman for your project, the more knowledge you have about your project and construction, the better your choice will be.
    - Cost
    - Availability
    - Work warranty
    - Timelines
    - Perimeters of work
    - Communications
- **Materials Purchasing and Storage:** You will learn when to order materials, where to source them, which ones will need delivery, how to store materials until required, and what to look for in the standards of materials. You may rent temporary storage units if you do not have adequate storage. These may be delivered to you on your site or off-site space, that you will have to get transported to your site.
- **Permit Acquisition:** You will need to know ahead of time if a permit is required for your project. You can find the requirements for a permit application online on your local government's Department of Development and Zoning CODES website for residential properties. In addition, most municipalities will have an outline on their website for what documents will be needed and downloadable applications to fill out and file with them.
- **Floor Plans and Drawings:** Being fully prepared BEFORE beginning a project will reduce the stress of a large or small renovation. We have shown you how to do your preliminary drawings to get a scaled drafted plan of your space. You have learned the proper placement of appliances and electrical and plumbing fixtures. The plan will let you see your space in your head and on paper to determine if what you are imagining will work for your home. You may want to use your Pre-Construction Team if the project is large enough. You will need drawings to help determine the quantities of the materials you need to purchase.
- **Equipment Rentals:** you may have to rent jackhammers, storage bins, excavators, or other tools needed to complete your project. You will need to factor in these costs as well for your project.

Section 2: Create Your Scope

Now that you have your drawings, you will create a scope of work to be done. Use each of the task categories as a header and list the work's details to be done under each heading. An example would be the following:

The following is just a **SAMPLE** of how it could look. It was created on an Excel spreadsheet. The prices are **NOT** a true reflection of the pricing. We will use this basic form to build your budget once we gather all the necessary information.

For each task category, write down a detailed description of the work for each room of the house. For example:

- Demolition:
    - Master bathroom: Remove the existing tub and faucets. Remove the existing toilet, vanity, sinks, faucets, and countertops.
    - Master bedroom: Remove the existing door entry and drywall to move the entry door.
- Foundation: Pour new foundation for bathroom extension.
- Framing:
    - Master bedroom: Frame new walls, ceiling, roof, and windows for new bathroom extension. Frame new shower walls and soap niches.
    - Master bedroom: Install new entry door to master bathroom.
- Roofing:
    - Master bath extension: Install new roofing to match the existing house.
- Siding: Install new Hardi lap siding on the bathroom extension.
- Insulation: Install new insulation in the exterior walls of the bathroom extension.
- Plumbing:
    - Master bath: Install new shower drain and supply lines. Install new vanity sinks (two) and a new toilet.
- Electrical:
    - Master bath: Install new switches, outlets, and lights: new wall vanity lights, new heat/light/vents, and new GFCI outlets for vanity. Place one outlet in the cabinet and the rest on the backsplash. Install new can lights in the bathroom on a separate switch.
        - Exterior: Install new security lights on the corners of the house.
- Drywall:
    - Master bathroom: Hang and float drywall on walls and ceilings where drywall was removed.
    - Master bedroom: Hang and float drywall where the entry door to the bathroom was removed.

- Painting:
    - Master bathroom: Prime and paint all walls, ceilings, trim, doors, and cabinetry.
    - Master bedroom: Prime and paint walls where new drywall was installed.
    - Exterior: Prime and paint all lap siding, trim soffit, and fascia.
- Tile Work:
    - Master bathroom: Tile primary flooring, shower walls, shower floor, shower bench, shower niche, and vanity backsplashes.
- Finish Carpentry:
    - Master bathroom: Install all new crown, baseboards, shoe molding, door trim, shower glass, cabinet hardware, bath hangers, and towel bars.
    - Master bedroom: Install new door hardware and door trim. Install new baseboards and shoe molding. Install new door threshold.

See Sample forms at the end of the Chapter

Project Scope

Property		
Email:		

Tasks	Materials	Labor
Demo		
Remove walls as needed		
Remove Flooring - wood or tile		
Pack & Remove furniture and cabinet contents		
Debris Removal Fees		
Foundation & Framing		
Frame out & pour foundation with vapor barrier		
Spray for termites on new foundation		
Frame out walls, roof, ceilings, windows, doors		
Roofing		
Install new roofing		
Siding		
Install new siding ; LAP		
Install new siding ; BRICK		
Insulation		
Install insualtion in ceilings		
Install insualtion in walls as needed		
HVAC		
Change out AC registers		
Plumbing		
Rough-in Plumbing: supply & drain lines		
Finish Plumbing: install components		
Electrical		
Rough -in Electrical: lines & boxes		
Finish Electrical: install componenets		
Wall Coverings/Painting		
Hang & Float walls and ceilings		
Prep, prime & paint cabinetry		
Prep, Prime & paint walls, ceilings, trim & doors: INTERIOR		
Prep, Prime & paint siding, trim & doors: EXTERIOR		
Tile Work & Flooring		
Tile Backsplash		
Tile Shower walls, floor and niches		
Tile primary flooring		
Install vinly plank flooring		
Cabinetry & Countertops		
Install kitchen cabinets: base & uppers		
Install Vent hood		
Install full height cabinet storage with adjustable shelving		
Install countertops : solid surface		
Finish Carpentry		
Install all trim: crown, base & shoe molding		
Install Wall paper		
Install Bath Hardware & Mirror		
Install cabinetry hardware		
Install appliances provided by client		
Sub-Totals		
Total		

The more detail you can offer to your scope of work, the more likely you will accurately price materials and communicate better with your tradesmen.

Again, you can use an Excel spreadsheet or a sheet (*following the outline presented to detail the work you need for your project*), so pricing for labor and materials can be added later. Following the task category outline will also help you determine which sub-contractors (*tradesmen*) you need to hire. It will also help you itemize the materials you need for your project according to each task category.

Using your drawings, calculate the measurements for each category and fill in your **resource schedule**. There is a form at the end of the Chapter. This resource schedule is designed to record all calculations for the quantities (*linear footage, square footage, and counts*) for materials needed in each category. With this resource schedule, you can build your materials list. Most tradesmen call this a "take off" or "take away" list.

The next step is to make your **materials list**. Again, there is a form at the end of the Chapter. Again, you will use the task categories as your guide and the chart listed before to determine which materials need to be listed.

To further help you determine the materials needed, we have created a chart for you to follow and use as a reference guide.

"Knowns / Known unknowns / Unknown unknowns."

In every project, there are a set of "knowns," "known unknowns," and "unknown unknowns."

"knowns" are the typical straightforward situations we expect to run into. Some examples would be having to remove a toilet to remove the tub next to it because the space may be small

"Known unknowns" - these are situations we are not sure exist, but all signs point to it. An example would be mold and mildew at the base of a shower pan, which may mean there is leaking, and we should anticipate replacing the rotted framework. However, we won't know for certain until demo day.

"Unknown unknowns" are conditions or situations that cannot be foreseen. Examples would be a nest of mice in a wall, termite damage in a wall that has just begun, and compromised pipes inside a wall—connections made by people who have remodeled the house over the years.

Every tradesman will prepare themselves for the "knowns" and will try to prepare themselves for the "known unknowns," but no one can prepare themselves for the "unknown unknowns."

Section 3: Making a Material List

This table may be used as a checklist to ensure you have considered all the materials you will need to purchase for any raw and design materials. It may also be referred to when talking to your subcontractor. The tradesmen (subcontractors) will buy some of these materials. This will be discussed in detail in Chapter 3.

Task Category	Material
Framing	Stick lumber, plywood, fasteners, posts, beams, windows, doors, house wrap
Roofing	Shingles, drip edge, flashing, roof jacks
Insulation	Insulation
Siding	Lap siding, brick, stucco, metal, fasteners, caulk if needed
HVAC	Units, trunk lines, registers
Plumbing—Rough-in	Rough-in valves, supply line drains, pipes
Plumbing—Finish	Finish fixtures for sinks and showers
Electrical—Rough-in	Rough-in lines, wire, boxes, panels, circuits, conduits
Electrical—Finish	Appliances, light fixtures, heat/light/vents, light/vents, outlets, switches
Drywall	Drywall, screws, mud, tape
Painting	Paint, primers, rollers, brushes, rags, cleaners
Cabinetry	Kitchen and Bath: base uppers, islands, peninsulas, storage, pantry
Countertops	Solid surface, tile, laminate, wood, concrete
Tile Work	Tile, trim pieces, waterproofing materials, thin-set, grout
Flooring	Carpet, wood, laminate, vinyl flooring, padding if needed *if tile flooring: see above for tile
Masonry	Siding, post caps, mailboxes, driveways, bricks, fasteners, mortar

Materials Room by Room

This section will discuss the materials needed in each room of the house and each task category required to purchase for a renovation project. Using this chart, you can focus on a singular room as a project or combine rooms for larger projects. Bathrooms and kitchens are the most complicated rooms. They require more permanently fixed items than any other room in the house. This also means more shopping and more questions to answer. Planning these two spaces will take more thought and time than your other rooms. The only exception to this would be planning the FULL outdoor patio with a kitchen, bathroom, and fireplace. Yes, we have done this a few times.

Interior Items

Task Category	Kitchen	Bathroom	Laundry	Living/ Dining/ Bedroom
Framing	walls, doors, windows, stick lumber	walls, doors, windows, stick lumber	walls, doors, stick lumber	walls, doors, windows, stick lumber
Insulation	exterior walls, ceiling, roll batten, sheets, blown-in, foam	exterior walls, ceiling, roll batten, sheets, blown-in, foam	exterior walls, ceiling, roll batten, sheets, blown-in, foam	exterior walls, ceiling, roll batten, sheets, blown-in, foam
HVAC	ceiling or floor registers, trunk lines	ceiling or floor registers, trunk lines	ceiling or floor registers, trunk lines	ceiling or floor registers, trunk lines
Plumbing	sink, dishwasher, fridge lines for ice makers, pot fillers, gas appliances, faucets	sinks, toilets, showers, tubs, faucets	clothes washer, utility sink, faucets	gas fireplace insert
Electrical	lighting: overhead, sink, feature lighting, outlets, switches, appliances	lighting: vanity, shower, HLV, LV, outlets, switches	lighting: overhead Appliances, outlets, switches	lighting: overhead, fans, outlets, switches
Drywall	walls and ceiling, drywall sheets, mud, screws, tape	walls and ceiling, drywall sheets, mud, screws, tape	walls and ceiling, drywall sheets, mud, screws, tape	walls and ceiling, drywall sheets, mud, screws, tape
Painting	paint, primer, caulk, rollers	paint, primer, caulk, rollers	paint, primer, caulk, rollers	paint, primer, caulk, rollers
Tile work	flooring, backsplash: tile, trim, thin-set, grout, grout-caulk	flooring, backsplash: shower walls	flooring: tile, trim, thin-set, grout, grout-caulk	flooring: tile, trim, thin-set, grout, grout-caulk

		tub surrounds: tile, trim, thin-set, grout, grout-caulk		
Flooring	wood, tile, concrete, laminate, vinyl	wood, tile, concrete, laminate, vinyl	wood, tile, concrete, laminate, vinyl	wood, tile, concrete, laminate, vinyl, carpet
Cabinets	base, uppers, pantry, island, peninsula	base, uppers, tower, linen	base, uppers, pantry	built-in entertainment, banquette, bars
Countertops	tile, solid surface, laminate	tile, solid surface, laminate	tile, solid surface, laminate	bar tops, dining hutch top
Hardware	cabinets, doors	cabinets, doors	cabinets, doors	doors, hutches, bar doors
Trim Carpentry	crown, base, shoe moldings, door, window, and cabinet trim, fasteners, caulk	crown, base, shoe moldings, door, window, and cabinet trim, fasteners, caulk	crown, base, shoe moldings, door, window, and cabinet trim, fasteners, caulk	crown, base, shoe moldings, door, window trim, fasteners, caulk
Accessories	towel hangers, window treatments	towel hangers, toilet paper hangers, robe hooks, mirrors, shower doors, shelving	window treatments	window treatments

Exterior Items

Task Category	Main House	Patio	Garage	Storage
Framing	Walls, ceilings, roofs, doors, windows, stick lumber, fasteners, plywood, house wrap, sealers	Roof, ceiling, stick lumber, posts, and beams	Walls, ceiling, roof, doors, windows, stick lumber, fasteners, plywood, house wrap, sealers	Wall, ceiling, roof, doors, windows, stick lumber, fasteners, plywood, house wrap, sealers
Siding	Exterior walls, soffit and fascia, brick, lap siding, stucco	Soffit and fascia Gable walls	Exterior walls: brick, lap siding, stucco, etc. interior walls: drywall, mud, tape, screws, or paneling and caulk	Exterior walls: brick, lap siding, stucco, etc. interior walls: drywall, mud, tape, screws, or paneling and caulk

Roofing	Shingles, metal,	Shingles, metal	Shingles, metal	Shingles, metal
HVAC	Exterior unit			Exterior unit, window unit
Plumbing	hose bibs	hose bibs, outdoor sinks, gas grills, burners	hose bibs	hose bibs
Electrical	lighting: sconces, lanterns, soffit lights, security, outlets, switches	lighting: fans, outlets, switches, tv outlets, sound systems	lighting: outlets, switches	lighting: outlets, switches
Painting	siding, soffit, fascia, door, and window trim	ceiling, soffit, fascia, posts, beams	exterior siding, interior walls, ceiling, door, and window trim	exterior siding, interior walls, ceiling, door, and window trim
Trim Carpentry	door and window trim, corners, top and bottom wall trim, railings, posts, columns, corbels	soffit, fascia, beams, posts, ceiling trim, corbels	door and window trim *crown and baseboard	door and window trim *crown and baseboard, shelving
Cabinetry		outdoor kitchen, tv cabinets, pool supply storage, hardware	storage cabinetry, hardware	storage cabinetry, hardware
Countertops		outdoor kitchen: tile or solid surface, granite	worktables: tile or solid surface, granite	worktables: tile or solid surface, granite
Tile Work	porch flooring: tile, trim, thin-set, grout, grout-caulk	flooring: tile, trim, thin-set, grout, grout-caulk	flooring: tile, trim, thin-set, grout, grout-caulk	flooring: tile, trim, thin-set, grout, grout-caulk
Accessories	hose reels, shutters, awnings,	TV, speakers, outdoor kitchen appliances	bike racks, tool storage	tool storage, bike racks,

Using these two charts and your material list outline: *at the end of the Chapter,* you can make your list, plug in your quantities, and get the total pricing for your materials. Suppose you need to determine the price for materials, especially raw materials. In that case, you can search online or visit your local lumberyard and tile, lighting, and plumbing retailers with your list and get a quote from them directly. Some building material retailers offer a service to price out your framing package, window and door package, trim package, drywall materials, etc., by merely giving them your drawings and plans. You will have to call around and ask if this service is available. Some may do it for a minimal cost or even free if you set up an account and purchase your materials through them.

Calculating Materials

You must determine the quantities for each material you need and/or have selected. The three most common measurements to calculate are as follows:

Length: The longest measurement of a given room.

Width: The shortest measurement of a given room.

Square Footage: Total square footage = length in feet x width in feet.

Linear Footage: The total length in feet.

Count: The number of items needed. The most common things you will use this for are the following:

   Windows, doors, and cabinet and door hardware

   Soffit Vents

   Lights: cans, heat/light/vent, light/vent, outlet, and switches

   Tile Trim Pieces

   Thresholds

Roofing:

Squares: This is a common term used in roofing to note the amount of roofing needed. Each square represents 100 square feet. Example: 1,200 square feet = 12 squares

Calculating the square footage of a roof for asphalt shingles or torch-down roofing:

Sqft = Length (*from the ridge to the roof's eave*) in feet x the width *(side to side of a single roof plane)* in feet. You will have to calculate that for each roof plane *(side of roofing)* and add them all together to have the total square footage.

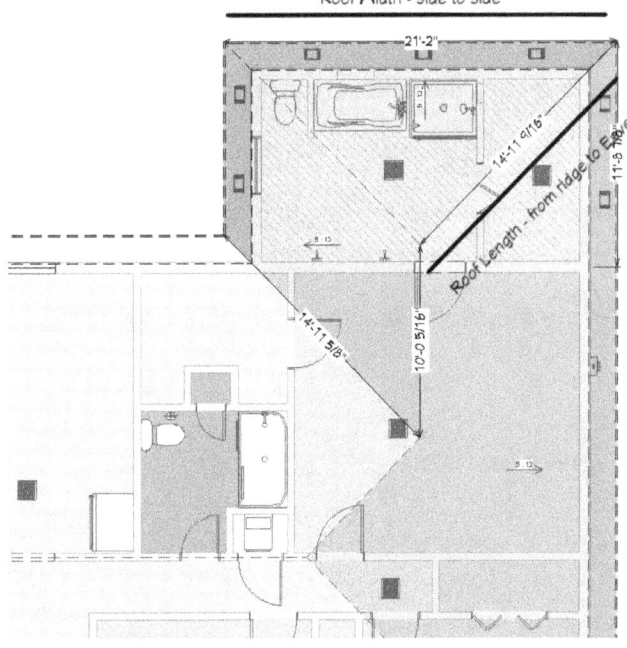

Metal Roofing: Metal roofing panels are sold in 16"–24" boards; you will have to know how many panels to buy.

- **16" Wide:** (the width of roof x 12÷16) + length of roof = total linear footage needed.

Framing: Calculating the number of stick framing lumber you need is time-consuming.

- **Studs:** If your studs are 16" on center—the **length of the wall x 12÷16 = the number of studs.**
  - Add two more studs for each corner, window, and door framing.

Rafters: If your rafters are 24" on center—**width of the roof ÷2 = the number of rafters.**

*Add all roof planes together for your total. *if rafters are 16" on center, use the formula above.*

Plywood:

- **Walls:** since plywood is installed vertically, the **length of the wall ÷4 = sheets of plywood.**
- **Roof:** Since the plywood is installed horizontally, **(the width of the roofline ÷ 8) + (length of the roof plane ÷ 4) = plywood sheets**. You will have to add up all roof planes to get your total.

Siding:

- **Brick:** Square footage needed x 5.5 = the number of bricks to order. You will need overage just in case of breakage and cut-off. So, multiply the total by 10% for your total.
- **Lap Siding:** Depending on the size of the lap siding you are getting, each board is sold in a specific length and width. Check the amount of square footage the board covers. **Example:** 8" wide lap siding at 12' long will cover about 7 sqft. The manufacturer will usually indicate the coverage. You can then calculate the square footage needed by the **length of the wall x the height of the wall = the sqft**.
- **Stucco: The length of the wall x the height of the wall = the sqft**.

Insulation:

- **Walls:** The length of the wall x the height of the wall = sqft needed. Add all walls together.

Ceiling: The width of the room x the width of the room = the sqft.

Drywall:

- **Walls:** The length of the wall x the height of the wall = the sqft needed. Add all walls together.
- **Ceiling:** The width of the room x the width of the room = the sqft.

Flooring: The width of the room x the length of the room = the sqft.

Tile:

- **Walls:** The wall's length of the wall x the height = the sqft needed. Add all walls together.
- **Floors:** The width of the room x the width of the room = the sqft.

Countertops: The length of the base cabinet x the base cabinet's depth = the sqft of materials needed.

Trim Work: Base, crown, shoe molding, casings, etc., are measured by total length.

Cabinetry: Is measured by the total length filling the space and individually by the cabinet size needed to fill every space depending on the cabinet's use.

Ceiling and Floor Square Footage

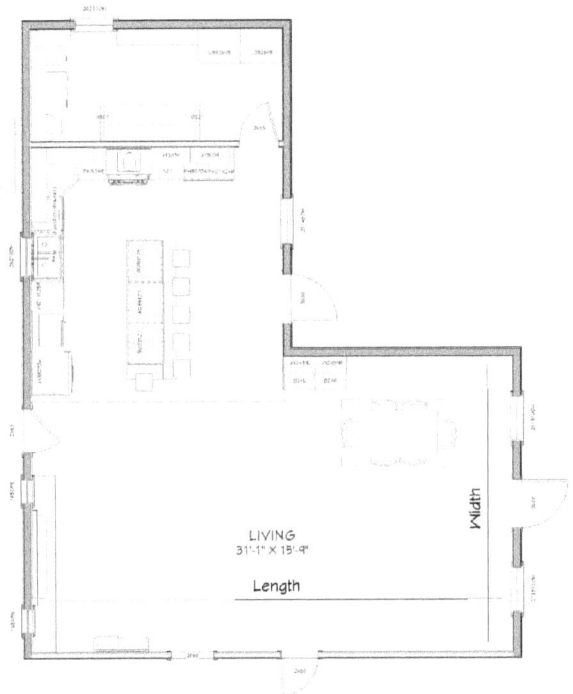

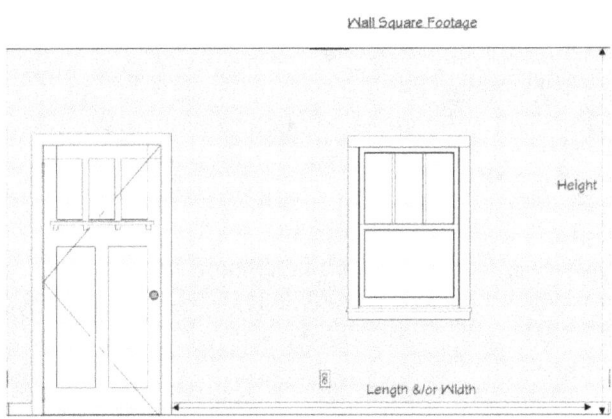

Making your Schedules

Schedules - a table defining your surfaces, locations and quantiles, and other relevant information. When making a schedule, always make it according to the surface or fixtures you are tracking. Now that you have learned how to calculate your materials, you can begin to make your schedules. Samples forms are at the end of the Chapter.

The following are the schedules you would typically need for your Surface & Fixtures:

- Paint Schedule
    - Room name / Square Footage/ Color name / Color number / Base & Sheen
        - Walls
        - Ceilings
        - Trim
        - Doors
        - Cabinetry
- Tile; always include 10% for waste for your square footage
    - Room (or Surface) name / Square footage / Color name/size of tile / Grout color
        - Shower walls, bench, niche
        - Shower floors and curb
        - Tub surrounds, niches
        - Primary floors
        - Backsplashes; kitchens, bathrooms, laundry rooms
- Flooring; always include 10% for waste for your square footage
    - Room name / Material / Square footage / Color name
        - Wood
        - Carpet & padding
        - Tile
        - Vinyl plank
        - Vinyl sheet
- Countertops; include your edging style and thickness for stone
    - Room name / Materials / Square footage
        - Stone
        - Laminate
        - Tile
- Plumbing
    - Room name / Color / Brand name / Model number / Count
        - Sinks - kitchen, baths, and utility
        - Sink fixtures - kitchen, baths, utility
        - Tubs
        - Tub faucet and spout
        - Shower valve, head, and sprayer
        - Toilets

- Lighting
    - Room name / Color / Brand name / Model number / Count
        - Pendant lights
        - Chandeliers
        - Fans
        - Sconce lighting
- Trim work
    - Room name / Linear feet / Size / Style
        - Crown molding
        - Base molding
        - Shoe base or Quarter round
        - Door casing
        - Window casing
        - Stair railing
        - Wainscoting
- Roofing
    - Style (architectural or 3 tab) / Manufacturer / Color / Square footage
- Siding
    - Style (lap, brick, stucco, etc.) / Size / Color / Square footage

Keeping these schedules will help you in the future with repairs, replacements, or warranty items. In addition, as previously stated, schedules are often referred to as a guide and checklist throughout your build. Therefore, you will need to keep them updated and handy for anyone needing information about a particular material or room.

Section 4: Project Journal

Planning a renovation project on your home is a big undertaking. Much like planning a wedding, you may have been thinking about this for quite a while. A renovation will require research, lists, and organization. In this next section, you will put together a **project journal**. It will be the hub of all the information needed to complete your project.

Depending on your project's size, buy a binder ½"–1½" wide, page protectors, and dividers that can be labeled. You will need at least nine sections, and you may split one or more sections into two parts. Each is as follows:

- Inspirational Pictures
- Project Scope and Budget—defining the work to be done
    - Material Lists
    - Drawings
- Vendor Selections and Quotes:
    - Specification Sheets
- Tradesmen Selections and Quotes
    - Contracts Signed
- Receipts Collected
- Change Orders

You may find a template or blank page project binders online or in any major bookstore. They are formatted already with blank pages for you to fill in for most of the categories you will need to stay organized for your project.

- **Inspirational Pictures:** This section will include all the pictures that have inspired you to do your Project. It is helpful to print them out or keep a file on your phone and/or computer to be shared with tradesmen to communicate the idea you have in mind for the project's focus. Inspiration pictures may consist of the following:
    - Paint Colors
    - Plumbing Fixtures
    - Lighting Fixtures
    - Wallcoverings: such as shiplap, paneling, and wallpaper
    - Countertops: Colors, materials, and thickness
    - Cabinets: Styles and colors
    - Hardware: Styles and sizes
    - Appliances
    - Siding preferences: Wood, brick, stucco, stone, etc.

- Roofing: Colors, textures, and styles (*shingle, metal, etc.*)
- Windows: Styles and colors
- Doors: Styles and colors
- Tile: Styles, colors, and sizes

It is important to know that when sourcing products from social media outlets such as Pinterest or internet images, some of those products may be limited in their availability. Other outlets will sometimes offer a method of purchasing.

Always try to get pictures comparable to the project you are undertaking. Such as a room with the same ceiling heights, room size, and, if possible, similar door and window placement. It will help you choose better products for your project. It gives you a more realistic idea of the result.

- **Project Scope and Budget:** To create a project journal, you must create a full scope of work, a detailed list of materials needed, quotes from vendors and tradesmen, and a timeline for the work to be completed.
    - **Drawings:** These will help you complete your scope of work.
    - **Surface & Fixture Schedule:** You will fill this out using your drawings as your reference. *See the* end of the Chapter. It will help you make a detailed list of items needed for each of the tasks for your project, complete with quantities, colors, textures, styles, etc.
    - **Project Scope:** Use the following task categories to fill in the project scope form *at the end of the Chapter.*
        - A detailed listing of each task using the task categories form above
        - A column for the materials cost
        - A column for the quote for labor
            - This information can be obtained once you have a work scope to share with the tradesmen and drawings to show them the work
    - **Materials List:** Build a detailed list, including the quantities for the above task categories. Knowing your measurements and counts will help you define the amount of each material you need.
        - List each item separately
        - List the quantity you will need for each item
        - Price each item at the vendor of your choice

- **Vendor Selection and Quotes:** Shopping for materials needed for your project can be overwhelming. A dedicated section in your binder will allow you to access the information needed to minimize stress. In this section of your project journal, there will be:
    - **Surface & Fixture Schedule:** A detailed list of materials, quantities, and colors of the material needed for each task category
    - **Vendor List:** A list of all vendors you will need to contact to purchase materials, including
        - Vendors listed by task category—space for 2–3 vendors
        - Vendor name and contact info
        - Vendor quote
        - Date given quote
        - Special notes
        - Timeline for arrivals.
    - **Spec Sheets:** Items that will require a certain power source or need fitting into cabinetry, openings, or stone, will need to have a specification sheet to ensure proper installation. Keeping these sheets in this section will make them readily available to share with your tradesmen when needed. In addition, you will need to download or request from your vendor specification sheets for the following:
        - **Appliances:** Kitchens, wine bars, outdoor kitchens, laundry, etc.
        - **Motorized Items:** Garage doors, disposals, blinds, shades, etc.
        - **Outdoor Kitchen Components:** Grills, burners, sinks, trash cans
        - **Sinks:** Bathrooms, laundry, kitchens
        - **Faucets:** Interior and exterior
        - **Drains:** Landscaping, showers, sinks
        - **Lights:** kitchen, living area, bedroom, bathrooms, patios, etc.
        - **Specialty Items:** Doors, window units, fire escapes, fire pits, fireplaces, etc.
- **Tradesmen Selections and Quotes:** This section of your project journal will track each professional tradesman you need to get the job done. There will be quite a lot of interviews and discussions. It will be difficult to make sure you remember who said what. The following forms will help you track your information in one place, so you can access it readily without chasing down pieces of paper. In addition, it will give you a good side-by-side comparison of each tradesman you will interview. This section should include the following:
    - **Project Scope:** The detailed list made previously for all the work to be done. It should have each task category and a list of what is needed in each section. It will help you and the tradesman stay on the same page before and during the process. You will be able to use the copy you made for your budget.

- **Tradesman Quote List:** A detailed list of all tradesmen interviewed that need to be contacted for the work to be completed. It will be an overview where you will see your side-by-side comparison. The list will include the following:
    - Tradesman list by task category
    - Tradesman name and contact information
    - Tradesman quote
    - Date given quote
- **Interview Form:** This form will help guide you in your interviews with your tradesmen and write down all the important information you need to know to make an informed decision. You may have multiple sheets (one for each interview) and transfer the necessary information to the quote list as your referral sheet. The interview sheet will contain the following information:
    - Contact information
    - Skill sets—what their area of expertise is and where they excel.
    - Expectations—availability, work hours, etc.
    - Homeowner Policies—cleanliness of work site, hours, tool storage, etc.
    - Documentation—insurance papers, licenses, etc.
- **Contracts:** This section is where you will keep all contracts between you and your tradesmen. You may also want to keep any written agreements from your vendors in this section, so you may refer to them to verify arrival times, costs, warranty outlines, etc. All contracts should outline the following:
    - **Cost:** This should include a deposit amount if any is required.
    - **Start Date:** The expected start date, with a variance allowance for the date moving.
    - **Responsibilities:** To include tradesmen's promise of work to complete and the homeowner's responsibility to make payments. If the homeowner is performing any work on the project, it should stipulate how this will affect the tradesmen's timeline.
    - **Signatures:** Both parties with the date.
- Some contracts are as informal as the quote given by the tradesman, signed and dated by both parties. However, getting something in writing stating the work and its cost is good practice. It will protect both you and the tradesman.
- **Receipts:** In this section you may want to split it into two sections—one for the items and products purchased and one for invoices from your tradesmen. Collecting your receipts can help you stay on budget and track it as you go along. You can also compare the quotes given to the invoices received.

- **Change Orders:** You may have split this section into sections according to the task categories. Most projects will incur a change order at some point. There are two different types of change orders:
    - **Necessity:** The structure may have unseen damage from past work or have defects. This damage will need repair before continuing. Several things will contribute to damage:
        - Past storm damage
        - Animal invasion
        - Termites
        - Faulty work in the past
        - Material or product failure
        - Materials and/or product requirement—the material or fixture chosen may require different wiring and/or structure than a standard fixture
    - **Design:** You may see a desired wall structure or placement change as the project takes shape. Some of the most common change orders are the following:
        - Wall placement—enlarge certain areas for use or to create privacy
        - Light placement—more light may be needed for task work or less light for ambiance
        - Additional space—such as a deck or closet space
        - Additional cabinetry and/or storage
        - Different wall coverings—paint, wallpaper, and wainscotting

Since there are so many moving parts in any renovation project, keeping your paperwork organized will keep you on top of everything. Having a central location for all this information is critical in maintaining order amid the moving parts and progress. You will need to keep your project journal up to date with only relevant information. Routinely go through your paperwork and throw out all unnecessary information. This purging will avoid any confusion in the process of renovation.

Section 5: Cleaning Out Your Project Journal

Clearing Out Your Journal: Now that you have done all your research, you will be able to clean up and clear out the unnecessary pages of your project journal. Each part of your journal will need to be gone through. You need to throw away all papers that are not relevant to the project. This will help you stay on task with your project, keep the end goal in mind, and cause less confusion.

- **Drawings:** You may have gone through a few project revisions by now. You have tried out as many plans as possible and settled on the best option for you and your family. You will need to get rid of the drawings you will not use. It will only confuse you and your tradesmen. It can lead to framing walls wrong, getting the incorrect quantities of materials, etc.
- **Budget Outlines:** Keep only the current.
    - **Surface & Fixture Schedule:** Filled out with the proper quantities, styles, and materials needed.
    - **Scope:** Detailed outline of the work needed for each task category.
    - **Materials List:** A detailed list of all materials needed with the quantities and the cost.
- **Vendor Selections and Quotes:**
    - **Selections:** Keep final choices and 2nd choices. Mark each one as the 1st choice or the 2nd choice. If you have pictures to go with these choices, be sure to mark the images appropriately. Get rid of the rest and stop looking.
    - **Quotes:** Keep quotes from your vendors with the 1st and 2nd choices. You can highlight your 1st and 2nd choices using your vendor quote sheet.
- **Tradesman Selections and Quotes:**
    - **Selections:** Using your tradesman quote sheet, highlight the 1st and 2nd choices of tradesmen you want to use.
    - **Quotes:** If the tradesman has given you any paperwork, an estimate, and/or pictures, keep them together with the quote sheet. Keep each quote in order of the task category.
- **Inspiration Pictures:** Clean out all pictures no longer relevant to the project. It will prevent you from second-guessing your choices and keep you focused on the end design you are trying to achieve. Mark each picture with the specific inspiration drawn from that picture. For EXAMPLE, a picture of the house's exterior; maybe the brick and lap siding combination is what you liked about the pictures. You may have found an image of a kitchen you wanted, so you will mark on the photo exactly what you liked about the kitchen: the cabinet style, cabinet color, the hardware on the cabinets, the countertop, the backsplash, etc.
- **Spec Sheets:** Keep only those sheets that are for the items you have chosen.
    - Plumbing Fixtures: To include tubs, faucets, sinks, shower faucets, toilets, and gas appliances.

- Lighting Fixtures: The ceiling fans, ceiling-mounted lights, wall sconce lights, and pendants for the interior and exterior.
- Appliances: For indoor and exterior refrigerators, freezers, sinks, grills, ranges, vent hoods, ovens, dishwashers, etc.
- Motorized Items: Are blinds, garage doors, disposals, etc.
- Doors and Windows: These will need to go to your framer and trim carpenter. Keep only the ones that apply to the final selection.

SAMPLE FORMS

Project Scope

Property:

Email:

Tasks	Materials	Labor
Demo		
Remove walls as needed		
Remove Flooring - wood or tile		
Pack & Remove furniture and cabinet contents		
Debris Removal Fees		
Foundation & Framing		
Frame out & pour foundation with vapor barrier		
Spray for termites on new foundation		
Frame out walls, roof, ceilings, windows, doors		
Roofing		
Install new roofing		
Siding		
Install new siding ; LAP		
Install new siding ; BRICK		
Insulation		
Install insualtion in ceilings		
Install insualtion in walls as needed		
HVAC		
Change out AC registers		
Plumbing		
Rough-in Plumbing: supply & drain lines		
Finish Plumbing: install components		
Electrical		
Rough -in Electrical: lines & boxes		
Finish Electrical: install componenets		
Wall Coverings/Painting		
Hang & Float walls and ceilings		
Prep, prime & paint cabinetry		
Prep, Prime & paint walls, ceilings, trim & doors: INTERIOR		
Prep, Prime & paint siding, trim & doors: EXTERIOR		
Tile Work & Flooring		
Tile Backsplash		
Tile Shower walls, floor and niches		
Tile primary flooring		
Install vinly plank flooring		
Cabinetry & Countertops		
Install kitchen cabinets: base & uppers		
Install Vent hood		
Install full height cabinet storage with adjustable shelving		
Install countertops : solid surface		
Finish Carpentry		
Install all trim: crown, base & shoe molding		
Install Wall paper		
Install Bath Hardware & Mirror		
Install cabinetry hardware		
Install appliances provided by client		
Sub-Totals		
Total		

Material List
Raw & Finished

Demo	QTY	$ Amount	Electrical	QTY	$ Amount
contractor bags			single gang boxes nail in		
visqueen			pancake ceiling boxes		
rags			single toggle switches w/ covers		
brown paper roll			duplex tamper proof outlets w/ covers		
painters tape			Bath room vanity light		
Foundation & Framing			dining room light		
2x4x14 treated bottom plates INT			island lights		
2x4x14 dead wood & top plates INT			under cabinet lighting		
2x6x14 treated bottom plates EXT			fan		
2x6x14 top plates EXT			LED can lights		
sill sealer roll @ 50'			hood vent insert		
8x8x10 treated posts			HLV		
2x8x12 treated pine			Light Vent		
2x12x12 headers			**Drywall**		
2x4x8 studs			½" drywall 4x8		
2x6x12 joists			1⅝" coarse thread screws		
2x8x12 rafters			self adhesive drywall tape		
2x10x8 ridge beams			mud		
30' laminated beams					
¾" CDX plywood for roof					
½" CDX plywood for walls			**Painting**		
joist hangers - 2x6			Ext. Primer		
rafter ties			Ext. Wall Paint		
plywood clips - large box- 5/8"			Ext. Trim Paint		
Nails & fasteners			Int. Primer		
Tyvek Tape			Int. Wall Paint		
housewrap			Int. Ceiling Paint		
lexel			Int. Trim Paint oil base		
permafelt					
1x8x16 echo wood facia					
1" brads			**Flooring**		
composite shims			flooring w/ 10% overage		
interior doors			flooring w/ 10 % overage		
exterior doors					
windows 3030			**Tile Work**		
window tape			shower pan, drain kit		
			Hydrobord 1/2" 3' x 5' boards		
Roof			hydroban screws		
ice & water sheild - 2:12 & lower			hydroban sealer		
architechual shingles			hydroban sheet membrane		
ridge capping			porcelain tile for shower walls		
starter row - 200 sqft minimum			porcelain tile for floors		
ridge vents - 4' long			mosaics for shower floor		
drip edge 10'			backsplash		
roll flashing			thinset		
roofing caulk			grout		
roofing nails			tile trim sticks		
			grout caulk		
Siding			**Cabinetry**		
hardi plank siding woodgrain 8" x 12' (7sqft)			kitchen base		
hardi vented soffit 24" x 8'			kitchen uppers		
cement screws			full height cabinet		
caulk			vent hood casing		
¼" hardi trim @ 10' sticks			closet shelving		
Insulation			**Countertops**		
R-19 roll insulation @ 50 sqft / roll			quartz		
R-30 insulation blow in @ 50 sqft / pack					
			Finish Carpentry		
Plumbing			Hardware for Int. doors		
toilet			Hardware for Ext. Doors		
kitchen sink			1x4 pre-primed radiator pine for trim		
kitchen sink faucet			soffit vents 6" x 12"		
vanity sink			½"AC plywood for soffit		
sink fixtures			cove molding - 16' sticks		
shower fixtures			3" crown - 16' sticks		
tub/shower fixtures			baseboards - 16' sticks		
tub			shoe base - 16' sticks		
shower pans			finishing nails		
rough-in valves			shower door		
			window trim - 8' sticks		
			Shower glass or door		
			mirrors		
			caulk		

Surface & Fixture Schedules

Tile & Flooring

Area	$ per SQFT	Square Feet	Count	Name:	Grout Color
MB shower walls					
MB shower floor					
MB main floor					
MB shower niche					
HB shower walls					
HB shower floors					
HB main floor					
HB shower niche					
Primary Flooring		SQFT			
Kitchen					
Living room					
Dining room					
Bedrooms					
BACSPLASH :		SQFT			
kitchen					
master bath vanity		0			
hall bath vanity		0			
laundry base		0			

Countertops:	$ per SQFT	Square Feet	Count	Name:	Grout Color
Countertops:		SQFT			
kitchen island		0			
master bath vanity		0			
guest bath vanity		0			
laundry base		0			

Plumbing Schedule

Fixture	$ EACH	Color	Qty	Model number	Room
toilet		White	0		
kitchen sink		White	0		
kitchen sink faucet		White	0		
vanity sink		satin nickle	0		
sink fixtures		satin nickle	0		
shower fixtures		White	0		
tub/shower fixtures			0		

Electrical Schedule

Fixture	$ EACH	Color	Qty	Model number	Room
single toggle switches w/ covers			0		
duplex tamper proof outlets w/ covers			0		
pendant lights					
dining room chandelier					
bath sconce lights			0		
fan			0		
LED can lights			0		
hood vent insert			0		
HLV			0		
Light Vent			0		

Window Schedule

Area	Qty	Size	Hang	Lites	Color

Door Schedule

Area	Qty	Size	Swing	Lites	Color

Roofing Schedule

Area	SQFT	SIZE		COLOR	Type

Siding Schedule

Area	SQFT	SIZE		COLOR	Type

Trim Schedule

Room	Crown	Base & Shoe	QTY	Door & Window	QTY
Kitchen	5 1/4" colonial	5" col / 1/4 rd		2" colonial	
Living Room	5 1/4" colonial	5" col / 1/4 rd		2" colonial	
Dining Room	5 1/4" colonial	5" col / 1/4 rd		2" colonial	
Master Bedroom	5 1/4" colonial	5" col / 1/4 rd		2" colonial	
Master Bath	5 1/4" colonial	5" col / 1/4 rd		2" colonial	
Guest Bed	5 1/4" colonial	5" col / 1/4 rd		2" colonial	
Guest Bath	5 1/4" colonial	5" col / 1/4 rd		2" colonial	
Laundry	5 1/4" colonial	5" col / 1/4 rd		2" colonial	

Paint Schedule

Area	Color		Sheen & Base
Kitchen			
walls:			latex eggshell
ceiling:			latex flat
trim: crown, base shoe			oil-base semi-gloss
doors & trim			oil-base semi-gloss
window trim			oil-base semi-gloss
Living Room			
walls:			latex eggshell
ceiling:			latex flat
trim: crown, base shoe			oil-base semi-gloss
doors & trim			oil-base semi-gloss
window trim			oil-base semi-gloss
Dining Room			
walls:			latex eggshell
ceiling:			latex flat
trim: crown, base shoe			oil-base semi-gloss
doors & trim			oil-base semi-gloss
window trim			oil-base semi-gloss
Laundry			
walls:			latex eggshell
ceiling:			latex flat
trim: crown, base shoe			oil-base semi-gloss
doors & trim			oil-base semi-gloss
window trim			oil-base semi-gloss
Master Bedroom			
walls:			latex eggshell
ceiling:			latex flat
trim: crown, base shoe			oil-base semi-gloss
doors & trim			oil-base semi-gloss
window trim			oil-base semi-gloss
Master Bathroom			
walls:			latex eggshell
ceiling:			latex flat
trim: crown, base shoe			oil-base semi-gloss
doors & trim			oil-base semi-gloss
window trim			oil-base semi-gloss
Guest Bathroom			
walls:			latex eggshell
ceiling:			latex flat
trim: crown, base shoe			oil-base semi-gloss
doors & trim			oil-base semi-gloss
Guest Bedroom			
walls:			latex eggshell
ceiling:			latex flat
trim: crown, base shoe			oil-base semi-gloss
doors & trim			oil-base semi-gloss
window trim			oil-base semi-gloss
Exterior			
Lap siding			latex Flat
Soffit & Fascia			latex Flat
Front Entry			oil-base Satin
door			oil-base Satin
door trim			oil-base Satin
Shutters			oil-base Satin

Vendor Quotes

Wooton Construction, LLC
Home Improvement Specialists

Customer										
Project Description										

Category	Item	Size	Price Per	Total	Date	Vendor	Email	Phone	Address
Demo		0	$ -	$ -					
Demo		0	$ -	$ -					
Foundation		0	$ -						
Foundation		0	$ -	$ -					
Foundation		0	$ -	$ -					
Framing		0	$ -	$ -					
Framing		0	$ -	$ -					
Framing		0	$ -	$ -					
Roofing		0	$ -	$ -					
Roofing		0	$ -	$ -					
Siding		0	$ -	$ -					
Siding		0	$ -	$ -					
Siding		0	$ -	$ -					
Insulation		0	$ -	$ -					
HVAC		0	$ -	$ -					
HVAC		0	$ -	$ -					
HVAC		0	$ -	$ -					
Insulation		0	$ -	$ -					
Plumbing		0	$ -	$ -					
Plumbing		0	$ -	$ -					
Plumbing		0	$ -	$ -					
Lighting Fixtures		0	$ -	$ -					
Lighting Fixtures		0	$ -	$ -					
Lighting Fixtures		0	$ -	$ -					
Drywall		0	$ -	$ -					
Drywall		0	$ -	$ -					
Painting		0	$ -	$ -					
Painting		0	$ -	$ -					
Painting		0	$ -	$ -					
Finish Carpentry		0	$ -	$ -					
Finish Carpentry		0	$ -	$ -					
Tile Work		0	$ -	$ -					
Tile Work		0	$ -	$ -					
Tile Work		0	$ -	$ -					
Flooring		0	$ -	$ -					
Flooring		0	$ -	$ -					
Flooring		0	$ -	$ -					
Cabinetry: kit upper		0	$ -	$ -					
kit base		0	$ -	$ -					
MB vanity		0	$ -	$ -					
MB linen		0	$ -	$ -					
HB vanity		0	$ -	$ -					
HB linen		0	$ -	$ -					
Living Area		0	$ -	$ -					
Countertops		0	$ -	$ -					
Countertops		0	$ -	$ -					
Countertops		0	$ -	$ -					
		0	$ -	$ -					
		0	$ -	$ -					
		0	$ -	$ -					

Tradesman Interview Checklist

Contact Information:
Name:
Address:
Phone Number:
Email :

Skill Sets

☐			

1. Foundation   2. Framing   3. Siding   4. Roofing   5. HVAC   6. Insulation
7. Plumbing   8. Electrical   9. Drywall   10. Painting   11. Tile Work   12. Finish Carpentry
13. Cabinetry

Expectations & Availability   Responses

- ☐ Work Hours – standard & special hours
  Years of Experience
  References
  Photos of work
- ☐ Pricing for Labor – hourly rate day rate, per job
- ☐ Guarantee of Workmanship
- ☐ Materials willing to purchase
- ☐ Tools & Transportation

Homeowner Policies

- ☐ Payment Expectations
- ☐ Site Set up
- ☐ Site Tool Storage
- ☐ Smoking Areas
- ☐ Phone Usage
- ☐ Change Orders

Documentation

- ☐ Certificate of Insurance
- ☐ Tax ID #
- ☐ Pictures

Tradesman Checklist / Quotes

Project Description

Site Schedule

Category	Item	Referral	Price Per	Total	Date	Tradesman	Email	Phone	Address
Demo			$ -	$ -					
Demo			$ -	$ -					
Foundation			$ -						
Foundation			$ -	$ -					
Foundation			$ -	$ -					
Framing			$ -	$ -					
Framing			$ -	$ -					
Framing			$ -	$ -					
Roofing			$ -	$ -					
Roofing			$ -	$ -					
Siding			$ -	$ -					
Siding			$ -	$ -					
Siding			$ -	$ -					
Insulation			$ -	$ -					
HVAC			$ -	$ -					
HVAC			$ -	$ -					
HVAC			$ -	$ -					
Insulation			$ -	$ -					
Plumbing			$ -	$ -					
Plumbing			$ -	$ -					
Plumbing			$ -	$ -					
Electrician			$ -	$ -					
Electrician			$ -	$ -					
Electrician			$ -	$ -					
Drywall			$ -	$ -					
Drywall			$ -	$ -					
Painting			$ -	$ -					
Painting			$ -	$ -					
Painting			$ -	$ -					
Finish Carpentry			$ -	$ -					
Finish Carpentry			$ -	$ -					
Tile Work			$ -	$ -					
Tile Work			$ -	$ -					
Tile Work			$ -	$ -					
Flooring			$ -	$ -					
Flooring			$ -	$ -					
Flooring			$ -	$ -					

Site Schedule

Category	Item	Referral	Price Per	Total	Date	Tradesman	Email	Phone	Address
Cabinetry: kit upper			$ -	$ -					
kit base			$ -	$ -					
MB vanity			$ -	$ -					
MB linen			$ -	$ -					
HB vanity			$ -	$ -					
HB linen			$ -	$ -					
Living Area			$ -	$ -					
Countertops			$ -	$ -					
Countertops			$ -	$ -					
Countertops			$ -	$ -					
			$ -	$ -					
			$ -	$ -					

Top Choices

Category	Tradesman	Start Date	Duration	Materials Needed	Area	Referred By
Demo						
Foundation						
Framing						
Roofing						
Siding						
Insulation						
HVAC						
Plumbing						
Electrician						
Drywall						
Painting						
Tile						
Cabinetry						
Cabinetry						

Chapter 5: Renovation Project Management
Section 1: Building the Timeline

Setting Timelines: Now that you have made your material and tradesman selections and obtained your permit, you can start developing your timelines for the labor and materials. I have often referred to this process as doing the "Double Dutch" jump rope. You will be scheduling materials to be delivered before the tradesmen arrive and the work according to the standard construction process.

Project Flow: In this section, we will outline the project's overall flow for you with a description of the task category along with the tradesmen, materials, and equipment needed for each.

Task Category	Tradesman	Materials	Equipment	Duration
Demolition: removal of any building products from roofing to flooring and slabs *Order framing materials including doors and windows	**Specialty:** demolition for whole building structures to include slab **Standard:** demolition for cabinets, walls, flooring, etc.	trash bags, brown paper, painter's tape	**Standard**: dumpsters, trash trailers, buckets, brooms, dustpans, pry bars, hammers, sledgehammers, **Specialty**: excavators, jackhammers, augers tradesman may provide*	one day–two weeks
Foundation Forming: Slab: excavate and form shape, install a vapor barrier, metal mesh and grounding wire Raised: level ground, install piers and pads with sills and joists	**Slab**: concrete masonry works **Raised:** framing carpenter	**Slab**: stick lumber; forms (2x6, 2x12 and stakes) grounding wire, metal mesh, Visquen; vapor barrier, rebar sticks; tying into existing **Raised**: stick lumber treated, concrete piers and pads, termite shields	**Slab**: excavators to level ground, levels, string, tape measure, hammers **Raised**: framing guns, excavators to level ground, bottle jacks and foundation jacks to hold beams in place before securing, levels, tape measure **the tradesman may provide***	**Slab:** 1–3 days **Raised:** 1–10 days

Rough-in Plumbing 1: the installation of the main sewer and drainpipes in the foundation	plumber: will usually provide these materials and equipment	drainpipe, varying sizes	shovels	one day
INSPECTION: Plumbing Inspection: must be completed BEFORE concrete is poured	**CODES OFFICE** the plumber will call in this inspection			same day as install or next day
Foundation: the base on which you will build your structure **Slab:** concrete **Raised:** platform off the ground	**Slab:** concrete masonry works **Raised:** framing carpenter	**Slab:** concrete plywood; the pathway of equipment **Raised:** subfloor, plywood sheathing, fasteners	**Slab:** concrete trucks, concrete screeding tools (*used to smooth out the concrete as it dries*) **Raised:** framing guns The tradesman may provide*	**Slab:** 1–2 days **Raised:** 1–3 days
INSPECTION: Foundation Inspection: after the concrete is poured	**CODES OFFICE** homeowner to call in this Inspection			when complete
Framing: walls, ceilings, roofs, doors, windows, fascia order roofing materials order siding materials order drywall materials	framing carpenter	stick lumber, plywood sheathing, fascia boards, house wrap, foam sill sealer, fasteners	framing guns, ladders, scaffolding, compressors and hoses for the framing guns, skill saws, chop saws, extension cords, levels, framing squares, tape measure	2–30 days depends on the size
Rough-in Plumbing 2: the installation of water and gas supply, and drain lines in walls in place for sinks, showers, tubs, hose bibs, appliances, etc.	plumber: will usually provide these materials and equipment	piping, drains, hoses, and connectors		1–2 days depends on the size

Task Category	Tradesman	Materials	Equipment	Duration
Rough-in Electrical: installation of panels, wiring, switch and outlet boxes, junction boxes, can lights in the ceiling, and wall sconce plates	electrician: will usually provide these materials and equipment	wires, gang boxes, junction boxes, can light housing, heat/light /vent unit, light/vent unit		1–7 days
HVAC: installation of indoor and outdoor units, trunk lines, register openings in ceilings	HVAC company			1–5 days
INSPECTION: Plumbing Electrical HVAC Open Wall	CODES OFFICE plumber to call his in, electrician to call his in, open wall—homeowner to call in			when complete
Roofing: installation of shingles, drip edge, roof jacks, ridge vents and/or turbine roof vents, ridge capping, valley flashing, etc. order insulation materials	Roofer: will usually provide these materials and equipment. You will select the color and type of shingle	shingles, roofing jacks, drip edge, flashing, ridge vents and/or turbine vents, ridge capping	nail guns, compressors, and hoses	1–3 days
Siding: installation of stucco, wood or Hardi lap siding, brick masonry, vinyl siding *any combination of the three as well	**Masonry:** brick and/or stucco **Lap Siding:** siding carpenter **Vinyl Siding:** vinyl siding installer	**Masonry:** bricks, sand and mortar, brick ties, metal breaks for windows and doors **Lap Siding:** lap siding or panels, fasteners, trim **Vinyl:** vinyl panels, trim, fasteners	**Masonry:** concrete mixer, trowels, hoses, hammers, levels **Lap:** finish guns, compressors and hoses for the finish guns, levels, tape measure, chop saws, skill saws **Vinyl:** vinyl cutters, hammers, levels, tape measure	**Masonry:** 1–10 days (size) **Lap:** 1–10 days (size) **Vinyl:** 1–5 days (depends on size)

Insulation: installation in walls and ceilings. roll, blown-in, foam	**Roll:** carpenter **Blown-in:** carpenter or insulation company **Foam:** insulation company	**Roll and Blown-in:** rolls, staples (roll) pkg. and machine (blown-in) **Blown-in and Foam:**	**Provided:** roll and/or blown-in utility knife **Foam:** provided by the Insulation company	1–3 days (depends on size)
Drywall: hang drywall on walls and ceilings, then float all seams with tape and mud order trim package order tile materials/flooring	**Drywaller:** to hang drywall and float; will be able to achieve any texture on the ceiling and/or walls you will need applying	drywall sheets, screws, tape, mud, sandpaper	**Provided:** trowels, mud pans, sanding poles, drywall knives, utility knives	1–7 days (depends on size)
Trim Carpentry 1: Installation of the crown, baseboards, door and window trim, any needed cabinetry trim as well, soffits and exterior trim needed	Trim Carpenter: soffit and fascia materials	crown, baseboards, door and window trim, nails	Tools: finishing gun, compressor, and hoses for the finish gun provided for by the trim carpenter Fasteners: will fit their tools	1–5 days (size)
Painting 1: prime all walls, ceilings, and trim. If there are any blemishes, refloat and prime again. First coat all walls, ceilings, and trim work	Painters: will provide the materials and equipment. You will have to give a paint schedule with the color choices	Provided: putty, caulk, primer, paint, rags, sandpaper, roller naps, brush cleaners	Provided: rollers, brushes, caulk guns, putty knives, scaffolding, ladders, brown paper, painter's tape for protection	1–3 days (size)
Cabinetry: installation of any cabinets for kitchens, bathrooms, laundry room, and/or utility storage	cabinet maker	all base, uppers, full units, and specialty items to include all shelves, doors and/or drawer fronts, hinges, and slides	**Provided:** the cabinet maker will provide all	4–8 weeks from template to install
Countertops 1: template for the tops in kitchen, baths, laundry, etc.	**Stone Distributors and Fabricators:** will provide the materials and equipment	stone and any under-mount sinks: you may have them delivered to the fabricator	**You** will give them a stone choice and provide any under-mount sinks and the faucet mounting specs	1-day template, 2–4 weeks from template to install

Tile Work 1: installation of shower walls, niches, and floor tiles, including grout	Tile Setter: will provide some materials: waterproofing materials, mortar, and thin-set	tile, motor thin-set, grout, backer materials, waterproofing materials, sealants	**Provided**: tile saw, trowels, sponges, buckets, cleaners	1–8 days (size)
Glass Works: template shower doors and enclosures	Glass Company: materials and equipment will be provided			One day 2–4 week for install
Flooring: installation of floors; wood, laminate, vinyl, and/or carpet	Flooring Installer: there are usually specialists for every type, wood, laminate, vinyl	**Wood or laminate:** paddings, thresholds, fasteners **Vinyl sheets, tiles, or planks,** padding, glue, and thresholds **Carpet:** tack strips, padding, thresholds	**Provided**: hammers, nail guns, trowels, stretchers, caulk guns, etc.	1–6 days (size)
Countertops 2: install the countertops	Stone fabricators: will provide the materials and equipment			1–2 days
Tile Work 2: install all backsplashes in kitchens, baths, laundry, etc.	Tile Setter: will provide some materials and all equipment; you will provide tile and grout	tile, motor thin-set, grout, backer materials, waterproofing materials, sealants	**Provided**: tile saw, trowels, sponges, buckets, cleaners	1–2 days (size)
Trim Carpentry 2: installation of shoe base and final specialty trim	Trim Carpenter: the equipment will be provided	shoe molding, fasteners, putty, caulk, rags	**Provided**: chop saw, finish gun, compressors, and hoses for the finish gun, putty knives	1–3 days (size)
Painting 2: 2nd coat all walls, ceilings, trim work, and/or cabinets interior and exterior	Painters: will provide the materials and equipment, you will have to give a paint schedule with the color choices	**Provided**: putty, caulk, primer, paint, rags, sandpaper, roller naps, brush cleaners	**Provided**: rollers, brushes, caulk guns, putty knives, scaffolding, ladders, brown paper, painter's tape for protection	1–3 days (size)
Plumbing 3: install all finish plumbing fixtures in kitchens, baths, laundry, etc.	Plumber: the equipment will be provided	**Finish fixtures**: sinks, sink faucets, shower, tub faucets, drain catches, gas appliances, etc.	**Provided**: all tools, fasteners, connection hoses, etc.	1–2 days (size)

Electrical 2: install all finish light fixtures, beauty rings, switches, and outlets, including cover plates	**Electrician:** the equipment will be provided	**Finish fixtures:** light bulbs, fixtures, cover plates, beauty rings, ceiling fans, appliances, etc.	**Provided:** beauty rings and cover plates may be provided, cover plates	1–3 days (size)
INSPECTIONS: PLUMBING: final ELECTRICAL: final HVAC final	**CODES** the plumber will call in the electrician will call in			
Finish Carpentry: installation of mirrors, accessories, hangers, shower doors, hardware for doors and cabinets, window treatments	**Finish Carpenter or Trim Carpenter:** the equipment will be provided	mirrors, bath hangers and accessories, door and cabinet hardware, window treatments	**Provided:** hammers, drills, utility knives, rags, caulk	1–6 days (size)
INSPECTION: FINAL	**CODES** homeowner to call in			
Clean up: final wipe down of all surfaces and mopping and/or vacuuming the floors	cleaning service or homeowner	**Cleaning supplies:** you may provide if you have specific cleaners you prefer to use.	**Provided**: rags, mops, brooms, vacuum, ladders, etc.	two days

As you can see, a lot is involved in ensuring everything lines up to keep your project moving along. It will require daily attention to every detail and patience as deadlines move. There are several reasons for deadlines to change:

- **Weather:** This can affect the foundation, framing, roofing, siding, exterior painting, etc.
- **Materials Delays:** Some materials will be on backorder. Some may be out of stock and need to be ordered.
- **Tradesman Schedules:** Your tradesman may have had a delay on another job, causing them to delay yours.
- **Change Orders:** More work will change the deadline if something changes even a little.
- **Health:** You or your tradesmen may experience an illness during the project.

Calendars: Using the chart and the information given to you by your tradesmen, you can begin to mark out your calendar. The durations shown in the chart are **ONLY** guidelines. The duration will depend significantly on the size of your project, weather conditions, and tradesman availability.

Ordering Materials: You will notice reminders to order different materials along the way. You should put together a list for the task category scheduled for the next part of the project to ensure you have everything you need for your tradesman so they can begin on time. Order all finish electrical light fixtures and appliances and all finish plumbing fixtures as soon as the project starts. They should be stored away until needed.

Walkthrough: You will also do a final walkthrough of the project and determine the necessary touch-up in painting, tile, flooring, and/or cabinetry. Call back your tradesman and schedule the touch-ups required at this time. If any door or hardware adjustments need to be made, point those out. You may want to mark all areas that need attention with a small piece (nickel size) of painter's tape. This type of tape is used because it will remove easily without damaging the material's surface. It would also be helpful to have a list of items you want to be addressed or which you have questions.

Section 2: Scheduling

- **Availability:** You will begin scheduling the first 3–4 tradesmen, trying to coordinate when they can start. You will continue to plan the next 2–4 Tradesmen and progress in this manner. Depending on the work you are doing, you will begin with this order:
  - **Demo:** If siding needs removing to tie into the existing foundation. Schedule the next few tradesmen to follow.
    - **Foundation:** Frame out and pour concrete slabs
    - **Framing:** All walls, ceilings, roof doorways, and windows.
    - **Plumber (Phase One):** Install drain lines in the slab, if needed.
    - **Cabinetry (Phase One):** Measure for cabinets.
  - **Roofer:** Schedule the next few tradesmen to follow.
    - **Siding:** Any exterior siding you have chosen.
    - **Electrician (Phase One):** Install the wires and boxes in the walls needed for the outlets, switches, lights, and/or fans.
    - **Plumber (Phase Two):** Rough-in lines in the walls for the showers, tubs, sinks, gas lines (appliances), and water heaters.
  - **Drywaller:** Hang and float interior sheetrock for walls and ceilings. Schedule the next few tradesmen to follow.
    - **Trim Carpenter:** Install all crown, base moldings, doors, and window trim.
    - **Cabinetry (Phase Two):** Install all cabinetry.
    - **Countertops (Phase One):** Template for the countertops.
  - **Painter (First Coat):** Prep, prime, paint walls, ceilings, trim work, doors, and cabinets. Schedule the next few tradesmen to follow.
    - **Tile Work:** Showers, floors, backsplashes.
    - **Countertops (Phase Two):** Install tops and backsplashes.
    - **Flooring:** Install floors.
  - **Finish Carpenter:** Install all hardware for doors, cabinets, shower doors, mirrors, accessories, door stops, and shoe moldings. Schedule the next few tradesmen to work alongside or to follow.
    - **Painter (Second Coat):** Second coat walls, ceiling, trim, doors and/or cabinets, and touch-ups.
    - **Plumber (Phase Three):** Install all finish fixtures.
    - **Electrician (Phase Two):** Install all finish fixtures.
- This is a condensed outline of the order in which the work generally gets done. You will have inspections along the way. *SEE Section 3*

- **Communication:** Once the first tradesman is scheduled, call the other tradesmen to alert them to the new schedule. Give at least 2–3 weeks advanced notice when you need them. In most cases, this is enough notice, but occasionally you may have to wait a little longer on a tradesman to become available. You should also call them every week and the day before to remind them and ensure they are still good to start on time.
- **Orders and Deliveries:** Begin to order your materials for your project. You will be ordering in the order of the work being done.
    - **Materials:**
        - **Framing:** To include doors, windows, and tile waterproofing.
        - **Siding:** Any bricks, vinyl, stucco base, and lap siding.
        - **Roofing:** Shingles, metal, drip edge, etc.
        - **Plumbing:** Order all finish products.
        - **Electrical:** Order all finish fixtures.
        - *Drywall*: Sheetrock, mud, and tape.
        - **Tile:** All tile, grout, and trim materials (this may take up to three weeks to come in).
        - **Paint:** You will need at least the painting schedule.
        - **Trim:** All crown, base, and shoe moldings.
    - **Equipment:**
        - Dumpsters or trash trailers
        - Port-o-lets
        - Scaffolding

- **Contingency Plans:** You will need to have a backup plan in place when the original plans change. For example, some things you may be aware of right away is existing rot or damage. Another reason the scope of work may change will be based on the cost and/or availability of tradesmen and products. The following are just a few reasons you may need a contingency plan:

- **Unseen Rot:** You may have spotted areas around your house that are suspect to rot issues. This rot may go a lot further than initially anticipated. As a result, it will require more work and cost to your budget. To compensate for this, you may do the following:
    - Plan a certain amount of money you are ready to spend on the repairs.
    - Reselect certain products to make up for the price difference. I.e., granite selection, siding selection, plumbing, and/or light fixture selection.
    - Decide to do work on the project yourself, such as painting, to make up the cost difference.
- **Material Costs:** You may have selected granite countertops, high-end plumbing, or a light fixture at a much higher price point than you initially expected, but it's just an item you are in love with or feel would complete the design you are trying to achieve. In every design, there is always one unique piece. In this case, you may change the selections to do some of the work yourself.
- **Delivery and Back Order Delays:** There may be other work that can be done while waiting on a particular product, but there are items that you cannot continue until that item arrives. If the delay is long enough, you may have all other works continue out of order and retrofit your item later. It will cost more because there will probably be rework involved. In some cases, you may change the product last minute for something carried in stock and continue with the project. Always check with your vendor for substitutions.
    - **Items You Wait On:**
        - **Lumber:** You will need your lumber in specific sizes. Check around at other vendors to see if it is in stock. You may end up paying more, but the job can continue.
        - **Windows and Doors:** These are also so specific in style, material, size, and color you will need to wait on them. Other work can be done without them, and you will have to have them retrofitted when they arrive. If you need to close in the hole where the windows and/or doors are installed, use a plywood sheet to put in its place until they arrive.
        - **Drywall:** Much like lumber, you need it. If your vendor is out of stock on drywall, you may call other vendors to see if they carry it. Again, you may pay more, but you can continue your project.
        - **Tile:** This choice is too important to the design; you will have to wait until it arrives to be able to tile. Other work can be done, such as painting and most trim work. If your tile for the shower walls is delayed, then the final plumbing will be delayed, and the installation of the shower door will also be delayed.
        - **Plumbing Finish Valve Sets:** These are incredibly important to your design; you will need to wait. If you have ordered a unique vessel vanity sink, you will need to stay on this. Vessel sinks are chosen because they add to the design and are not meant to disappear into the background. If your sinks, tubs, and/or toilets are a

special-order color, you will need to wait on them. If the delay is long enough, you may get with your vendor and look at purchasing your second choice if they are available to arrive sooner. All other work can be done without the plumbing fixtures, so the wait will be worth it. You will have to wait to use your kitchen and/or bathroom until the fixtures are installed.
- **Lighting Fixtures:** These are important to the overall design as well. If the delay is long enough, you may want to get with your vendor and order your second choice if it will be available sooner. All other work can be done without the lighting fixtures, so the wait will be worth it.
- **Hardware:** The hardware for both doors and cabinets is generally essential to the overall design. However, you may have found more than one option attractive. Waiting on the hardware is acceptable. The cabinets still function without them.
- **Items That Can Be Replaced Easily:**
    - **Standard Vanity Sinks and Toilets:** These everyday items come in limited styles and colors. There may be similar sinks and/or toilets in stock that you can substitute for another one so the project can continue.
    - **Standard Lighting Fixtures and Fans:** Check with your vendor; there may be similar lighting fixtures in stock so your project can continue. All other work can be done without the lighting fixtures, so the wait may be worth it.
- **Weather:** There is little that can be done about delays in work because of the weather. Your tradesmen will be scrambling to catch up on work, and you will be anxious to get the project going again. In some rare cases, the weather may cause damage to the project requiring rework. Having a set amount of your budget dedicated to any damage caused by the weather is a good idea. It will depend significantly on where you live and the time of year you are working on your renovation. Be aware of the possible weather conditions you may incur when planning your project. A few examples of this would be the following:
    - **Snowstorms:** A heavy downfall can delay any outside work getting done, but also, the weight of the snow can break lumber, cave in roofs, damage plumbing lines, and break electrical supply lines. If the snow is not gotten rid of fast enough, it can also cause flooding issues as it melts.
    - **Tropical Storms:** May be tree limbs that damage roofs or break windows, doors, or siding. If windows, roofs, or doors are broken, water damage from the rain coming into the structure could also be water damage. It could also occur in a separate part of the house away from the renovation. It will be additional work you did not plan on this initially.
    - **Hurricanes:** If there happens to be a hurricane during your renovation, take the necessary precautions to secure your property, including any tools, materials, and

debris on site. With hurricanes, there comes enough warning for you to make the required preparations. In some cases, you will need to evacuate. Make a plan with your tradesmen to secure any tools or materials necessary and when to resume work after the hurricane has passed. Since hurricanes have high winds, heavy rainfall, and tornados, there could be significant damage to your property, or there could be truly little. Check with your insurance company to see if you are covered if there is damage to your property even though you are doing renovations. Take pictures before the hurricanes make landfall and any needed photos after the hurricane to show your insurance company if you need to make a claim.

- **Earthquakes:** Depending on the size of the earthquake, damage can occur in the aftermath. If you live in an area where this may be possible, you will need to check with your insurance company to ensure they are covered even though you are renovating if damage occurs during the earthquake. Take pictures, if you can, of any damage that occurred.

Section 3: Inspections and Expectations

- **Checkpoints:** Times to look at the work completed and the quality of work and check the project's overall progress. There will be several times to check in with your tradesmen, CODES office, and vendors. Some of these will be crucial to ensuring the work's quality and integrity as it progresses so it does not throw off a different task of the project, creating more work to be done later. On the other hand, it will be considerably less work than removing several layers of work completed to correct the original problem while adding more time. The following are a few of the critical checkpoints to follow. You may adapt this to your project and create any new ones where you think necessary.

- **Permits:** Always look at the CODES permit office as a part of your team in building your project. They are NOT the enemy; they are there to ensure that the tradesman you hire is completing work that is sound and of good quality. It is important to note that the CODES standards are the MINIMUM requirements. You may have a tradesman that goes above and beyond CODE for you.
    - **Beginning:** Make an appointment with your local permits office to talk to an inspector about your project. Give a brief description of your project and a rough drawing to let the inspector know what you are planning. Bring a list of questions about the work you are doing.
        - What are your property easements?
        - What are the electrical requirements?
        - What are the plumbing requirements for your project?
        - What are the structural requirements for your project?
        - Do they have any recommendations for your project?
        - How much advanced notice is required for an inspection?
    - **During:** If you have questions about any project phase, always call your local permit office. They are happy to answer questions ahead of time so you don't fail an inspection.

- **Mandated Inspections:** These inspections require a call to the permits office to schedule an inspector. You will need to talk to the tradesman performing the work to find out when they will need the inspection to be scheduled so that you may call it in on time. Most inspections will happen the same day if called in the morning. However, if the inspection is called for in the afternoon, it may not occur until the next day. Remember, these inspections must pass before proceeding with the next phase of work.
    - **Plumbing One:** The outside form for the slab is in place, and the drain lines, stacks, and sewage pipes are in place; your plumber should call this in himself.
    - **Foundation One:** The form is in place; the metal mesh visqueen and the grounding rod are in place. You will call this in for the foundation.
    - **Foundation Two:** The concrete is poured and set. You will call this in at this time.
    - **Plumbing Two:** The drain and supply lines are in the walls and/or ceilings. Water heaters are in place, and/or gas supplies. Your plumber will call this one in himself.

- **Electrical One:** All the panels, wiring, outlet and switch boxes, outlets, switches, can light housing, HLV housing, LV housing, and lighting boxes in ceilings and walls for interior and exterior lighting is in place. Your electrician will call this one in himself.
- **HVAC/Mechanical:** Inspection of all components that will be covered prior to final inspection. Items such as vents, drains, wiring, copper tubing, etc.
- **Open Wall:** All stick framing for walls, ceilings, roofs, and windows. Doors in place with plywood sheathing and house wrap in place. You will call for this one when this is complete.
- **Plumbing Three:** All finished plumbing fixtures are installed, including sinks, faucets (*valve sets*), toilets, water spigots, and appliances for water and gas. Your plumber will call this in himself.
- **Electrical Two:** All finish lighting fixtures and covers are installed. Your electrician will call this one in himself.
- **Final HVAC/Mechanical:** Ensure proper installation and operation of all Mechanical components. (Does not include standard appliances)
- **Final Building:** Completing the project with all flooring, painting, and installations completed. You will call this in at the end of the project.
- **Suggested Inspections:** These are inspections you would like to do yourself or have someone you trust help you at specific points in the project. These inspections will help to catch mistakes BEFORE they happen. It is suggested to do this after the tradesman has left for the day. This will allow you to thoroughly inspect the site and avoid offending the tradesman while closely examining his work. It will also allow you to make a list of anything you may have a question about to ask your tradesman the next day.
  - **Foundation:** Check for level and see if it is the same level as the existing home foundation.
  - **Framing:**
    - **Walls:** Check the walls for wobble and individual framing studs being equidistant apart. Use a long level or a straight board (about 4' in length), place it horizontally across the studs and move it from ceiling to floor, then from side to side. If there are any *significant* inconsistencies in the stud placement, the level or board will wobble like a seesaw. Mark any areas with this error and talk to your framer the next morning to correct this. *Slight* inconsistencies will occur because the wood studs are rough material and are not perfectly consistent with one another. Wood is a porous natural product that can expand and contract with temperature changes and humidity levels while being stored in warehouses before arriving. Also, look for any stud that may have significant "crowning." The board will be warped and will bow from top to bottom. You will see it right away.
    - **Ceilings:** Checking for wobble. It may not be possible for you to hold a board against the ceiling surface, but you may be able (with the help of a trusted person) to hold a string tight against the boards from wall to wall. Again, if there are any *significant* inconsistencies with the joists crowning (warping), make a note to talk to your framer in the morning.

- **Windows:** Check the window frame for level and proper support. Using a level, place it on the sill of the window and make sure it is level. Make sure the window is adequately supported with the stud work around it. Using the diagrams in the terminology and standards supplemental booklet—in the framing section—you will be able to compare it to the framework in your home. If not correctly framed in, it could lead to leaking, warping the window, and eventually rot issues later if it allows water to penetrate.
- **Doors:** Check the door frame for level and proper support. Using a level, hold it up against the side jambs and the top sill to ensure its level. Then, using the diagrams in the terminology and standards booklet under the framing section, you can compare it to the framework in your home. If it is not framed correctly, the door will not operate correctly. It can also cause warping of the door over time.
- **Plumbing:** Check the placement of the supply and drain lines. Make sure you have all the water sources you desire. Even though the supply and drain lines can be changed later, it will be more costly. Drywall and cabinetry may have to be redone and/or modified to move these lines. It is best to catch any changes that need to be made BEFORE drywall goes up. ****NOTE**: If you want a design change order in the placement of lines, this is the time to do it.
    - Kitchen sink supply and drain
    - Kitchen refrigerator water line (if needed)
    - Kitchen gas lines for appliances (if needed)
    - Bathroom vanity sink supply and drains
    - Bathroom shower supply lines and drains
    - Bathroom toilet supply (in-wall) and drain (in the floor)
    - Laundry room washer supply
    - Outdoor gas lines for grills
    - Water heaters
- **Electrical:** Check the placement of all switches, outlets, light fixtures, and can lighting. Even though the boxes and lines may be changed later, it will be more costly. Drywall and cabinetry may have to be redone and/or modified to move these lines and boxes. It is best to catch any changes that need to be made BEFORE drywall goes up. ****NOTE**: if you want a design change order in placing fixtures or outlets, this is the time to do it.
- **Drywall:** Check the drywall for any wobble. Much like the framing, use a long level or a straight board (about 4′ in length), place it horizontally across the drywall and move it from ceiling to floor, then from side to side. The level or board will wobble like a seesaw if there are any significant inconsistencies in the drywall. Mark any areas with this error and talk to your Drywaller the next morning to correct this. There will be *slight* inconsistencies because the wood studs are made of a rough material that the drywall is attached to and are not perfectly consistent. Look for tight seams where the boards butt against each other and around the outlet and switch boxes. If there are significant gaps around the boxes, the covers may not cover them,

and you will have an exposed hole in the wall. While this may be corrected later, it is best to catch it now to not require painting again.

- **Trim Work:** Look for tight seams with no more than a 1/8" gap. This allows for expansion and contraction in the heat and cold.
  - **Crown:** It should be tight to the wall and the ceiling (if the ceiling has no texture).
  - **Baseboards:** Should be tight to the wall and have a small gap between the bottom of the board and the floor. You will cover this gap with the shoe molding. Check to ensure the baseboard's top is level and straight and not just following the floor. Sometimes if you are using an existing slab, there can be inconsistencies in the slab with slight dips and bumps. Walking on the floor, you may never feel it, but it will show as a line on the wall if the baseboards follow the dips and bumps. Again, the shoe molding will hide this when the gap is left at the bottom.
  - **Door and Window Trim:** Check for straight lines around the door and/or window. Following the lines of the door or window unit, if significant corrections need to be made (if it's not straight), make a note of this and discuss options with your trim carpenter in the morning.
- **Cabinetry:** You will be checking for level and correct placement.
  - **Base Cabinets:** Using a level, place them on top of the base cabinets, and make sure they are level; this will be very important to ensure that the countertops are level. If significant corrections need to be made, make a note and talk to your cabinet installer in the morning. They may not finish the installation on their list to tackle. You will see gaps in the back of the base cabinets where they meet the wall. This ensures the fronts of the cabinets are flush, making sure the countertops are straight in the front.
  - **Upper Cabinets:** Check to ensure the bottom of the upper cabinets is level. The backsplash will meet this part and will ensure level lines in the grout lines. There will be gaps at the top of the cabinet where it meets the ceiling. Crown molding will hide this.
- **Countertops:** Check your seams, level, and the seal on the stone. You can check this with a glass of water. Fill the glass (*preferably a clear glass*) halfway with water and place it on the counter. You will immediately see if the counter is level. You can also pour a little water on the counter (*about the size of the bottom of the glass*); if the water runs off in a direction, it may not be level. Wipe off the water; if the stone is darker in that spot where the water sat, taking a while for the color to return, and the stone's seal may need to be rehoned. Get with the stone distributor/fabricator with pictures of the situation, so you get the right solution. They can often come out to your home and buff the area of concern.

Tile Work:
- **Wall Tiles (*Showers and Backsplashes*):** This one is a little tough because you may have chosen a tile with a lot of texture, and it will not have a smooth surface, no matter how "flat" the tile is installed. If significant tiles poke out and need resetting, take note of this and talk to your tile setter in the morning. Usually, there will only be one, MAYBE two tiles that need resetting, that's if there are any. If there are any issues with how the tile has been installed, it will be OBVIOUS. It is best to correct this before grouting. Once grouted, look for "holes" in the grout. Sometimes there are air bubbles in the grout when applied, and once it dries, it will leave a void. Ask your tile setter to re-grout where needed.
- **Floor Tiles (*Floors and Shower Floors*):** These tiles should be reasonably level; it depends on your chosen tile. Using a tile puck, slide it across the floor. This will reveal any tiles that stick up on the edges where they should not. Note any significant corrections that need to be made and talk to your tile installer in the morning.

- **Final Electrical:**
  - **Cover Plates:** Look for your cover plates to be flush with the wall and straight. If the cover plate is on top of the tile, it may not be completely flush, depending on the texture of the tile you have chosen and if the cover crosses over grout lines.
  - **Light Fixtures:** Your light fixtures should be level and straight, depending on the design of your light fixture.

- **Final Plumbing:**
  - **Valve Sets:** Should be flush to the surface (*wall or countertop*) and not move or spin. This will also depend on the design of your chosen valve set.
  - **Sinks:** Should be level and have a tight seam in between the top edge and the countertop.

There may be more inspections you would like to do during the project. Just know that if you are the contractor, you should inspect each tradesman's work before you sign off on completing their work. Doing inspections in front of your tradesman can cause tension and make it more challenging to get any corrections made. Not impossible, just a little more complicated. It is very human to become defensive when an imperfection is pointed out to us, which is no different in this situation. You are directly judging his work and craftsmanship; you must handle it as politely as possible. Allow the tradesman to explain the situation while being open to suggestions for a different solution but remain firm if the current situation is just not acceptable to you. Most of the time, it can be corrected without fuss and is already on their punch list. There may not have been a chance to discuss it the day before.

Process: It is essential to know your tradesman's process for completing his work. This way, you will understand the progress of the work being completed. Every tradesman has a process they follow. It may be how they first learned how to do their trade or a process they have adapted to make it more efficient. It may not make sense to you when you see it, but that does not necessarily make it "wrong." It is just a different method of arriving at the same place. If the necessary steps of structural support, proper insulation, waterproofing, and fixture installation have a quality result, it is best to let them follow their process. Discuss the process with them and ask why they feel it is a better method for them and why it works so well. They will be happy to share with you their experience and expertise. It will ease your mind about their methods and help you understand what you should expect to see as the project progresses.

Delays: Delays are inevitable. You will need patience for them. Communication between you, your tradesman, and/or vendor will be crucial with each delay. There are several reasons for delays in any project. Making this a part of your discussion at the beginning will help you to prepare for future incidents.

- **Failed Inspections:** Corrections to work performed will have to be done before the rest of the work can continue. Some may only take a few minutes by your tradesman, and others may take a day or two.
- **Rework:** Work may have been done incorrectly, or a product may have failed once installed. Therefore, the work completed will have to be redone before moving on with the remaining outline.
- **Weather:** If you have any terrible weather issues (*rain, snow, hailstorms, high winds, etc.*) when doing any exterior work, this will delay the tradesmen for however long the bad weather lasts. It is ESPECIALLY important to keep in touch with the tradesmen during this time and hold them to when they will resume work. Some may take on a job in another town where the weather is not bad, so your job's delay may end up being longer than the bad weather.
- **Change Orders:** Some minor change orders, if caught in time, may not change the timeline for more than a day. Other larger change orders will alter the timeline and budget anywhere from a day to weeks, depending on the change order.
- **Shipment Delays:** You may end up with shipment delays for products. There may be back orders or assembly problems, or even trouble with the trucks and/or airlines delivering your product. Your vendor should be able to give you an ETA. You will then need to notify your tradesmen of all delays in the products arriving. It will have a ripple effect on your timeline. If the delay is significant enough, it will completely alter the schedule for your tradesmen. They will take another job to fill in the time; they need to keep working to earn their paycheck. Ask when they will be able to reschedule you.
- **Illness:** You or your tradesmen may get sick enough that you may have to reschedule the work. It is rare, but it has been known to happen.
- **Communication:** The LACK of communication with your tradesmen and/or vendors regarding delays and deliveries can lead to other uncertainties in work. The act of communication cannot be stressed enough.

Section 4: Setting the Site Plan

This section will help you to set up your home as a work site. The key to keeping your sanity throughout his project will be to remember that your home is now temporarily a work site. You will share this space with others for a short time while owning your home. In sharing the space, your home and property will have to be organized so that you and your family can still use the home daily, keeping the routine as "normal" as possible while creating adequate working space for all your tradesmen.

Workstations: The first thing to establish are your workstations. Each tradesman will ask you where they can set up to do their work. The following are the areas you will need to establish for your tradesmen and yourself:

- **Cutting Stations:** This area will be set up to cut wood for framing, roofing, carpentry work, and trim carpentry work. Things to take into consideration when choosing a place for the cutting stations are the following:
    - **Sawhorses:** The stands on which the saw will be set up. Usually, a sheet of plywood is used as a temporary tabletop.
    - **Saws:** For cutting all the wood. There may be more than one type of saw set up at this location: chop or miter saws, skill saws, jigsaws, and routers.
    - **Extension Cords:** Provided the power for the saws being used, they will need a power source close.
    - **Sawdust:** The shavings from the wood. It should be cleaned up at the end of the day by either collecting it in a trash bag or raking through the grass to spread it out. You may request to keep it as mulch for any plant beds.
    - **Cut-offs:** The pieces of wood cut off the larger portion of the wood that will not be used. These may accumulate during the day but should be cleaned up at the end of every workday and not left lying around.
- **Water Station:** You will need to pick a place on your property that will temporarily take some abuse and get dirty. This area will be near a water source and be used for the following tasks:
    - **Tile Saws:** These saws need a water source to cut the tiles. It does make a mess on the ground. None of the runoff will cause any damage to your grass or concrete, but you will need to pressure wash the concrete after the tradesman is finished to clean off the residue.
    - **Washout:** This will be used to clean all tools used by your tradesman. There may be a remote grassy area or an area with landscape gravel that would be better suited for cleaning out around your house.
        - **Shovels:** Are used in foundation and landscaping. It can sometimes cause temporary dead spots when used in a grassy area, and other times it will not affect the landscaping.

- **Painting:** Paint brushes, rollers, pans, etc. It is usually best to pick out an area that may discolor the grass temporarily. However, it will grow out after a few cuts.
- **Drywall:** Trowels and pans used for the drywall mud usually have no effect area.
- **Tile Work:** Will use the tile saws, trowels, buckets, and sponges, used to lay the tile down and fill in the grout.
- **Debris Removal:** You will have to designate an area for your tradesmen to eliminate any debris. You usually will have one of the following:
    - **Dumpster:** Place on concrete because during the dumpster's delivery and pickup, it can dig into the grass and leave ruts that need to be filled in later.
    - **Trash Trailer:** It is good to place on grass or concrete because the trailer has wheels that are not as damaging to grass and will easily roll on concrete. The trash trailer provider will either put a hub lock on the trailer's hitch or deflate one or more tires to prevent theft.
- **Smoking Areas:** You will need to find an area for the workman to smoke. Try setting out a bucket for the cigarette butts. It will help keep down the amount you see around the property and designate the area you tolerate as the smoking area. Be firm and clear about your personal preferences for the smoking areas.
- **Port-o-lets:** You will need to find a place on your property you're comfortable with the placement of the port-o-let that has easy access for the provider of the port-o-let to service the unit.

- **Storage and Delivery Areas:** You will need designated areas for storing and delivering materials. Your stored materials will be kept for an extended period, and your deliveries will be materials used almost immediately. Your areas for the different types of materials, tools, and equipment will be essential to keeping everyone safe and on task. Work progress will not slow if you and your tradesmen can find the materials, tools, and equipment they need upon arrival. Time can be wasted looking for materials, tools, or equipment, so the following is a guideline for storing and delivering items and the placement that will be the most advantageous for each.

- **Storage:** These items will be kept in either a climate-controlled or non-climate-controlled environment. Tyr to organize the materials in the order they will be needed. EX: your lights may be to the back of the storage container, and the framing materials are to the front.
    - **Climate Control:** This would be a room in your house. The temperature and humidity can be controlled. The materials you may want to store here are as follows:
        - **Materials:**
            - Paint
            - Wood flooring
            - Wood paneling
            - Trim boards

- Drywall
- Glues and cleaners
- Grout

- **Tools:** You will need a designated place to store any tools that need to stay on-site overnight for your tradesmen. Your tools will need to be locked away as well. Most tools do not need a climate-controlled environment but must stay out of the rain and out of sight of passersby.
    - **Hand Tools:** Hammers, pry bars, screwdrivers, tape measures, etc.
    - **Power Tools:** Drills, skill saws, table saws, tile saws, etc.
- **Equipment:** You will need a designated place to store any equipment that will need to stay on-site for an extended time by your tradesmen. This equipment will usually not need a climate-controlled environment but must be kept out of the rain and out of sight from a passerby.
    - **Ladders and Scaffolding:** Should be broken down and put away every day to ensure that no one who is not authorized will use them. It will lessen your liability by preventing anyone from climbing on them and getting hurt.
    - **Excavators and Any Driven Machinery:** Should be parked in a designated area out of any passersby's sight, and the keys should be stored in the house overnight. You may have to leave the house key for your tradesmen in a particular location every morning so that he can use the equipment until it is returned. This may be gone over in the contract when you rent the machinery. When you rent the machinery, you will need to clarify this with the vendor. If you do not have a covered area for the machinery, you may need to purchase a tarp to cover the machinery overnight.

- **Non-climate Controlled:** You may store items in a garage, shed, or rental unit. Try to organize your materials as they will be needed and have easy access to them.
    - **Materials:**
        - Windows
        - Doors
        - Paint
        - Drywall
        - Tile and/or brick
        - Light fixtures
        - Plumbing fixtures

- **Tools:** You will need a designated place to store any tools that need to stay on-site overnight for your tradesmen. Your tools will need to be locked away as well. Most tools do not need a climate-controlled environment but must stay out of the rain and out of sight of passersby.
  - **Hand Tools:** Hammers, pry bars, screwdrivers, tape measures, etc.
  - **Power Tools:** Drills, skill saws, table saws, tile saws, etc.
- **Equipment:** Use the same procedure as the climate-controlled equipment.

Site Access: Most tradesmen will arrive early to work on your project. You will be able to let them into the house to work for the day and instruct them to lock up when they leave. However, you may work during the day and leave earlier than your tradesmen; arrangements may need to be made for your tradesmen to access your home as the work site. You will have to allow access to the house's interior and exterior.

- **Interior:**
  - You may have a lockbox set up for the tradesmen to access a key to the home.
  - A designated hidden area to keep the key.
  - A code for a coded entry lock.
  - A neighbor or relative to let them in.
  - Rooms must be cleared of unnecessary items, furniture, and personal effects.
  - If the furniture does not need complete removal, it may be enough to move it to the room's interior.
  - Arrange rooms so your family can operate in a regular daily routine as much as possible, sleeping, eating, getting dressed in the morning or evening, etc.

- **Exterior:**
  - Gates will need to be left unlocked.
  - Garage doors must be left open and/or given a remote to unlock.
  - A neighbor or relative to allow them in.
  - All areas near the work area will have to be cleared of unnecessary items such as outdoor furniture, potted plants, yard equipment, etc. If you cannot move these items, you may pay your tradesmen to move the items for you.
  - Make sure you arrange equipment, tool, and materials storage to park in the evening and leave in the morning so as not to interfere with your regular schedule.

- **Setting Expectations:** To naturally use your home, you will need to develop an expectation with your tradesman on how the site should look at the end of every day, end of the week, and even throughout the day.

- **Throughout the Day:**
    - Tools and equipment should be kept to the area of work.
    - Materials should be brought out of storage and used as needed. Most materials will be stored as close to the work site as possible.
    - Debris should be bagged and/or thrown into the trash trailer or dumpster as they are used and discarded.

- **The End of the Day:**
    - Tools and equipment should be picked up and stored in a designated area.
    - Materials should be stored away in the designated area.
    - Debris should be bagged up and thrown into the trash trailer or dumpster. Interior floors should be swept and/or vacuumed up. Exterior surfaces should be swept off or blown off with a leaf blower. All nails, screws, etc., should be picked up.

- **End of the Week:**
    - Tools and equipment should be safely stored away in cases (*if applicable*); all cords wound up and stored in a designated area.
    - Materials should be boxed and stored away in the designated area.
    - All debris should be removed from the site and thrown into the trash trailer and/or dumpster. All interior surfaces are swept, vacuumed, and/or wiped down. All exterior surfaces are swept and/or blown off with a leaf blower.

*Debris includes all paper trash, plastic wrap trash, empty containers, unused fasteners, wood cut-offs, material dust, tile pieces, food items, and cigarette butts.

Sometimes communicating your expectations to your tradesmen can be uncomfortable. What you need to remember is that while it is their job site, it is YOUR property. You have a right to expect a certain level of cleanliness, order, and respect given to your home. At the same time, the tradesmen and their crew members will make a mess during the workday. There is a balance between expectations and actions. You will find that fit with your tradesmen during the interview process.

Site Management: During your project planning, you will need to plan how the site (*your property*) will function as the storage and worksite. If you have a plan for these items, you will lessen stress during the process. Hold your guidelines as closely as possible while working with your CODES office, HOA, and tradesmen, to make a clean and safe work environment for everyone.

A few things to consider:

- **HOA Requirements For:**
    - Dumpsters and/or trash trailers
        - Placement and duration of the placement
    - Parking work vehicles and the duration of stay
    - Materials deliveries
        - Drop off locations
        - Service truck parking
- **Debris Locations:** Where and how you want trash removed—trash trailer or dumpster.
    - Ease of throwing out the trash—not having to haul too far
    - Ease of access for pick up and drop off for the service vehicles
    - Not easily accessed by neighbors throwing out debris
- **Smoking Areas:** A smoking area will need to be established and enforced.
- **Material Storage:** Even though not all materials will arrive on the first day, ensure you have room for materials to be stored for at least a week before being used as needed.
- **Tool and Equipment Storage:** Designate an area where the workers can cut wood, clean tools, and store them safely and securely.
- **House Rules and Expectations:**
    - Ensure each Tradesman and crew knows what is acceptable and what is NOT regarding behavior and language.
    - The removal of any food debris and drink cups
    - The expectation of material storage and usage during and after work hours
    - **Exceptional Circumstances:** Children and/or pets with special needs, disabled persons, or anything they may need to work around that is unique to your home.
- **Communication:** The key to keeping everyone working is communication. There will need to be daily communication between you, your tradesmen, and your vendors. The essential communication components are documentation, timing, methods, and attitude.
- **Documentation:** Included in this course are several forms for you to document. These should all be in your project journal.
    - **Scope of Work:** A detailed outline of the renovation project using task categories.
    - **Surface & Fixture Schedule:** A detailed listing of all the material resources for each task category with the quantities (square footage, linear footage, pieces, and counts) for each item needed. It includes different plumbing, electrical, tile, doors, windows, and paint

schedules. ***There are forms to help you keep each one of these separate so that you use only the ones you need.*
- **Materials Lists:** A detailed list of the materials you will need, quantities of each, and the cost totals.
- **Quotes From Vendors:** Detailed costs on the items you will be buying for your project and will include the item cost, vendor contact information, delivery options, and any special notes needed for each item.
- **Quotes From Tradesman:** Detailed list of quotes received by tradesmen to include contact information for each tradesman, a brief description of the work needed from them, the quote received, and any special notes to be made for every tradesman.
- **Overall Budget:** A combined estimate lists the scope of work, your material costs, and the quotes received from your tradesmen. It includes a place to combine all these to see what your project should cost. In addition, you will need to factor in a contingency amount (extra monies) to allow changes to be made.
- **Timelines:** Using the chart found at the beginning of this module and the estimated times given to you by your tradesmen, you can put together a calendar timeline. Remember to provide a day or two buffer between some tradesmen (*especially those doing exterior work*) to accommodate bad weather and unforeseen events.
- **Change Orders:** Record every change order for you and your tradesmen to stay on track with the cost and the work to be done. Each change order should include:
  - Quote for the additional labor.
  - Quote for the additional materials.
  - An estimated time frame for the work to be done, so you can adapt your timeline to reflect this change.

You are not locked into using these forms; use them as guidelines for the information you need to document. Documenting all these things will allow you to refer to them when questions arise to clarify the outline of required work, materials that need to be purchased, and who is responsible for them.

- **Rescheduling:** Any time there is a change in the schedule of work to do, via change order, delivery delays, weather, illness, etc., you should always notify your tradesman scheduled for the changes. The two of you should discuss the rescheduling and settle on a date for the work to resume. Do not leave it up in the air without a set date. The tradesman may schedule something else and not get back to you for a while. Also, if you must put the tradesman off for your reasons, be considerate of his time to reschedule the work. He is running a business and must keep it going. No company can put everything on hold indefinitely; it will fail, but no matter the situation, you should have an obvious and specific target to resume the project.

- **The Tradesman and Scheduling:** Some change orders will affect multiple tradesmen. Each one of them will need to be notified of the changes. Again, inform them of the updated timeline once you have rescheduled the original tradesman. Look at your calendar and make the necessary adjustment.
- **Methods of Communication:** During your interviews with your tradesmen, you will need to establish the preferred communication method.
    - **Texting and Email:** Highly effective for documentation purposes. It is a place to have it in writing that can be printed or stored digitally for reference. You can also send necessary pictures back and forth to ensure you are on the same page.
    - **Phone Calls:** This is also effective in relaying information but can create confusion. There will be no visual to go with it if needed, and you may resort to texting.
    - **Written Notes:** This has sometimes proven to be an effective form of communication as well. Trading notes with your tradesmen in the morning or evening and updating each other on any questions, concerns, or progress is another form of documentation.
- **Openness:** Keeping an open mind and open-door policy with your tradesmen will allow information to flow back and forth easily. The more understanding you can be of the situation, the more likely the tradesmen will get the job done for you. However, you do not want to be a total pushover and have them take advantage of your understanding. Therefore, you should always get a firm date with the tradesmen explaining that you will need to reschedule other people around this event, and it would only be fair to everyone if we could firm up a new schedule.

Using the forms provided to you in the previous chapters and this chapter, you should be able to build the full scope of work to include the following:

Drawings
Budget (Labor and Materials)
Material Lists
Vendor Quotes
Tradesman Quotes
Timeline
Change Order Contingency

Site Plan

Project Owner & Address
-
-
-

Project Description

Site Layout

Task	Contractor/Vendor	Delivery / Storage	Storage Area	Clean Out Area	Cut Station
Permit					
Trash					
Foundation					
Framing					
Roofing					
Siding					
Insulation					
Plumbing					
Electrical					
Drywall					
Painting					
Trim Work					
Cabinetry					
Countertops					
Flooring					
Tile Work					
KEEP ITEMS					
Smoking Area					

Special Requests

Sub Lists ON SITE		Notes
Trash		
Port a let		
Foundation		
Framing		
Roofing		
Siding		
Insulation		
HVAC		
Plumbing		
Electrical		
Drywall		
Painting		
Tile Work		
Cabinetry		
Countertops		
Flooring		
Finish Carpentry		

Other Notes

Section 5: Change Orders

We have covered Change orders before, but now we go into greater detail. This is covered multiple times because every job has change orders and can be a source of frustration and confusion for both you and the tradesman. Understanding what these changes can do to your project and budget is necessary.

Change Orders: Most projects will have change orders either out of necessity or design change. How well your tradesmen can deal with change orders will be important. Also, what will the change order do to your **timeline**, **cost**, and budget, and when is it too late for a change order?

Necessity: This change order is because there is a circumstance that was not seen before by you or your tradesman and must be corrected before proceeding with other work. Several things can contribute to these circumstances; these are just a **few** examples:

- **Foundation:**
    - A weak spot in the foundation and breaks.
    - Sinkhole under foundation, leaking, breaking, and separations in the foundation.
    - Bad aggregate (concrete) breaks and cracks.
    - No vapor barrier was installed, leading to condensation and "sweating" of the concrete, forcing the flooring to come up.
    - Improper sloping of the slab, causing the wall plates to be the wrong height.

- **Framing:**
    - Walls out of plumb; the wall turns, causing doors not to work or being framed improperly, and drywall cracks.
    - Doors and windows have improper support, causing the improper function of the door and/or window.
    - Improper wall support is racking in the framework, drywall cracking doors, and windows don't function correctly. Or sagging in the ceiling or roof.
    - Improper support in roofing is causing sagging and future leaking.
    - Rot issues in walls, causing siding and drywall to break and fall.
    - Past storm damage: weakness in the wall, racking of the framework, doors, and window breakage.
    - Termites: weak framework and bracing, which support the roof and siding.

- **Roofing:**
  - Bad shingles causing leaking issues.
  - Rotted plywood sheathing, causing rotted rafters.
  - Drip edge installed improperly, causing the soffit and fascia to rot.
  - Past storm damage, leaking issues, and rotted sheathing.

- **Insulation:**
  - Not enough insulation, causing condensation issues and damage to drywall, trim, and interior finishes.
  - Too much, causing condensation issues and damage to drywall, trim, and interior finishes.

- **Siding:**
  - Improper installation causes rot, sagging, cracking, or breakage.
  - Animal invasion causes rot issues in the wall and insulation, causing breaking or cracking of interior finishes.
  - Material availability: the existing materials may not match the look and/or style of the new materials because they are out of date and not available anymore; there may need to be more siding removed and replaced than initially budgeted.

- **Plumbing:**
  - Material failure (*new or old*), causing leaks, leading to rot issues, and damage to interior finishes such as drywall and flooring.
  - Wrong fittings will cause materials failure in fixtures as they are used, as well as plumbing supply and drain line failure, leading to leaks, damage to interior finishes, and rot of framework.
  - Material selection: the newly selected faucet may need special fittings other than the standard fittings.

- **Electrical:**
  - Improper wiring causes fire hazards with arching and overheating, non-working lights, switches, outlets, appliances, etc.
  - Improper circuit load causes fire hazards or non-working lights, switches, outlets, appliances, etc.
  - Improper junction boxes cause fire hazards or non-working lights, switches, outlets, appliances, etc.

- Out-of-date materials need replacing because they cannot handle the same energy loads as newer appliances and electronic devices.
- Materials selection: the newly selected fixture may need special wiring or load capacities different from the standard.

- **Wall Coverings:**
    - Multiple layering, more demo to be done, walls out of plumb. A new wall covering will not line up; it will have to be shimmed to the same thickness or add a layer to the wall to achieve the same consistency.
    - Installed incorrectly, causing cracking and new wall covering not to line up. More may have to be removed and reinstalled to get a smooth finish.
    - Old paneling install that can't be matched. It will have to change to a new wall covering or accept the difference in the look.
    - Drywall covering solid concrete walls; will need more time in electrical work or hanging accessories.
    - Animal infestation behind existing drywall; this will have to be dealt with by an exterminator before putting drywall back up

- **Doors and Windows:**
    - The new doors and windows may not be standard sizing, requiring framing to be done that was not anticipated.
    - Unexpected rot of the sills and/or headers has not been seen before and will have to be replaced.

Design Change Orders: These change orders usually happen during the project process. You may see the desired change as you and/or the designer see the project come together. The following are just a few examples of what some of the most common design change orders would be

- **Framing:**
    - Wall placement and/or size of the wall. Perhaps it should be cut short of the original outline or longer to offer privacy to a room.
    - Additional space, adding on a deck, closet, room, etc.
    - Door and/or window sizing, causing framing to change from the original plan and new materials to be purchased. Sometimes there may be an open casing you want to enlarge or lessen.

- **Roofing:**
    - Change color and type.
    - Change the roof lines to the addition.
    - Adding dormers to the front of the house.

- **Siding:**
    - Changes in materials chosen will affect labor pricing and materials pricing.
    - Adding exterior trim work or completing a look such as corbels or shutters will add more to the labor and materials.

- **Plumbing:**
    - Depending on the selection, different fixtures may also affect your countertops and sinks.
    - Placement of fixtures may require plumbing to be redone; valves and drains may need to be moved.

- **Electrical:**
    - The selection of the lights may change, requiring different wiring or placement due to design and size.
    - Additional lighting and switches.
    - Changing the placement of the lighting.

- **Cabinetry:**
    - Additional cabinetry will also cost more in hardware.
    - Placement of cabinetry can also affect countertops and flooring.

- **Countertops:**
    - The materials chosen may change the cost. It may also change the base cabinets if the thickness varies.
    - The appliances chosen may affect the cut out of the stone, requiring the fabrication to change.

- **Wall Coverings:**
    - The materials chosen are changed out. An example would be drywall for paneling; this will affect the labor and material costs and may also change the tradesman required.
    - Additional wall covering is added if extra space is added in framing.
    - Wallpaper—used as an accent wall or, if preferred, instead of paint. It usually requires a specific tradesman and only requires priming the wall. It may be painted, and wallpaper hung later if the design changes.

- **Painting:**
    - Change of the colors, requiring additional coats of paint.
    - Additional wall covering requires more painting.
    - Additional cabinetry and/or trim; when old meets new, sometimes the old needs to be freshened up with a new paint coat.

Dealing With Change Orders: Ask the following questions to prepare for when a change order comes up and what protocol will follow.

- **Necessity:**
    - Are pictures taken to show the reason for the need for the change order?
    - How quickly can the work be done? An exact time will not be determined until the tradesman looks at what needs to be done to fix the problem.
    - Will they provide you with the cost of the change order before performing the work? In most cases, it will have to be billed to you as time and materials.
    - Will the change order require a different tradesman to complete the work before moving forward?
- **Design:**
    - Are they willing to work with you if a design change order arises?
    - Will they be able to give you a cost for the change order before performing the work? In most cases, it will need to be billed to you as time and materials.
    - How much advance notice would they need for the change order?
    - When is it too late to change the design?

Chapter 6 Budget Management & Record Keeping

Section 1: Creating a Statement

To keep your budget under control, you will need to keep good records and compare these to the original scope. This will involve having a copy of the original budget you created, keeping your receipts (*both for materials and your subcontractor invoices*), and having a running tally.

We will discuss further the payment plans you may set up with your vendors and subcontractors, when to expect to make payments, and how payments are generally handled.

You will first need to create a detailed statement to track your spending. This statement should include rows and columns. The rows will indicate the task categories you are spending money on, and the columns will represent the invoices you are paying. The last three columns should be the estimated budget, the amount paid, and the expected remainder. Knowing how to use an Excel spreadsheet will make it easier in the tracking process, but it can still be managed manually; it will take a little extra time. It should look something like the following chart.

	Week 1	Week 2	Week 3	Week 4	Week 5	Paid Total	Budget	Remaining
Demo Labor						= Invoices From Each Week	Original Budget $ Created	Subtract Paid from Budget $
Demo Materials & Equipment								
Foundation								
Framing Labor	$7000	$5500				$12500	$12500	0
Framing Materials & Equipment	$10000	$2500				$12500	$12000	-$500
Roofing Labor								
Roofing Materials								
Siding Labor								
Siding Materials								
HVAC								
Insulation Labor								
Insulation Materials								

	Week 1	Week 2	Week 3	Week 4	Week 5	Paid Total	Budget	Remaining
Plumbing Labor								
Plumbing Materials								
Electrical Labor								
Electrical Materials								
Drywall Labor								
Drywall Materials						= Invoices From Each Week	Original Budget $ Created	Subtract Paid from Budget $
Painting Labor			$6000		$5500	$11500	$12000	$500
Painting Materials			$1000		$500	$1500	$1200	-$300
Cabinetry								
Countertops								
Tile Labor								
Tile Materials								
Flooring Labor								
Flooring Materials								
Finish Carpentry Labor								
Finish Carpentry Materials								

You will first place the money amount for the budget in the budget column. Then, you will need to sit down once a week and fill in your receipts and invoices in the appropriate columns. When you enter receipts, subtract what you have paid from the Budget money, and you should see the amount left to pay. If you end up with a positive number when the work is complete, you have come under budget. If you end up with a negative number in the remaining column, you have gone over the budget.

You may add a section that accounts for your change orders as they arise, and you know that you are making them as the job progresses.

	Week 1	Week 2	Week 3	Week 4	Week 5	Paid Total	Budget	Remaining
Change Order Description EX: Upgraded Doors			$550			= Invoices from each week	Original Budget $ Created	Subtract Paid from Budget $
Change Order 2: Removed the 5th Window		-$750						

Section 2: Record Keeping & Receipts

Record Keeping and Receipts: Keep all receipts for every task category, even for stick lumber. You will need these to log in to your detailed statement to track your ongoing budget. You also never know if you must do a return or exchange. Most vendors will require proof of purchase. Some items can be returned if you have purchased too much. Keep in mind these items will have to be whole and not partial. Some items will usually be taken back for a refund. You will have to make sure with your vendor of their policy for returns. The following are the most common items that may be returned for a credit or refund.

- **Framing:**
    - Full sheets of plywood
    - Full-length boards; 8′, 10′, 12′ 14′ 16′ etc.
    - Full boxes of nails and other fasteners
    - Full rolls of house wrap
- **Roofing:**
    - Full packs of shingles
    - Full rolls of drip edge
    - Full boxes of fasteners
    - Plumbing jacks
    - Full ridge vents
    - Turbine vents
    - Power vents
- **Siding—keep some for replacement in the future:**
    - Half and full pallets of bricks
    - Full bags of mortar
    - Any full lap siding boards
    - Any full wood or Hardie panels
    - Full buckets of stucco base coat (*without color*)

- **HVAC:**
    - Ceiling and/or floor register covers
    - Filters
- **Plumbing:**
    - Drains
    - Faucets
    - Valve sets
- **Electrical:**
    - Outlets
    - Switches
    - Cover plates
    - Light fixtures
    - Can lights
- **Drywall:**
    - Full sheets of drywall
    - Full boxes of mud
    - Full rolls of tape
    - Full boxes of screws
- **Paint:**
    - Full cans of primer
    - Full tubes of caulk
- **Trim Carpentry:**
    - Full sticks of any base, crown, or shoe molding
    - Full boxes of fasteners
- **Tile Work:** it is always a good idea to keep at least one box of each tile used in your project for any future repairs.
    - Full boxes of tile—check with your vendor about returns of tile. Certain ones may require a minimum number of complete packages for a return and have a restocking fee.
    - Full bags of thin-set mortar and grout

- **Finish Carpentry:**
    - Bath accessories
    - Mirrors
    - Hardware for doors or cabinets
- **Contracts and Subcontractor Invoices:** Keep only the contracts you need for the tradesmen you are using. Keep these with the tradesmen's quotes. Then, you can compare their invoices to the quote or bid given when making up your budget.
- **Change Orders:** You will need to keep track of all change orders for your project. You can use the change order forms at the end of the chapter, or you can track them digitally on a form of your own. Make sure you have the following information:
    - The labor cost
    - The material costs
    - Date of the change order
    - Description of the change order

Remember to keep only essential documents relating to your project. You may want to keep a folder of receipts for each task category in your project journal. It will help you to look up receipts if or when needed later.

Section 3: Financial Expectations

Financial Expectations: In this section, we will discuss expectations of the work, the duration of the project, and the result of the craftsmanship, as well as expectations of payments, processes, purchases, and change orders. You, your tradesmen, and your vendors all have expectations of how the process will work, and this is usually where tensions grow, and miscommunications happen. Therefore, it is essential to clarify your expectations from the beginning. Do not worry about hurting feelings. It can be made clear and firm without offending anyone. It is your home, and you are the one cutting the checks. You will also need to be open to the expectations of the tradesmen and vendors you hire. They are running a business, and they employ other people. It is a joint effort to create an atmosphere of teamwork from the beginning to quash arguments and/or confusion later. There should be no "power" struggle. You need each other to make this project come to fruition. You each have a function in this renovation, and each relies on the other for something.

You rely on the vendor to know about the products they are selling. You also depend on the tradesmen to do the work and know how to install your materials correctly. The tradesmen rely on the vendor to deliver quality products for them to install. They also depend on you for the design and overall vision of the project to perform their craft. The vendor relies on the tradesmen to install their product correctly to give you the best experience and satisfaction in using the products. The vendor will also depend on you to have the project's design and overall vision so you can use their products to their full potential. It is a relationship you are building, however temporary. Your project may have different phases to it in which you will repeat this experience. Let us discuss some of the expectations involved in a home renovation.

- **Payments:** Be open and direct about the payment expectations. Your vendors and tradesmen will be set up differently for payments and accept different compensation forms. The following are only guidelines of the timing and format of payments received by both. You will have to have a candid and direct discussion about both with your vendors and tradesmen.

  - **Vendors Payment Schedule:**

    - **Deposits:** 50% upfront and the remaining upon arrival.
    - **Payment Plans:** A percentage paid at the time of the order and a set payment schedule for the remaining.
    - **Accounts:** Set up an account and make no payments until the product comes in.
    - **Full Payment:** Will expect full payment at the time of order.

- **Vendors' Form of Payment:**
    - Cash
    - Checks
    - Credit cards
    - PayPal accounts

- **Tradesmen Payments Schedule:**
    - **Deposits:** Need a percentage of the quote to begin (*usually because they are purchasing materials right away*) and the remaining amount of the quote upon completion of the job.
    - There is nothing down to begin, a partial payment at the end of the week (and every week) for the work completed that week until the entire job is complete.
    - Nothing to begin the job with full payment upon completing the work.

- **Tradesmen Form of Payments:**
    - Cash
    - Checks
    - Credit cards usually come with an additional charge for whatever the credit card company charges them for the transaction.

- **Purchases:** There will be some purchases you will make and some the tradesmen will be making. Make a list of the materials you will need to purchase and a list the tradesmen will purchase. Go through it with the tradesmen and ensure you understand what is expected. There will also be materials that will need purchasing during the work progression, fasteners, extra wood, drywall, etc. It is crucial to establish who will need to purchase these materials as they come up. You can have the tradesmen make a list for you to purchase what they will need, or you can ask if they would like to buy the items and add it to their bill. If the tradesmen buy the material for you, there will be an added charge for them to go and purchase them. The value for you is that you will not travel to buy the materials, and you know that the correct item will be purchased.
- **Change Orders:** We have talked a lot about change orders, and there is more to come. They seem to be just a part of every renovation, small or large. They are also a significant source of tension because they affect the budget and timeline. Both are precious commodities to you and your tradesmen. The next module deals entirely with change orders in detail.

Subcontractor Payment Schedules:

Even though most people are uncomfortable talking about money, you must establish a payment schedule with your tradesmen. Not every tradesman will have the same payment schedule. You will need to understand what they will expect or need. The most common methods of payment are as follows:

- **Deposit:** To pay for the materials they will be purchasing themselves.
    - **Weekly Payments:** For the work, usually performed on Fridays to cover labor.
    - **Final Invoice:** For completion of work.
- **Draw:**
    - The 1st draw is to cover materials purchased.
    - The 2nd draw is to cover labor costs.
    - The 3rd and final draw—completion of work.
- **Half and Half:**
    - First half of the quote to begin work.
    - Second half of the quote at the completion of work.

Getting the payment plan set up in advance will help you and the tradesmen feel comfortable moving forward with the work knowing the expectations. You will also be able to set your budget in order by knowing how and when the money is going out. It is best to have all the money you need for the entire project secured, plus any contingency amount you think you may spend on change orders and beyond.

Section 4: Revisiting Your Budget

Materials:

At this time, you should take the time to revisit the budget materials. This is a place where the budget can go off track very easily. As a project progresses, we may change design choices, resulting in a change in the budget. Often, we find a different or new product that we "fall in love with," this does not cause a change in the labor but will make the budgeted materials go up or down. Some of the tools to help you have already been put in place.

- Use the detailed statement and your project journal to compare your actual spending to your budgeted pricing.
- Track your change order receipts for materials and labor. Your vendor and subcontractor should clarify when a charge is added to the original scope of work and budget.

Labor:

Your labor costs should stay relatively the same as the original budget since you will receive bids and quotes from your subcontractors. The items that will change these prices are any unforeseen circumstances in the structure or any design changes you make.

If you intend to make design changes, please track them in the form of your Surface & Fixture Schedules. Every time you would like to discuss a change from the original plan with a designer, subcontractor, and/or architect, know that there is a cost difference associated with this. Whenever asking for a change to the original plan, it alters the work schedule and the materials to purchase. It is also a change in the timeline. New plans must be made that take time, which must be conveyed to the work crews. If new materials need to be purchased, these materials may have additional wait times. It also eats up time.

Change Orders:

We discussed making a section for change orders in your project journal. It is suggested to separate this section into two sections: necessity and design. Keeping an eye on your budget will require keeping track of the changes as they come. It can get away from you and become overwhelming. Having a place to keep them so you can refer to the changes as they happen will help you keep your job on track. It may not be the path you initially designed but on a path no less. Daily communications with your tradesmen will help you track all your change orders. Using your detailed statement will also let you see the change orders, and in which task category it happened.

- **Necessary Changes:**
  - Take pictures of the needed changes. Examples would be rot, burst pipes, or cracked foundations. These pictures will help you and your tradesmen know the need for the change order.
  - Keep a record of the work outline for the change order and take notes of your discussion with your tradesmen when the change order occurs. You may refer to it when it comes up again, the need to tell an insurance agent (*if it is storm-related and can be covered under your policy*), or another tradesman that needs to adjust their work outline because of the change order. For example: siding may have to be changed out because you must reframe a wall due to rot.
  - Keep a record of the labor cost. The larger the job, the more overwhelming all the details can seem. As a result, the budget can feel like it's out of hand; with noted changes in the labor costs, you will see how these changes affect your overall budget.
  - Keep a record of the material cost, if any. There may be some changes that can be handled using materials that have already been purchased. However, most of the time, it will require additional materials to be purchased to complete the work. Keep receipts and mark them as a change order material and what task category they are related.
  - Alert any other tradesmen if their schedule may be affected. If the change order is significant enough, the workload may have grown for other tradesmen or, in some cases, (*rarely*) eliminated. If the workload has increased, your cost will increase, but it will also affect the tradesmen's schedule. They may need to break up the work into phases, but they will take it on all at once more often than not. **EXAMPLE**: there is more rot in a wall than anticipated, and there will be significantly more drywalling and painting to do. You will also have to replace more trim work (crown, base, and/or shoe molding, and possibly door and/or window trim). You will be buying more materials and must alert your drywaller, painter, and trim carpenter of the change in the scope of work previously outlined and discussed.
- **Design Changes:**
  - Track your design changes on a separate change order sheet. Keep a record of it with your initial scope outline. You may also want to keep a copy of the change order with the tradesman's original quote. It will remind you why this bill is higher.
  - Take notes while discussing the design change order with your tradesmen. Then, have them walk you through the new process so that you can alter the expectations of your timeline and budget.
  - Ask your tradesmen to invoice for the design change order separately from the original quote if possible. This way, it's easier to see the increase in your budget.
  - Establish who will be purchasing the newly needed materials for the change order. Sometimes, you will put in an order for more drywall, trim, flooring, etc. Other times, it may be your framer, plumber, or electrician supplying more back-end materials. Ask them to mark any new materials and fees clearly on the billing for the change order so you can track it.
  - Alert any other tradesmen if their schedule will be affected. It will alter your timeline as well. If the change order is significant enough, it may have grown the workload for other tradesmen or, in some

cases (*rarely*) eliminated. If the workload has increased, your cost will increase, but it will also affect the tradesmen's schedule. They may need to break up the work into phases, but they will take it on all at once more often than not. **EXAMPLE**: you may have decided to do an accent wall with wallpaper. This will change the scope of work for your painter, not having to paint the wall (just prime), and depending on the schedule of the wallpaper hanger, the electrician may not be able to hang any light fixtures that may be on the wall, etc.

Impact: Change orders have one of the most significant impacts on your project. They will affect every part of the project, including the budget, timeline, and the tradesmen's schedules.

- **Budget:** The cost will go up 99% of the time for labor and materials for any changes made.
  - **Necessity:** These are usually unexpected by you and the tradesmen. If there are structural, electrical, or plumbing problems, while it can feel unpleasant to spend the money and time on this being corrected, it is best to catch it now and have it corrected, rather than redo it the work you are doing now.
  - **Design:** These changes may be more predictable, manageable, and pleasant. It will be worth it to have your home just how you like it and function for you and your family in the best possible way. You are spending a good deal of money for the project to be completed; you do not want things to be "*fine*" when they are complete; you want them to be **EXCEPTIONAL**! Improving the quality of your life is never the wrong decision. Being able to come home to your sanctuary and release the tensions of the world so you can face them again is the best reward.

Sample Form

Alternative Work Orders

Contractor	Wooton Construction
	111 Row One
	Lafayette, LA 70508

No. _____

| DATE | |
| PREPARED BY | |

Client

Work Request Description

Items Added to & Removed	Budget	Actual	Difference
			$0.00
			$0.00
			$0.00
			$0.00
			$0.00
			$0.00
			$0.00
			$0.00
			$0.00
			$0.00
			$0.00
			$0.00
			$0.00
			$0.00
Total Change to Project			**0.00**

This Total represents the total amount that will will charged to the client for the work requested.
The work covered by this order shall be performed under the same terms and conditions as
that included in the Original Budget.
Credits are applied from the original Budget as a substitution or deletion of work where it is applicable.
All other work requsted that is not outlined in the Original Budget is considered additional work and therefore an additional charge.
NOTE: It is understood and agreed that this change order constitutes compensation in full to contractor for all costs and markups directly
or indirectly attributable to the changes ordered herein, for all delays related therto, and for any impact on other work.

NOT VALID UNTIL SIGNED BY THE CONTRACTOR AND OWNER

_____ _____
CONTRACTOR (Firm Name)   OWNER (Customer)

_____ _____
BY (Signature)   BY (Signature)

_____ _____
DATE   DATE

Section 5: Course Review

We will wrap up what you have learned throughout this course by going through the process from beginning to end, and reviewing each step. This will reinforce the necessary measures in preparing you to take on your renovation project with great confidence and preparedness.

In the first part of the process, we will review your planning. Then, we will begin with your **drawings**. Whether you completed your drawings or had them professionally made when you began your space planning process.

Once your space planning is complete, you can do your **scope of work**.

You could make a Surface & Fixture schedule and a materials list from this.

With the materials list and scope in hand, you could get your **vendor pricing**, subcontractor bids, and **quotes.**

Now you have completed your initial **budget**. From this, you were able to begin building your **project journal**.

The **project journal** was crucial to keeping your project's details in order. In a large project, the details will become overwhelming and confusing. This project journal will assist in keeping stress and anxiety to a minimum.

Project Journal: A binder containing all the details and important documents you will need for your project to begin and stay on track.

- **Drawings:** Detailed drawings to include measurements and/or elevations for construction. The measurements will help you acquire quotes and pricing for your scopes and budget.
- **Budget Outlines:** To include the following:
  - **Scope:** A detailed outline of the work to be done according to task categories and each trade.
  - **Surface & Fixture Schedules:** A detailed list outlining all materials needed in the quantities required that includes colors, styles, and any special notes and/or preferences.
  - **Individual Material Schedules:** A detailed list of materials needed for ordering and/or handing out to tradesmen during the installation process.
  - **Material Lists:** These are detailed material lists with descriptions, quantities, and pricing according to each task category.
  - **Budget Scopes:** Will include the work's detail to be done, with quotes from tradesmen, vendors, and material pricing.
- **Vendor Selections:** Detailed lists to include multiple quotes, contact information, arrival times, material descriptions, and any special notes needed from at least three different vendors.

- **Tradesmen Selections:** Detailed lists that include multiple quotes, contact information, start dates, task descriptions, and any special notes needed from at least three tradesmen.
- **Pictures and Spec Sheets:** A collection of inspiration pictures for your project, specific material choices, and any instructional and/or spec sheets for materials needing electrical, plumbing, and/or framing installations.
- **Receipts:** Any receipts for orders and purchases made.
- **Contracts:** All tradesmen, vendors, and rental agreements are written and signed.
- **Change Orders:** A single listing of all change orders or individual change order forms detailing any changes to your project, including any labor and material pricing.

After building your project journal, the **timeline** was set with **purchases** of materials, **scheduling** subcontractors, making deposits, and signing contracts.

Next, you began to set your **site plans** for your project. Along with workstations, delivery, and storage areas, you also began to develop realistic expectations.

At the onset of the project, you should have begun a **detailed statement,** which allows you to track your ongoing project cost. It outlines your original budget, the actual costs, and the remaining costs. You will also track any change orders along the way.

Final Checklist

The following is a simple checklist to let you know you are on track and have covered your bases.

	Task
	Drawings: self, architect, draftsman, interior designer
	Space Planning: self, interior designer
	Scope: detailed list of work to be done by task category
	Resource Schedule: list of quantities, styles, and colors for all materials
	Design Schedules: a listing of all the design elements required for your project
	Materials List: all materials, raw and design, needed and priced for your project
	Detailed Statement
	Subcontractor Quotes: bids and labor pricing from tradesmen performing work
	Budget: completed scope and pricing put together
	Project Journal: your complete binder with all the above items and a place for spec sheets, receipts, and change orders
	Timeline: an outline of the work to be done, including inspections, allotted time by the subcontractor, and contingencies.
	Purchasing: all needed raw and design Materials
	Scheduling: all materials deliveries and subcontractors
	Site Plans: getting your property ready for work with workstation, storage areas, debris removal site, and delivery areas

Course Goals:

After taking this course, you will walk away with a new knowledge and a skill set that improves your home renovation project. What you will take away from the completion of this course are the following:

To have knowledge in making the soundest choices for your project. You will now be confident that you have thoroughly researched each product that will go into your home. You will purchase your products, knowing each has its pros and cons. You will add value to your home's worth and lifestyle by improving your use of the house and the quality of the lifestyle you and your family have together while living in the home. Doing thorough research will also help lessen any change orders after the build has begun.

You will understand what it takes to construct a home from the ground up. This insight will help you understand any tradesmen or vendors when discussing the renovation and bridging the communication gap. Knowing what goes into getting the work done will also help you feel more confident that your home is built soundly and understand what you are looking at when a tradesman talks to you during construction. In addition, it will help you see any warning signs and verify work with inspections during the process. It will also allow you to know *which* changes can be made, should be made, and *when* they can be made.

Don't forget that you will repeat the reviewing process throughout your project build. This will be done before a task begins and as each task is completed. Follow through with your inspections for quality control. Keep the lines of communication open with each tradesman and ask for their advice if you think you have a situation that requires their expertise and experience. You are a team.

Your home is your sanctuary, and it deserves your attention and time. Planning for a renovation is not unlike any other major life choice like marriage or family vacations! Prepare yourself for the impact, keep your purpose in mind and stay curious. Always reach out and ask questions. Remember, you get to live here!

www.ingramcontent.com/pod-product-compliance
Lightning Source LLC
Chambersburg PA
CBHW060303010526

44108CB00042B/2656